A Final Reckoning
A Tale Of Bush Life In Australia

By

G. A. Henty

Double 9
BOOKS

A Final Reckoning
A Tale Of Bush Life In Australia
by G. A. Henty

ISBN: 978-93-61424-70-0

Published by

DOUBLE 9 BOOKS

2/13-B, Ansari Road
Daryaganj, New Delhi – 110002
info@double9books.com
www.double9books.com
Tel. 011-40042856

ABOUT THE AUTHOR

English author and war correspondent George Alfred Henty lived from 8 December 1832 to 16 November 1902. He is most well-known for his historical fiction and adventure books, including The Dragon & The Raven (1886), For The Temple (1888), Under Drake's Flag (1883), and in Freedom's Cause (1883). (1885). He was a British journalist who served as G. A. Henty's war correspondent. He was raised in Cambridge and finished his education there at Gonville and Caius College. He continued to cover important wars that followed, such as the Italian and Austro-Italian Wars. He wrote 122 books, most of which were geared toward young readers. He also wrote non-fiction, adult fiction, and short tales. In Henty's stories, the main character is a boy or young man who is going through a challenging situation. His characters are consistently low-key, astute, courageous, truthful, and resourceful with a lot of "pluck." The date was put at the bottom of the title page of each of Henty's 122 historical fiction works in their first printings.

CONTENTS

Preface 7

Chapter 1
The Broken Window 8

Chapter 2
The Poisoned Dog.. 20

Chapter 3
The Burglary At The Squire's.. 33

Chapter 4
The Trial.. 44

Chapter 5
Not Guilty!.. 58

Chapter 6
On The Voyage... 71

Chapter 7
Gratitude... 85

Chapter 8
A Gale... 99

Chapter 9
Two Offers 111

Chapter 10
An Up-Country District 123

Chapter 11
The Black Fellows 135

Chapter 12
The Bush Rangers 147

Chapter 13
Bush Rangers.. 155

Chapter 14
An Unexpected Meeting... 168

Chapter 15
At Donald's.. 181

Chapter 16
Jim's Report 194

Chapter 17
In Pursuit 207

Chapter 18
Settling Accounts... 221

Preface

In this tale I have left the battlefields of history, and have written a story of adventure in Australia, in the early days when the bush rangers and the natives constituted a real and formidable danger to the settlers. I have done this, not with the intention of extending your knowledge, or even of pointing a moral, although the story is not without one; but simply for a change—a change both for you and myself, but frankly, more for myself than for you. You know the old story of the boy who bothered his brains with Euclid, until he came to dream regularly that he was an equilateral triangle enclosed in a circle. Well, I feel that unless I break away sometimes from history, I shall be haunted day and night by visions of men in armour, and soldiers of all ages and times.

If, when I am away on a holiday I come across the ruins of a castle, I find myself at once wondering how it could best have been attacked, and defended. If I stroll down to the Thames, I begin to plan schemes of crossing it in the face of an enemy; and if matters go on, who can say but that I may find myself, some day, arrested on the charge of surreptitiously entering the Tower of London, or effecting an escalade of the keep of Windsor Castle! To avoid such a misfortune—which would entail a total cessation of my stories, for a term of years—I have turned to a new subject, which I can only hope that you will find as interesting, if not as instructive, as the other books which I have written.

G. A. Henty.

Chapter 1
The Broken Window

"You are the most troublesome boy in the village, Reuben Whitney, and you will come to a bad end."

The words followed a shower of cuts with the cane. The speaker was an elderly man, the master of the village school of Tipping, near Lewes, in Sussex; and the words were elicited, in no small degree, by the vexation of the speaker at his inability to wring a cry from the boy whom he was striking. He was a lad of some thirteen years of age, with a face naturally bright and intelligent; but at present quivering with anger.

"I don't care if I do," he said defiantly. "It won't be my fault, but yours, and the rest of them."

"You ought to be ashamed of yourself," the master said, "instead of speaking in that way. You, who learn easier than anyone here, and could always be at the top of your class, if you chose. I had hoped better things of you, Reuben; but it's just the way, it's your bright boys as mostly gets into mischief."

At this moment the door of the school room opened, and a lady with two girls, one of about fourteen and the other eleven years of age, entered.

"What is the matter now?" the lady asked, seeing the schoolmaster, cane in hand, and the boy standing before him.

"Reuben Whitney! What, in trouble again, Reuben? I am afraid you are a very troublesome boy."

"I am not troublesome, ma'm," the boy said sturdily. "That is, I wouldn't be if they would let me alone; but everything that is done bad, they put it down to me."

"But what have you been doing now, Reuben?"

"I have done nothing at all, ma'm; but he's always down on me," and he pointed to the master, "and when they are always down on a fellow, it's no use his trying to do right."

"What has the boy been doing now, Mr. White?" the lady asked.

"Look there, ma'm, at those four windows all smashed, and the squire had all the broken panes mended only a fortnight ago."

"How was it done, Mr. White?"

"By a big stone, ma'm, which caught the frame where they joined, and smashed them all."

"I did not do it, Mrs. Ellison, indeed I didn't."

"Why do you suppose it was Reuben?" Mrs. Ellison asked the master.

"Because I had kept him in, half an hour after the others went home to dinner, for pinching young Jones and making him call out; and he had only just gone out of the gate when I heard the smash; so there is no doubt about it, for all the others must have been in at their dinner at that time."

"I didn't do it, ma'm," the boy repeated. "Directly I got out of the gate, I started off to run home. I hadn't gone not twenty yards when I heard a smash; but I wasn't going for to stop to see what it was. It weren't no business of mine, and that's all I know about it."

"Mamma," the younger of the two girls said eagerly, "what he says is quite true. You know you let me run down the village with the jelly for Mrs. Thomson's child, and as I was coming down the road I saw a boy come out of the gate of the school and run away; and then I heard a noise of broken glass, and I saw another boy jump over the hedge opposite, and run, too. He came my way and, directly he saw me, he ran to a gate and climbed over."

"Do you know who it was, Kate?" Mrs. Ellison asked.

"Yes, mamma. It was Tom Thorne."

"Is Thomas Thorne here?" Mrs. Ellison asked in a loud voice.

There was a general turning of the heads of the children to the point where a boy, somewhat bigger than the rest, had been apparently studying his lessons with great diligence.

"Come here, Tom Thorne," Mrs. Ellison said.

The boy slouched up with a sullen face.

"You hear what my daughter says, Tom. What have you to say in reply?"

"I didn't throw the stone at the window," the boy replied. "I chucked it at a sparrow, and it weren't my fault if it missed him and broke the window."

"I should say it was your fault, Tom," Mrs. Ellison said sharply—"very much your fault, if you throw a great stone at a bird without taking care to see what it may hit. But that is nothing to your fault in letting another boy be punished for what you did. I shall report the matter to the squire, and he will speak to your father about it. You are a wicked, bad boy.

"Mr. White, I will speak to you outside."

Followed by her daughters, Mrs. Ellison went out; Kate giving a little nod, in reply to the grateful look that Reuben Whitney cast towards her, and his muttered:

"Thank you, miss."

"Walk on, my dears," Mrs. Ellison said. "I will overtake you, in a minute or two.

"This will not do, Mr. White," she said, when she was alone with the master. "I have told you before that I did not approve of your thrashing so much, and now it is proved that you punish without any sufficient cause, and upon suspicion only. I shall report the case at once to the squire and, unless I am greatly mistaken, you will have to look out for another place."

"I am very sorry, Mrs. Ellison, indeed I am; and it is not often I use the cane, now. If it had been anyone else, I might have believed him; but Reuben Whitney is always in mischief."

"No wonder he is in mischief," the lady said severely, "if he is punished, without a hearing, for all the misdeeds of others. Well, I shall leave the matter in the squire's hands; but I am sure he will no more approve than I do of the children being ill treated."

Reuben Whitney was the son of a miller, near Tipping. John Whitney had been considered a well-to-do man, but he had speculated in corn and had got into difficulties; and his body was, one day, found floating in the mill dam. No one knew whether it was the result of intention or accident, but the jury of his neighbours who sat upon the inquest gave him the benefit of the doubt, and brought in a verdict of "accidental death." He was but tenant of the mill and, when all the creditors were satisfied, there were only a few pounds remaining for the widow.

With these she opened a little shop in Tipping, with a miscellaneous collection of tinware and cheap ironmongery; cottons, tapes, and small articles of haberdashery; with toys, sweets, and cakes for the children. The profits were small, but the squire, who had known her husband, charged but a nominal rent for the cottage; and this was more than paid by the fruit trees in the garden, which also supplied her with potatoes and vegetables, so that she managed to support her boy and herself in tolerable comfort.

She herself had been the daughter of a tradesman in Lewes, and many wondered that she did not return to her father, upon her husband's death.

But her home had not been a comfortable one, before her marriage; for her father had taken a second wife, and she did not get on well with her stepmother. She thought, therefore, that anything would be better than returning with her boy to a home where, to the mistress at least, she would be most unwelcome.

She had, as a girl, received an education which raised her somewhat above the other villagers of Tipping; and of an evening she was in the habit of helping Reuben with his lessons, and trying to correct the broadness of dialect which he picked up from the other boys. She was an active and bustling woman, managed her little shop well, and kept the garden, with Reuben's assistance, in excellent order.

Mrs. Ellison had, at her first arrival in the village three years before, done much to give her a good start, by ordering that all articles of use for the house, in which she dealt, should be purchased of her; and she highly approved of the energy and independence of the young widow. But lately there had been an estrangement between the squire's wife and the village shopkeeper. Mrs. Ellison, whose husband owned all the houses in the village, as well as the land surrounding it, was accustomed to speak her mind very freely to the wives of the villagers. She was kindness itself, in cases of illness or distress; and her kitchen supplied soups, jellies, and nourishing food to all who required it; but in return, Mrs. Ellison expected her lectures on waste, untidiness, and mismanagement to be listened to with respect and reverence.

She was, then, at once surprised and displeased when, two or three months before, having spoken sharply to Mrs. Whitney as to the alleged delinquencies of Reuben, she found herself decidedly, though not disrespectfully, replied to.

"The other boys are always set against my Reuben," Mrs. Whitney said, "because he is a stranger in the village, and has no father; and whatever is done, they throw it on to him. The boy is not a bad boy, ma'm—not in any way a bad boy. He may get into mischief, like the rest; but he is not a bit worse than others, not half as bad as some of them, and those who have told you that he is haven't told you the truth."

Mrs. Ellison had not liked it. She was not accustomed to be answered, except by excuses and apologies; and Mrs. Whitney's independent manner of speaking came upon her almost as an act of rebellion, in her own kingdom. She was too fair, however, to withdraw her custom from the shop; but from that time she had not, herself, entered it.

Reuben was a source of anxiety to his mother, but this had no reference to his conduct. She worried over his future. The receipts from the shop were sufficient for their wants; and indeed the widow was enabled, from time to time, to lay by a pound against bad times; but she did not see what she was to do with the boy. Almost all the other lads of the village, of the same age, were already in the fields; and Mrs. Whitney felt that she could not much longer keep him idle. The question was, what was she to do with him? That he should not go into the fields she was fully determined, and her great wish was to apprentice him to some trade; but as her father had recently died, she did not see how she was to set about it.

That evening, at dinner, Mrs. Ellison told the squire of the scene in the school room.

"White must go," he said, "that is quite evident. I have seen, for some time, that we wanted a younger man, more abreast of the times than White is; but I don't like turning him adrift altogether. He has been here upwards of thirty years. What am I to do with him?"

Mrs. Ellison could make no suggestion; but she, too, disliked the thought of anyone in the village being turned adrift upon the world.

"The very thing!" the squire exclaimed, suddenly. "We will make him clerk. Old Peters has long been past his work. The old man must be seventy-five, if he's a day, and his voice quavers so that it makes the boys laugh. We will pension him off. He can have his cottage rent free, and three or four shillings a week. I don't suppose it will be for many years. As for White, he cannot be much above sixty. He will fill the place very well.

"I am sure the vicar will agree, for he has been speaking to me, about Peters being past his work, for the last five years. What do you say, my dear?"

"I think that will do very well, William," Mrs. Ellison replied, "and will get over the difficulty altogether."

"So you see, wife, for once that boy of Widow Whitney's was not to blame. I told you you took those stories on trust against him too readily. The boy's a bit of a pickle, no doubt; and I very near gave him a thrashing, myself, a fortnight since, for on going up to the seven-acre field, I found him riding bare backed on that young pony I intended for Kate."

"You don't say so, William!" Mrs. Ellison exclaimed, greatly shocked. "I never heard of such an impudent thing. I really wonder you didn't thrash him."

"Well, perhaps I should have done so, my dear; but the fact is, I caught sight of him some time before he saw me, and he was really sitting her so well that I could not find it in my heart to call out. He was really doing me a service. The pony had never been ridden, and was as wild as a wild goat. Thomas is too old, in fact, to break it in, and I should have had to get someone to do it, and pay him two or three pounds for the job.

"It was not the first time the boy had been on her back, I could see. The pony was not quite broken and, just as I came on the scene, was trying its best to get rid of him; but it couldn't do it, and I could see, by the way he rode her about afterwards, that he had got her completely in hand; and a very pretty-going little thing she will turn out."

"But what did you say to him, William? I am sure I should never stop to think whether he was breaking in the pony, or not, if I saw him riding it about."

"I daresay not, my dear," the squire said, laughing; "but then you see, you have never been a boy; and I have, and can make allowances. Many a pony and horse have I broken in, in my time; and have got on the back of more than one, without my father knowing anything about it."

"Yes, but they were your father's horses, William," Mrs. Ellison persisted. "That makes all the difference."

"I don't suppose it would have made much difference to me," the squire laughed, "at that time. I was too fond of horse flesh, even from a boy, to be particular whose horse it was I got across. However, of course, after waiting till he had done, I gave the young scamp a blowing up."

"Not much of a blowing up, I am sure," Mrs. Ellison said; "and as likely as not, a shilling at the end of it."

"Well, Mary, I must own," the squire said pleasantly, "that a shilling did find its way out of my pocket into his."

"It's too bad of you, William," Mrs. Ellison said indignantly. "Here is this boy, who is notoriously a scapegrace, has the impertinence to ride your horse, and you encourage him in his misdeeds by giving him a shilling."

"Well, my dear, don't you see, I saved two pounds nineteen by the transaction.

"Besides," he added more seriously, "I think the boy has been maligned. I don't fancy he's a bad lad at all. A little mischief and so on, but none the worse for that. Besides, you know, I knew his father; and have sat many a time on horseback chatting to him, at the door of his mill; and drank more than one glass of good ale, which his wife has brought out to me. I am not altogether easy in my conscience about them. If there had been a subscription got up for the widow at his death, I should have put my name down for twenty pounds; and all that I have done for her is to take eighteen pence a week off that cottage of theirs.

"No, I called the boy to me when he got off, and pretty scared he looked when he saw me. When he came up, I asked him how he dared to ride my horses about, without my leave. Of course he said he was sorry, which meant nothing; and he added, as a sort of excuse, that he used from a child to ride the horses at the mill down to the ford for water; and that his father generally had a young one or two, in that paddock of his by the mill, and he used often to ride them; and seeing the pony one day, galloping about the field and kicking up its heels, he wondered whether he could sit a horse still, and especially whether he could keep on that pony's back. Then he set to, to try.

"The pony flung him several times, at first; and no wonder, as he had no saddle, and only a piece of old rope for a bridle; but he mastered him at last, and he assured me that he had never used the stick, and certainly he had not one when I saw him. I told him, of course, that he knew he ought not to have done it; but that, as he had taken it in hand, he might finish it. I said that I intended to have it broken in for Kate, and that he had best get a bit of sacking and put it on sideways, to accustom the pony to carry a lady. Then I gave him a shilling, and told him I would give him five more, when he could tell me the pony was sufficiently broken and gentle to carry Kate."

Mrs. Ellison shook her head in disapprobation.

"It is of no use, William, my talking to the villagers as to the ways of their boys, if that is the way you counteract my advice."

"But I don't always, my dear," the squire said blandly. "For instance, I shall go round tomorrow morning with my dog whip to Thorne's; and I shall offer him the choice of giving that boy of his the soundest thrashing he ever had, while I stand by to see it, or of going out of his house at the end of the quarter.

"I rather hope he will choose the latter alternative. That beer shop of his is the haunt of all the idle fellows in the village. I have a strong suspicion that he is in league with the poachers, if he doesn't poach himself; and the first opportunity I get of laying my finger upon him, out he goes."

A few days later when Kate Ellison issued from the gate of the house, which lay just at the end of the village, with the basket containing some jelly and medicine for a sick child, she found Reuben Whitney awaiting her. He touched his cap.

"Please, miss, I made bold to come here, to thank you for having cleared me."

"But I couldn't help clearing you, Reuben, for you see, I knew it wasn't you."

"Well, miss, it was very kind, all the same; and I am very much obliged to you."

"But why do you get into scrapes?" the girl said. "If you didn't, you wouldn't be suspected of other things. Mamma said, the other day, you got into more scrapes than any boy in the village; and you look nice, too. Why do you do it?"

"I don't know why I do it, miss," Reuben said shamefacedly. "I suppose it's because I don't go into the fields, like most of the other boys; and haven't got much to do. But there's no great harm in them, miss. They are just larks, nothing worse."

"You don't do really bad things?" the girl asked.

"No, miss, I hope not."

"And you don't tell stories, do you?"

"No, miss, never. If I do anything and I am asked, I always own it. I wouldn't tell a lie to save myself from a licking."

"That's right," the girl said graciously.

She caught somewhat of her mother's manner, from going about with her to the cottages; and it seemed quite natural, to her, to give her advice to this village scapegrace.

"Well, try not to do these sort of things again, Reuben; because I like you, and I don't like to hear people say you are the worst boy in the village, and I don't think you are. Good-bye," and Kate Ellison proceeded on her way.

Reuben smiled as he looked after her. Owing to his memory of his former position at the mill, and to his mother's talk and teaching, Reuben did not entertain the same feeling of respect, mingled with fear, for the squire's family which was felt by the village in general. Instead of being two years younger than himself, the girl had spoken as gravely as if she had been twenty years his senior, and Reuben could not help a smile of amusement.

"She is a dear little lady," he said, as he looked after her; "and it's only natural she should talk like her mother. But Mrs. Ellison means well, too, mother says; and as for the squire, he is a good fellow. I expected he would have given it to me the other day.

"Well, now I will go up to the pony. One more lesson, and I think a baby might ride it."

As he walked along, he met Tom Thorne. There had been war between them, since the affair of the broken window. Reuben had shown the other no animosity on the subject as, having been cleared, he had felt in no way aggrieved; but Tom Thorne was very sore over it. In the first place, he had been found out; and although Reuben himself had said nothing to him, respecting his conduct in allowing him to be flogged for the offence which he himself had committed, others had not been so reticent, and he had had a hard time of it in the village. Secondly, he had been severely thrashed by his father, in the presence of the squire; the former laying on the lash with a vigour which satisfied Mr. Ellison, the heartiness of the thrashing being due, not to any indignation at the fault, but because the boy's conduct had excited the squire's anger; which Thorne, for many reasons, was anxious to deprecate. He was his landlord, and had the power to turn him out at a quarter's notice; and as there was no possibility of obtaining any other house near, and he was doing by no means a bad trade, he was anxious to keep on good terms with him.

Tom Thorne was sitting on a gate, as Reuben passed.

"You think you be a fine fellow, Reuben, but I will be even with you, some day."

"You can be even with me now," Reuben said, "if you like to get off that gate."

"I bain't afeared of you, Reuben, don't you go to think it; only I ain't going to do any fighting now. Feyther says if I get into any more rows, he will pay me out; so I can't lick you now, but some day I will be even with you."

"That's a good excuse," Reuben said scornfully. "However, I don't want to fight if you don't, only you keep your tongue to yourself. I don't want to say nothing to you, if you don't say nothing to me. You played me a dirty trick the other day, and you got well larruped for it, so I don't owe you any grudge; but mind you, I don't want any more talk about your getting even with me, for if you do give me any more of it I will fetch you one on the nose, and then you will have a chance of getting even, at once."

Tom Thorne held his tongue, only relieving his feelings by making a grimace after Reuben, as the latter passed on. In the various contests among the boys of the village, Reuben had proved himself so tough an adversary that, although Tom Thorne was heavier and bigger, he did not care about entering upon what would be, at best, a doubtful contest with him.

Contenting himself, therefore, with another muttered, "I will be even with you some day," he strolled home to his father's ale house.

The change at the school was very speedily made. The squire generally carried out his resolutions while they were hot and, on the very day after his conversation with his wife on the subject, he went first to the vicar and arranged for the retirement of the clerk, and the instalment of White in his place; and then went to the school house, and informed the master of his intention. The latter had been expecting his dismissal, since Mrs. Ellison had spoken to him on the previous day; and the news which the squire gave him was a relief to him. His emoluments, as clerk, would be smaller than those he received as schoolmaster; but while he would not be able to discharge the duties of the latter for very much longer, for he felt the boys were getting too much for him, he would be able to perform the very easy work entailed by the clerkship for many years to come. It was, too, a position not without dignity; and indeed, in the eyes of the village the clerk was a personage of far greater importance than the schoolmaster. He therefore thankfully accepted the offer, and agreed to give up the school as soon as a substitute could be found.

In those days anyone was considered good enough for a village schoolmaster, and the post was generally filled by men who had failed as tradesmen, and in everything else they put their hands to; and whose sole qualification for the office was that they were able to read and write. Instead of advertising, however, in the county paper, the squire wrote to an old college friend, who was now in charge of a London parish, and asked him to choose a man for the post.

"I don't want a chap who will cram all sorts of new notions into the heads of the children," the squire said. "I don't think it would do them any good, or fit them any better for their stations. The boys have got to be farm labourers, and the girls to be their wives; and if they can read really well, and write fairly, it's about as much as they want in the way of learning; but I think that a really earnest sort of man might do them good, otherwise. A schoolmaster, in my mind, should be the clergyman's best assistant. I don't know, my dear fellow, that I can explain in words more exactly what I mean; but I think you will understand me, and will send down the sort of man I want.

"The cottage is a comfortable one, there's a good bit of garden attached to it, and I don't mind paying a few shillings a week more than I do now, to get the sort of man I want. If he has a wife so much the better. She might teach the girls to sew, which would be, to nine out of ten, a deal more use than reading and writing; and if she could use her needle, and make up dresses and that sort of thing, she might add to their income. Not one woman in five in the village can make her own clothes, and they have to go to a place three miles away to get them done."

A week later the squire received an answer from his friend, saying that he had chosen a man, and his wife, whom he thought would suit.

"The poor fellow was rather a cripple," he said. "He is a wood engraver by trade, but he fell downstairs and hurt his back. The doctor who attended him at the hospital spoke to me about him. He said that he might, under favourable circumstances, get better in time; but that he was delicate, and absolutely needed change of air and a country life. I have seen him several times, and have been much struck with his intelligence. He has been much depressed at being forbidden to work, but has cheered up greatly since I told him of your offer. I have no doubt he will do well.

"I have selected him, not only for that reason, but because his wife is as suitable as he is. She is an admirable young woman, and was a dressmaker before he married her. She has supported them both ever since he was hurt, months ago. She is delighted at the idea of the change for, although the money will be very much less than he earned at his trade, she has always been afraid of his health giving way; and is convinced that fresh air, and the garden you speak of, will put new life into him."

The squire was not quite satisfied with the letter; but, as he told himself, he could not expect to get a man trained specially as a schoolmaster to accept the post; and at any rate, if the man was not satisfactory his wife was likely to be so. He accordingly ordered his groom to take the light cart and drive over to Lewes, the next day, to meet the coach when it came in; and to bring over the new schoolmaster, his wife, and their belongings.

Mrs. Ellison at once went down to the village, and got a woman to scrub the cottage from top to bottom, and put everything tidy. The furniture went with the house, and had been provided by the squire. Mrs. Ellison went over it, and ordered a few more things to be sent down from the house to make it more comfortable for a married couple and, driving over to Lewes, ordered a carpet, curtains, and a few other little comforts for it.

James Shrewsbury was, upon his arrival, much pleased with his cottage, which contrasted strongly with the room in a crowded street which he had occupied in London; and his wife was still more pleased.

"I am sure we shall be happy and comfortable here, James," she said, "and the air feels so fresh and pure that I am convinced you will soon get strong and well again. What is money to health? I am sure I shall be ten times as happy, here, as I was when you were earning three or four times as much, in London."

The squire and Mrs. Ellison came down the next morning, at the opening of the school; and after a chat with the new schoolmaster and his wife, the squire accompanied the former into the school room.

"Look here, boys and girls," he said, "Mr. Shrewsbury has come down from London to teach you. He has been ill, and is not very strong. I hope you will give him no trouble, and I can tell you it will be the worse for you, if you do. I am going to look into matters myself; and I shall have a report sent me in, regularly, as to how each of you is getting on, with a special remark as to conduct; and I can tell you, if any of you are troublesome you will find me down at your father's, in no time."

The squire's words had considerable effect, and an unusual quiet reigned in the school, after he had left and the new schoolmaster opened a book.

They soon found that his method of teaching was very different to that which they were accustomed to. There was no shouting or thumping on the desk with the cane, no pulling of ears or cuffing of heads. Everything was explained quietly and clearly; and when they went out of the school, all agreed that the new master was a great improvement on Master White, while the master himself reported to his wife that he had got on better than he had expected.

Chapter 2
The Poisoned Dog

The boys soon felt that Mr. Shrewsbury really wished to teach them, and that he was ready to assist those who wanted to get on. In the afternoon the schoolmaster's wife started a sewing class for the girls and, a week or two after he came, the master announced that such of the elder class of boys and girls who chose to come, in the evening, to his cottage could do so for an hour; and that he and the boys would read, by turns, some amusing book while the girls worked. Only Reuben Whitney and two or three others at first availed themselves of the invitation, but these spoke so highly of their evening that the number soon increased. Three quarters of an hour were spent in reading some interesting work of travel or adventure, and then the time was occupied in talking over what they had read, and in explaining anything which they did not understand; and as the evenings were now long and dark, the visits to the schoolmaster soon came to be regarded as a privilege, and proved an incentive to work to those in the lower classes, only those in the first place being admitted to them.

Reuben worked hard all through the winter, and made very rapid progress; the schoolmaster, seeing how eager he was to get on, doing everything in his power to help him forward, and lending him books to study at home. One morning in the spring, the squire looked in at Mrs. Whitney's shop.

"Mrs. Whitney," he said, "I don't know what you are thinking of doing with that boy of yours. Mr. Shrewsbury gives me an excellent account of him, and says that he is far and away the cleverest and most studious of the boys. I like the lad, and owe him a good turn for having broken in that pony for my daughter; besides, for his father's sake I should like to help him on. Now, in the first place, what are you thinking of doing with him?"

"I am sure I am very much obliged to you," Mrs. Whitney said. "I was thinking, when he gets a little older, of apprenticing him to some trade, but he is not fourteen yet."

"The best thing you can do, Mrs. Whitney. Let it be some good trade, where he can use his wits—not a butcher, a baker, or a tailor, or anything of that sort. I should say an upholsterer, or a mill wright, or some trade where his intelligence can help him on. When the time comes I shall be glad to pay his apprentice fees for him, and perhaps, when you tell me what line he has chosen, a word from me to one of the tradesmen in Lewes may be a help. In the meantime, that is not what I have specially come about. Young Finch, who looks to my garden, is going to leave; and if you like, your boy can have the place. My gardener knows his business thoroughly, and the boy can learn under him. I will pay him five shillings a week. It will break him into work a little, and he is getting rather old for the school now. I have spoken to Shrewsbury, and he says that, if the boy is disposed to go on studying in the evening, he will direct his work and help him on."

"Thank you kindly, sir," Mrs. Whitney said. "I think it will just be the thing, for a year or so, before he is apprenticed. He was saying only last night that he was the biggest boy in the school; and though I know he likes learning, he would like to be helping me, and feels somehow that it isn't right that he should be going on schooling, while all the other boys at his age are doing something. Not that I want him to earn money, for the shop keeps us both; but it's what he thinks about it."

"That's natural enough, Mrs. Whitney, and anything the boy earns with me, you see, you can put by, and it will come in useful to him some day."

Reuben was glad when he heard of the arrangement; for although, as his mother had said, he was fond of school, he yet felt it as a sort of reproach that, while others of his age were earning money, he should be doing nothing. He accepted the offer of the schoolmaster to continue to work at his studies in the evening, and in a week he was installed in Tom Finch's place.

The arrangement was not the squire's original idea, but that of his younger daughter, who felt a sort of proprietary interest in Reuben; partly because her evidence had cleared him of the accusation of breaking the windows, partly because he had broken in the pony for her; so when she heard that the boy was leaving, she had at once asked her father that Reuben should take his place.

"I think he is a good boy, papa," she said; "and if he was clever enough to break in my pony, I am sure he will be clever enough to wheel the wheelbarrow and pull weeds."

"I should think he would, lassie," her father said, laughing, "although it does not exactly follow. Still, if you guarantee that he is a good boy, I will see about it."

"Mamma doesn't think he is a very good boy," Kate said; "but you see, papa, mamma is a woman, and perhaps she doesn't understand boys and girls as well as I do. I think he's good, and he told me he never told stories."

The squire laughed.

"I don't know what your mamma would say to that, puss; nor whether she would agree that you understand boys and girls better than she does. However, I will take your opinion this time, and give Reuben a chance."

The subject was not mentioned again in Kate's hearing, but she was greatly pleased, one morning, at seeing Reuben at work in the gardens.

"Good morning, Reuben," she said.

"Good morning, miss," he replied, touching his hat.

"I am glad you have come in Tom's place, and I hope you will be good, and not get into scrapes, for I told papa I thought you would not; and you see, if you do, he will turn round and blame me."

"I will try not to get into scrapes, Miss Kate," Reuben said. "I don't do it often, you know, and I don't think there will be much chance of it, here."

Kate nodded and walked on, and Reuben went about his work.

There was, however, much more opportunity for getting into scrapes than Reuben imagined, although the scrapes were not of the kind he had pictured. Being naturally careless, he had not been there a week before, in his eagerness to get home to a particularly interesting book, he forgot to carry out his orders to shut the cucumber frames and, a sharp frost coming on in the night, the plants were all killed; to the immense indignation of the gardener, who reported the fact, with a very serious face, to the squire.

"I am afraid that boy will never do, squire. Such carelessness I never did see, and them plants was going on beautifully."

"Confound the young rascal!" the squire said wrathfully, for he was fond of cucumbers. "I will speak to him myself. This sort of thing will never do."

And accordingly, the squire spoke somewhat sharply to Reuben, who was really sorry for the damage his carelessness had caused; and he not only promised the squire that it should not occur again, but mentally resolved very firmly that it should not. He felt very shamefaced when Kate passed him in the garden, with a serious shake of her head, signifying that she was shocked that he had thus early got into a scrape, and discredited her recommendation.

The lesson was a useful one. Henceforth Reuben paid closer attention to his work, and even the gardener, who regarded boys as his great trial in life, expressed himself satisfied with him.

"Since that affair of the cucumbers I must own, squire," he said a month later, "that he is the best boy I have come across. He attends to what I say and remembers it, and I find I can trust him to do jobs that I have never been able to trust boys with, before. He seems to take an interest in it, and as he is well spoken and civil, he ought to get on and make a good gardener, in time."

"I am glad to hear a good account of him," the squire replied. "He is sharp and intelligent, and will make his way in life, or I am mistaken. His father was an uncommonly clever fellow, though he made a mess of it, just at the end; and I think the boy takes after him."

Among Reuben's other duties was that of feeding and attending to the dogs. These consisted of two setters, a pointer, and a large house dog, who was chained up at the entrance to the stables. Reuben was soon excellent friends with the sporting dogs, but the watchdog, who had probably been teased by Reuben's predecessor, always growled and showed his teeth when he went near him; and Reuben never dared venture within the length of his chain, but pushed the bowl containing his food just within his reach.

One day, he had been sent on an errand to the stables. He forgot the dog and ran close to the kennel. The animal at once sprang out. Reuben made a rush, but he was not quick enough, and the dog caught him by the leg. Reuben shouted, and the coachman ran out and, seizing a fork, struck the dog and compelled him to loose his hold.

"Has he bit you badly, Reuben?"

"Well, he has bit precious hard," Reuben replied. "I think he has nearly taken a piece out of my calf," as, on pulling up his trousers, he showed his leg streaming with blood.

"Put it under the pump, lad. I will pump on it," the coachman said. "He's a bad-tempered brute, and I wonder the squire keeps it."

"The brute ought to be killed," Reuben grumbled angrily. "I have never teased it or worried it, in any way. I wish you had stuck that fork into him, instead of hitting him with it. If you hadn't been within reach, he would have taken the bit out of me. He will kill somebody some day, and it were best to kill him, first."

The gardener pumped for some time on Reuben's leg; and then, going into the kitchen, he got some strips of rag from the cook and bound it up.

"You had best go home now," he said. "I will tell the gardener, when he comes round, what has happened to you. I doubt you will have to lay up, for a day or two."

As Reuben limped home, he met Tom Thorne walking with another boy.

"Hello, Reuben!" the latter exclaimed. "What's come to you? Yer trousers bee all tore."

"That brute of a house dog at the squire's has had hold of me," Reuben answered. "The savage beast has had a try, a good many times; but this time he got hold, and he has bit me pretty sharp."

Reuben had to keep his leg quiet for three days but, the third evening, he was well enough to go down the village to the schoolhouse. After the lesson was over he walked for some distance up the road, for his leg was very stiff; and he thought it would be a good thing to try and walk it off, as he intended to go to work next morning. On getting up early in the morning, however, he found it was still stiff and sore; but he thought he had better go and try to work for a bit.

"I am glad you are back again," the gardener said, when he saw him, "for there's a lot of work on hand; but I see you are still lame. The coachman tells me it were a nasty bite."

"It's pretty sore still," Reuben replied, "and I don't think I can walk about much; but I thought I might help in some other way."

"Very well," the gardener said. "There are a lot of plants which want shifting into larger pots. You do them, and I will take up the fork and dig up that piece of ground I want to put the young lettuces into."

Reuben worked hard till half-past eight, and then went off to his breakfast. On his return, he was told the squire wished to speak to him.

"It's about that dog, I expect," the gardener remarked. "I suppose you know he were poisoned last night."

"No, I didn't know," Reuben replied; "but it's a precious good job. I wish he had been poisoned before he got his teeth into me."

Reuben, on going round to the back door, was shown into the library, where the squire was sitting. The coachman was with him.

"Now then, Reuben," the squire said, "I want you to tell me the truth about this matter. The coachman told me, three days ago, that you had been bitten by the yard dog, and I made up my mind to get rid of him, on the first opportunity; but I find he was poisoned, yesterday evening."

He stopped as if expecting Reuben to say something; but the boy, having nothing to say, merely replied:

"Yes, sir, so the gardener has told me."

"What do you know about it, Reuben?"

"I don't know anything about it, sir," Reuben replied, opening his eyes.

"Now, look here, lad," the squire said gravely, "I am disposed to think well of you; and although I consider it a serious offence your poisoning the dog, I shall consider it very much worse if you deny it."

"But I didn't poison it, sir," Reuben affirmed. "I never dreamt of such a thing."

The squire set his lips hard together.

"Just tell me your story over again," he said to the coachman.

"Well, yesterday evening, squire, I went down into the village to buy some 'bacca. Just as I got back to the gate, out runs a boy. It was too dark for me to see his face, but I naturally supposed it were Reuben, so I said, 'Hello, Reuben, how's the leg?' But the moment I spoke, he turned off from the path and ran away.

"Well, I thought it was queer, but I went on to the stable. About a quarter of an hour afterwards, and as I was a-cleaning up the bits, I heard Wolf howl. He kept on at it, so I took a lantern and went out to see what was the matter. He was rolling about, and seemed very bad. I stood a-looking at him, wondering what were best to do, when sudden he gave a sort of yell, and rolled over, and he was dead. I thought it was no good telling you about it till this morning; and thinking it over, and seeing how sudden like it was, I come to the 'pinion as how he had been poisoned; and naturally thinking that, as he had bit Reuben, and as how Reuben said he ought to be killed, and seeing as I had met the boy a quarter an hour afore the dog was took bad, it came to me as how he had done it.

"This morning I knew for certain as the dog had been poisoned, for just outside of the reach of his chain there was that piece of paper a-lying, as you have got before you."

It was a piece of blue paper, about four inches square, on which was printed: "Rat poison."

"You hear that, Reuben? What have you to say?" the squire asked.

"I have got nothing to say, sir," Reuben answered, "except that whoever the boy was, it wasn't me, and that I know nothing about it."

"Well, Reuben, it will be easy for you to clear yourself, by saying where you were at the time.

"What o'clock was it, Robert, that you saw the boy?"

"It was just a quarter past eight, squire. The quarter struck just as I opened the gate."

"Were you out or at home at that hour, Reuben?"

"I was out, sir. I went to the schoolmaster's."

"What time did you leave there?"

"I left at eight, sir."

"Then if you got in just after eight, it is clear that you were not the boy," the squire said. "If your mother tells me that you were in at five minutes past eight, that settles the question, as far as you are concerned."

"I didn't get in till half-past eight, sir," Reuben said. "I walked about for a bit, after I came out from school, to try and get the stiffness out of my leg, so as to be able to come to work this morning."

"Was anyone with you, Reuben? Is there anyone to say what you did with yourself, between eight and half-past eight?"

"No, sir," Reuben said quietly. "I didn't speak to a soul; and didn't see a soul, so far as I know, from the time I came out of the gate of the schoolhouse till I got home."

"Does your mother sell packets of this poison?" the squire said, pointing to the paper.

Reuben looked at the paper.

"Yes, sir; I believe she does."

"Well, my lad," the squire said, "you must acknowledge that the case looks very ugly against you. You are known to have borne bad feelings against the dog; naturally enough, I admit. A boy about your size was seen by Robert in the dark, coming out of the gate; and that he was there for no good purpose is proved by the fact that he ran away when spoken to. A quarter of an hour later, the dog dies of poison. That poison you certainly could get at home and, by your own admission, you were out and about at the time the dog was poisoned. The case looks very bad against you."

"I don't care how bad it looks," Reuben said, passionately. "It wasn't me, squire, if that were the last word I ever had to speak."

"Very well," the squire said coldly. "In my mind, the evidence is overwhelming against you. I have no intention of pursuing the matter further; nor will I, for your father's and mother's sake, bring public disgrace upon you; but of course I shall not retain you here further, nor have anything to do with you, in the future."

Without a word, Reuben turned and left the room. Had he spoken, he would have burst into a passion of tears. With a white face, he walked through the village and entered his mother's shop.

"What? Back again, Reuben?" she said. "I thought your leg was too bad to work."

"It isn't my leg, mother," he said, in a choking voice. "The squire has dismissed me. He says I have poisoned his dog."

"Says you poisoned his dog, Reuben! Whatever put such an idea into his head?"

"The coachman saw a boy coming out of the yard, at a quarter past eight last night. It was too dark for him to say for certain, but he thought it was me. A quarter of an hour later the dog died of poison, and this morning they picked up a cover of one of those rat powders you sell. I couldn't say where I was at a quarter past eight, when the coachman saw the boy; for as you know, mother, I told you I had walked out a bit, after I came out from the school, to get the stiffness out of my leg. So, altogether, the squire has made up his mind 'tis me, and so he has sent me away."

Reuben had summed up the points against himself in a broken voice, and now broke into a passion of tears. His mother tried in vain to pacify him; but indeed her own indignation, at her boy being charged with such a thing, was so great that she could do little to console him.

"It's shameful!" she exclaimed, over and over again. "I call it downright wicked of the squire to suspect you of such a thing."

"Well, mother, it does look very bad against me," Reuben said, wiping his eyes at last, "and I don't know as the squire is so much to be blamed for suspecting me. I know and you know that it wasn't me; but there's no reason why the squire should know it. Somebody has poisoned his dog, and that somebody is a boy. He knows that I was unfriendly with the dog so, putting things together, I don't see as he could help suspecting me, and only my word the other way. It seems to me as if somebody must have done it to get me in a row, for I don't know that the dog had bit anyone else. If it is anyone, I expect it's Tom Thorne. He has never been friends with me, since that affair of the school window."

"I will go at once and speak to his father," Mrs. Whitney said, taking down her bonnet from the wall.

"No, mother, you can't do that," Reuben exclaimed. "We have got nothing against him. The squire has ten times as good reason to suspect me, as I have to suspect Tom Thorne; so as we know the squire's wrong, it's ten times as likely we shall be wrong. Besides, if he did it, of course he would deny it, he is the worst liar in the village; and then folks would say I wasn't satisfied with doing it myself, but I wanted to throw the blame on to him, just as he did on me before. No, it won't do, mother."

Mrs. Whitney saw that it wouldn't do, and sat down again. Reuben sat thinking, for some time.

"I must go away, mother," he said at last. "I can't stop here. Every one in the village will get to know of it, and they will point at me as the boy as poisoned the squire's dog, and then lied about it. I couldn't stand that, mother."

"And you sha'n't stand it, my boy," Mrs. Whitney said, "not a day. I will give up the cottage and move into Lewes, at once. I didn't go there before, for I am known there, and don't like folk to see how much I have come down in the world."

"No, mother, you stop here, and I will go up to London. They say there is lots of work there, and I suppose I can get on as well as another."

"I will not hear of your doing such a thing. I should never expect to hear of you again. I should always be thinking that you had got run over, or were starving in the streets, or dying in a workhouse. No, Reuben, my plan's best. It's just silliness my not liking to settle in Lewes; for of course it's better going where one is known, and I should be lost in a strange place. No; I daresay I shall find a cottage there, and I shall manage to get a living somehow—perhaps open a little shop like this, and then you can be apprenticed, and live at home."

An hour later, Mrs. Ellison called. Reuben had gone upstairs to lie down, for his leg was very painful. Mrs. Whitney did not give her visitor time to begin.

"I know what you have called about, Mrs. Ellison, and I don't want to talk about it with you. The squire has grievously wronged my boy. I wouldn't have believed it of him, but he's done it; so now, ma'm, I give a week's notice of this house, and here's my rent up to that time, and I will send you the key when I go. And now, ma'm, as I don't want any words about it, I think it will be better if you go, at once."

Mrs. Ellison hesitated a moment. Never, from the time she entered the village as the squire's wife, had she been thus spoken to; but she saw at once, in Mrs. Whitney's face, that it were better not to reply to her; and that her authority as the squire's wife had, for once, altogether vanished. She therefore took up the money which Mrs. Whitney had laid on the counter and, without a word, left the shop.

"I do believe, William," she said as, greatly ruffled and indignant, she gave an account of the interview to the squire, "that the woman would have slapped my face, if I had said anything. She is the most insolent creature I ever met."

"Well, my dear," the squire said seriously, "I can hardly wonder at the poor woman's indignation. She has had a hard time of it, and this must be a sad blow. Naturally she believes in her son's innocence, and we must not altogether blame her, if she resents his dismissal. It's a sad business altogether, and I know it will be a worry and trouble to me for months. Mind, I don't doubt that the boy did it; it does not seem possible that it should be otherwise. Still, it is not absolutely proved; and upon my word, I wish now I had said nothing at all about it. I like the boy, and I liked his father before him; and as this story must get about, it cannot but do him serious damage. Altogether it is a most tiresome business, and I would give a hundred pounds if it hadn't taken place."

"I really do not see why you should worry about it, William. The boy has always been a troublesome boy, and perhaps this lesson may do him good."

The squire did not attempt to argue the question. He felt really annoyed and put out and, after wandering over the ground and stables, he went down to the schoolhouse after the children had been dismissed.

"Have you heard, Shrewsbury, about that boy Whitney?"

"No, sir, I have heard nothing about him," the schoolmaster said. "He was here yesterday evening, as usual. His leg is no worse, I hope. Those dog bites are always nasty things."

"I wish it had been worse," the squire said testily; "then he would have been laid up quietly at home, instead of being about mischief."

"Why, what has he done, sir?" the schoolmaster asked, in surprise.

The squire related the history of the dog's death, and of his interview with Reuben. The schoolmaster looked serious, and grieved.

"What do you think of the matter, Shrewsbury?" the squire asked, when he had finished.

"I would rather not give any opinion," the schoolmaster replied quietly.

"That means you think I am wrong," the squire said quickly. "Well, say it out, man; you won't offend me. I am half inclined to think I was wrong, myself; and I would as lief be told so, as not."

"I don't say you are wrong, sir," the schoolmaster said, "except that I think you assumed the boy's guilt too much as a matter of course. Now, I have seen a great deal of him. I have a great liking for him, and believe him to be not only a singularly intelligent and hard-working lad, but a perfectly truthful and open one. I allow that the circumstances are much against him; but the evidence is, to my mind, completely overbalanced by his absolute denial. You must remember that he saw that you were quite convinced of his guilt; and that, in your eyes, his denial would be an aggravation of the offence. Therefore you see he had no strong motive for telling a lie.

"Who killed your dog I do not know but, from my knowledge of his character and assurance of his truthfulness, I am perfectly convinced that Reuben Whitney did not do it. The boy is, in some ways, very superior to the other lads I teach. I hear that his father was in a good position, as a miller; and his mother is of a different class, altogether, to the other women of the village. The boy has a certain refinement about him, a thoughtfulness and consideration which set him apart from the others. Mischievous and somewhat inclined to be noisy as he generally is, on days when I have not felt quite equal to my work he would notice it at once and, without saying a word, would, by his quietness and attention to his work, try to save me trouble; and I have heard him try to quiet the others, as they trooped out. The boy has a good heart as well as a good intellect, and nothing save his own confession would make me believe that he poisoned your dog."

"But he said he wished it was killed," the squire urged, as in defence of his own opinion.

"He said so, squire, at the time he was smarting with the pain of a severe bite; and I think probably he meant no more than a man who, under the same circumstances, would say, 'Confound the dog!' or even a stronger oath."

Mr. Ellison was silenced, for when in wrath he was, himself, given to use strong expressions.

"I don't know what to say, Shrewsbury," he said at last. "I am afraid I have made a mess of it; but certainly, as I first heard it, the case seemed to admit of no doubt. 'Pon my word, I don't know what to do. My wife has just been up to see Mrs. Whitney, and the woman blazed out at her, and wouldn't let her say a word, but gave notice that she should give up the house at the end of the week. If it hadn't been for that, I might have done something; but Mrs. Ellison was very much aggrieved at her manner. Altogether, it's one of the most annoying things I ever had to do with."

In the evening the schoolmaster put on his hat and went up, with his wife, to Mrs. Whitney. The women had seen a good deal of each other, as they both stood somewhat apart from the rest of the village and, in thought and speech, differed widely from the labourers' wives; and on evenings when the sewing class did not meet, the schoolmaster's wife often went up for an hour or two to Mrs. Whitney's, or the latter came down to the Shrewsburys' cottage.

"We have come up, Mrs. Whitney," the schoolmaster said as they entered, "to tell you how sorry we are to hear that you are going to leave, and that we are still more sorry for the cause. Of course, neither my wife nor myself believe for a moment that Reuben poisoned the squire's dog. The idea is preposterous. I told the squire as much, today."

Mrs. Whitney burst into tears. She had kept up all day, sustained partly by indignation, and partly by the desire that Reuben should not see that she felt it; but the thought that all the village would believe Reuben guilty had cut her to the heart, and she had felt so unwilling to face anyone that, as soon as Mrs. Ellison had left, she had closed the shutters of her little shop; but she broke down, now, from her relief at hearing that someone besides herself believed the boy to be innocent.

"I don't know what I shall do without you, Mrs. Whitney," Mrs. Shrewsbury said, when the widow recovered her composure. "I shall miss you dreadfully. Is it quite settled that you will go?"

"Quite settled, Mrs. Shrewsbury. I wouldn't stop in the squire's house for an hour longer than I could help, after his believing Reuben to be guilty of poisoning his dog, and not believing the boy when he said he had nothing to do with it. He ought to have known my boy better than that. And he coming up only the other day, and pretending he felt a kindness for my dead husband."

"I think the squire was too hasty, Mrs. Whitney," the schoolmaster said. "But you see, he did not know Reuben as we do; and I think, if you will excuse my saying so, you have been a little hasty, too. The squire came in to me to tell me about it, and I could see he was not satisfied in his mind, even before I gave him my positive opinion that Reuben was innocent; and I do think that, if you had not given Mrs. Ellison notice so sharply, the squire would have taken back his words, and said that at any rate, as there was nothing absolutely proved, he would hold his judgment in suspense until the matter was cleared up."

"And having everyone pointing the finger at my boy in the meantime! No, thank you, Mr. Shrewsbury, that would not do for me. I was not a bit hasty. Mrs. Ellison came in here prepared to talk to me about Reuben's wickedness; I saw it in her face, so I wouldn't let her open her lips. If she had, I should have given her a piece of my mind that she wouldn't have forgot, in a hurry."

"I can quite understand your feelings, Mrs. Whitney," the schoolmaster said, "and I have no doubt I should have acted as you did, if a son of mine had been suspected in the same way. Still, I think it's a pity; for if Reuben had stayed here, there would have been more chance of the matter being cleared up. However, we won't talk about that now. Now tell me, what are your plans?"

Mrs. Whitney told her visitors what she had determined upon. As Lewes was only four miles off, the schoolmaster said that he and his wife would sometimes come over to see her; and that he hoped that Reuben, whatever trade he was apprenticed to, would still go on with his studies. He would give him any advice or assistance in his power.

The next day Mrs. Whitney and Reuben moved, with all their belongings, to Lewes.

Chapter 3
The Burglary At The Squire's

"What is that woman Whitney going to do with her boy?" the squire asked the schoolmaster, when he happened to meet him in the village about a month after she had left. "Have you heard?"

"Nothing is settled yet, sir. My wife had a letter from her, two or three days ago, saying that she had been disappointed in getting Penfold the mill wright to take him. He wanted fifty pounds premium, and she could only afford to pay twenty, so she is looking out for something else. You have heard nothing more that would throw any light on that affair, squire?"

"No, and don't suppose I ever shall. Have you any opinion about it?"

"My opinion is that of Reuben, himself," the schoolmaster said. "He believes that someone did it who had a grudge against him, on purpose, to throw suspicion on him."

"Who should have a grudge against him?" the squire asked.

"Well, squire, there was one boy in the village who had, rightly or wrongly, a grudge against Reuben. That is Tom Thorne. Reuben has not a shadow of evidence that it was this boy, but the lad has certainly been his enemy ever since that affair of breaking the windows of the school, just before I came here. Thorne, you know, did it, but allowed Reuben to be punished for the offence; and the truth would never have been known had it not been, as I heard, that your daughter happened to see the stone thrown. Since that time there has been bad blood between the boys. I do not for a moment say that Thorne poisoned your dog. Still, the boys are near enough of a size for one to be mistaken for the other in the dark; and Thorne knew that Reuben had been bitten by the dog, for Reuben spoke to another boy about it, that afternoon, while Thorne was standing by. Of course, this is but the vaguest suspicion. Still, if you ask my opinion, I should say that I consider, from what I have heard of the character of Tom Thorne, that he would be much more likely to poison the dog, in order to get Reuben into disgrace, than Reuben would be to do so out of revenge because the dog had bitten him."

The squire took off his hat, and passed his hands through his hair, in perplexity.

"I don't know what to think, Shrewsbury," he said. "It may be as you say. I look upon Thorne as the worst character in the village, and likely enough his son may take after him. That ale house of his is the resort of all the idle fellows about. I have strong reason to believe he is in alliance with the poachers. The first time I get a chance, out he goes. I have only been waiting, for some time, for an opportunity. I can't very well turn him out of his house without some excuse.

"What did you say was the name of the mill wright at Lewes Mrs. Whitney was wanting to get her son with?"

The schoolmaster repeated the name, which the squire jotted down in a notebook.

"Look here, Shrewsbury," he said, "don't you mention to Mrs. Whitney that you spoke to me about this matter. Do you understand?"

"I understand, sir," the schoolmaster said.

And he was not surprised when, a few days afterwards, his wife received a letter from Mrs. Whitney, saying that Mr. Penfold had come in to say that he had changed his mind, and that he would take Reuben as his apprentice for twenty pounds; adding, to her surprise, that he should give him half a crown a week for the first year, and gradually raise his pay, as he considered that boys ought to be able to earn a little money for themselves.

Reuben, therefore, was going to work on the following week. The half a crown a week which he was to earn was an important matter for his mother. For although she had found a cottage and opened a little shop, as before, her receipts were extremely small, and she had already begun to fear that she should be obliged to make another move, Lewes being too well supplied with shops for a small concern like hers to flourish. The half crown a week, however, would pay her rent; and she expected that she should make, at any rate, enough to provide food for herself and Reuben.

Mrs. Whitney had hoped that, although Lewes was but four miles from the village, the story about the dog would not travel so far; for it was not often that anyone from the village went over to the town. In this, however, she was mistaken for, a week after Reuben had gone to work, the foreman went to his master and said:

"I don't know whether you are aware, Mr. Penfold, about that new boy; but I hear that he had to leave Tipping, where he was employed by Squire Ellison, for poisoning the squire's dog."

"How did you hear it?" Mr. Penfold asked.

"William Jenkins heard it from a man named Thorne, who belongs to the village, and whom he met at a public house, yesterday."

"William Jenkins had best not spend so much time in public houses," Mr. Penfold said shortly. "I heard the story before I saw the boy and, from what I hear, I believe he was wrongfully accused. Just tell Jenkins that; and say that if I hear of him, or any of the hands, throwing the thing up in the boy's face, I will dismiss them instantly."

And so Reuben did not know, till long after, that the story of the killing of the dog was known to anyone at Lewes.

For three years he worked in Mr. Penfold's yard, giving much satisfaction to his employer by his steadiness and handiness. He continued his studies of an evening, under the advice of his former master; who came over with his wife, three or four times each year, to spend a day with Mrs. Whitney. Reuben was now receiving ten shillings a week and, although the receipts of the shop failed, he and his mother were able to live in considerable comfort.

One day, about three years after coming to Lewes, he was returning to work after dinner when, as he passed a carriage standing in front of one of the shops, he heard his name pronounced, and the colour flushed to his cheek as, looking up, he saw Kate Ellison. Timidly he touched his cap, and would have hurried on, but the girl called to him.

"Stop a minute, Reuben. I want to speak to you. I am glad I have met you. I have looked for you, every time I have come to Lewes. I wanted to tell you that I am sure you did not kill Wolf. I know you wouldn't have done it. Besides, you know, you told me that you never told stories; so when I heard that you said you didn't, I was quite sure about it."

"Thank you, miss," Reuben said gratefully. "I did not kill the dog. I should never have thought of such a thing, though every one seemed against me."

"Not every one, Reuben. I didn't think so; and papa has told me, since, that he did not think so, and that he was afraid that he had made a mistake."

"I am glad to hear that, miss," Reuben said. "The squire had been very kind to me, and it has always grieved me, very much, that he should think me capable of such a thing. I felt angry at the time, but I have not felt angry since I have thought it over quietly; for the case seems so strong against me that I don't see how the squire could have thought otherwise.

"Thank you, miss. I sha'n't forget your kindness," and Reuben went on with a light heart, just as Mrs. Ellison and her elder daughter came out from the shop.

"Who were you speaking to, Kate?" she asked, as she took her seat in the carriage.

"I was talking to Reuben Whitney, mamma. He was passing, so I called him to tell him that I did not believe he had killed Wolf."

"Then it was very improper behaviour on your part, Kate," her mother said angrily, for she had never quite recovered from the shock Mrs. Whitney had given to her dignity. "You know my opinion on the subject. I have told you before that it is one I do not care to have discussed, and that I consider it very improper for a girl, of your age, to hold opinions different to those of your elders. I have no doubt, whatever, that boy poisoned the dog. I must beg of you that you will never speak to him again."

Kate leaned back in the carriage with a little sigh. She could not understand why her mother, who was so kind to all the village people, should be so implacable on this subject. But Kate, who was now between fourteen and fifteen, knew that when her mother had taken up certain opinions they were not to be shaken; and that her father himself always avoided argument, on points on which he differed from her. Talking alone with his daughter the squire had, in answer to her sturdy assertion of Reuben's innocence, owned to her that he himself had his doubts on the subject, and that he was sorry he had dismissed the boy from his service; but she had never heard him do more than utter a protest, against Reuben's guilt being held as being absolutely proved, when her mother spoke of his delinquency.

But Kate was not one to desert a protege and, having been the means of Reuben's introduction to her father's, she had always regarded herself as his natural protector; and Mrs. Ellison would not have been pleased, had she known that her daughter had seldom met the schoolmaster without inquiring if he had heard how Reuben was getting on. She had even asked Mr. Shrewsbury to assure him of her belief in his innocence, which had been done; but she had resolved that, should she ever meet him, she would herself tell him so, even at the risk of her mother's displeasure.

Another year passed. Reuben was now seventeen, and was a tall, powerfully-built young fellow. During these four years he had never been over to Tipping, in the daytime; but had occasionally walked over, after dark, to visit the Shrewsburys, always going on special invitation, when he knew that no one else would be there. The Thornes no longer occupied the little public house. Tom Thorne had, a year before, been captured with two other poachers in the squire's woods, and had had six months' hard labour; and his father had at once been ejected from his house, and had disappeared from that part of the country. Reuben was glad that they had left; for he had long before heard that Thorne had spread the story, in Lewes, of the poisoning of the dog. He felt, however, with their departure all chance of his ever being righted in that matter was at an end.

One evening in winter, when Reuben had done his work, he said to his mother:

"I shall go over and see Mr. Shrewsbury tonight. I have not been over for some time and, as it is not his night for a class, I am pretty sure not to find anyone there. I told him, when I was there last, that I would take over a few tools and fix up those shelves for him.

"I don't suppose he will stay very much longer at Tipping. His health is completely restored now, and even his wife admits that he could work at his own business again. He has already been doing a little, for some of the houses he worked for in town, so as to get his connection back again. I expect, every time I see him, to hear that he has made up his mind to go. He would have done it, two years back; but his wife and the two little ones are so well that he did not like the thought of taking them up to London, till he was sure that his health was strong enough to stand steady work. I shall miss them very much. He has been a good friend, indeed, to me."

"He has indeed," Mrs. Whitney said. "I think anyhow, Reuben, you would have got on at your trade; but you would never have been what you are now, if it hadn't been for him. Your poor father would be proud of you, if he could see you; and I am sure that, when you take off that workman's suit and put on your Sunday clothes, you look as well as if the mill had never gone wrong, and you had been brought up as he intended you to be. Mrs. Tyler was saying only the other day that you looked quite the gentleman, and lots of people have said the same."

"Nonsense, mother," Reuben answered, "there is nothing of the gentleman about me. Of course, people say things that they think will please you, knowing that you regard me as a sort of wonder. I hope I shall make my way some day, and the fact that I have had a better education than most young fellows, in my position of life, of course may make some little difference; and will, I hope, help me to mount the ladder, when once I put my foot upon it."

But although, no doubt, Mrs. Whitney was a partial judge, her opinion as to her son was not an incorrect one; for with his intelligent face, and quiet self-assured bearing, he looked very much more like a gentleman than many young fellows in a far better position in life.

The stars were shining brightly when he started, at seven o'clock in the evening; and he walked with a brisk step, until he arrived within half a mile of the village. As he passed by the end of a lane which ran into the road, he heard a horse impatiently pawing the ground; the sound being followed by a savage oath, to the animal, to stand quiet. Reuben walked on a few steps, and then paused. The lane, as he knew, only led to some fields a short distance away. What could a horse be doing there? And who could be the man who spoke to it? There had, lately, been several burglaries on lonely houses, in that part of the country; and the general belief was that these had been perpetrated by men from London.

"I daresay it's nothing," Reuben said to himself. "Still, it is certainly curious and, at any rate, there can be no harm in having a look."

Walking upon the grass at the side of the road, he retraced his steps to the end of the lane, and then stood and listened. He heard a murmur of voices, and determined to follow the matter up. He walked quietly down the lane. After going about a hundred yards, he saw something dark in the road and, approaching it very cautiously, found that it was a horse harnessed to a gig. As he was standing wondering what to do next he started, for the silence was broken by some voices near him.

"It was a stupid thing to get here so early, and to have to wait about for four hours in this ditch."

"It was the best plan though," another voice replied. "The trap might have been noticed, if we had been driving about the roads after dark; while in the daylight no one would give it a second thought."

"That's right enough," the first speaker said, "but it's precious cold here. Hand me that flask again. I am blest if the wind does not come through the hedge like a knife."

The voices came from the other side of the hedge, on the opposite side of the lane. Reuben crossed noiselessly. There was a gate just where the cart had stopped, and the men had evidently got over it, to obtain the shelter of the hedge from the wind. Reuben felt the gate, which was old and rickety; then cautiously he placed his feet on the lower bar, and leaned forward so as to look round the hedge.

"What time are the others to be here, Tom?"

"They said they would be here at nine o'clock. We passed them about six miles on the road, so they ought to be here to time."

"I suppose there's no doubt about this here being a good business?"

"I will answer for that," the other said. "I don't suppose as there's much money in the house, but there's no end of silver plate, and their watches, and plenty of sparklers. I have heard say as there's no one in the county as has more jewels than the squire's wife."

"You know the house well, don't you?"

"I never was inside," the other said, "but I have heard enough, from them that has, to know where the rooms lie. The plate chest is in the butler's pantry and, as we are going to get in by the kitchen window, we are safe to be able to clear that out without being heard. I shall go on, directly the others come, and chuck this meat to the dogs—that will silence them. I know the way there, for I tried that on once before."

Reuben had thought that the voice was familiar to him, and the words gave him the clue—the speaker was Tom Thorne—and he, and those with him, were going to commit a burglary at the squire's. He was hesitating whether to make off at once, to warn the squire of what was intended; or to listen and learn a little more of their plan, when suddenly a light shone behind him, and a voice exclaimed with an oath:

"Who have we here?"

He leapt down, and was in the act of turning round to defend himself, when a heavy blow with a cudgel struck him on the head, and felled him insensible to the ground. While he had been listening to the conversation, two men had come quietly up the lane, walking on the grass as he had done; and their footsteps had been unheard by him, for the horse continued, at times, impatiently to paw the ground. The sound of their comrades' voices had told them where they were sitting and, turning on a bull's-eye lantern to show them the gate, they had seen Reuben leaning over it, in the act of listening.

When Reuben recovered consciousness, he found that he was lying in the ditch, his hands tightly bound to his sides, and a handkerchief stuffed into his mouth. The four men were gathered close by, talking in low tones.

"I ain't going to give up the job, now we come so far to do it," one said, with an oath. "Besides, it's not only the swag, but the grudge I owe the squire. If I am ready to go on, I suppose you needn't be afraid; besides, he don't know us."

"Best cut his throat and a done with it," a voice, which Reuben recognized as that of his old enemy, said. "I owe him one, and it will be safest to stop his mouth."

"No, no," a third voice protested; "I ain't going to have nothing to do with cutting throats. I don't mind running the risk of Botany Bay, but I ain't going to run the chance of being scragged. But let's move a bit away from here, while we settle it. You hit him pretty hard, but he will be coming round presently. I thought at first that you had killed him, but he's bleeding too free for that."

The men moved some little distance away, and for some time Reuben could hear a murmured talk, but could make out nothing of what had been said. It was, he judged, a quarter of an hour before the conversation ceased. They did not return to him but remained at some distance off, and Reuben thought that he heard the footsteps of one of them going down the lane. He could feel, by a warm sensation across his cheek, that the blood was flowing freely from the wound he had received on his temple. A dull torpid feeling came over him, and after a time he again lost consciousness.

How long he remained in this state he did not know, but he was at last aroused by being lifted and thrown into the bottom of the cart. Four men then climbed up into it and the horse was started. They drove at a quick pace, and Reuben wondered why they were taking him away with them. His head ached terribly, and he suffered much from the tightness of the cords which bound his arms. The men seemed in high good humour, and talked and laughed in low tones; but the noise of the vehicle prevented Reuben hearing what was said.

It was, as far as he could judge, full two hours before the vehicle stopped. He was roughly taken out of the cart, his arms were unbound; and the men, leaping up, drove away at full speed. The spot where he had been left was very dark, for trees overshadowed it on both sides. Where he was he had no idea, but he judged that he must be fully twenty miles from the village.

His first impulse was to take the handkerchief from his mouth, and he then walked slowly along the road, in the direction from which he had come. It was, he felt sure, no use shouting; for they would have been certain to have selected some lonely spot to set him down, and there would be no chance of awakening the inhabitants of any distant cottage. He walked slowly, for he was faint with loss of blood.

After proceeding about a quarter of a mile, he emerged from the wood and came upon a spot where the road forked. Having no clue whatever as to the direction in which Lewes lay, he sat down upon a heap of stones and waited patiently for morning. He had no doubt that the burglary had been a successful one, and he bitterly regretted his neglect to keep a watch down the lane, to see that he was not surprised by the men he had heard were coming. At any rate, he hoped that he should be able to give such information as would set the constables upon the track.

It seemed to him that some three hours passed before a faint light began to dawn in the sky. By this he knew that it must be about half-past six, and calculated, therefore, he must have set out in the trap about half-past one. He now started to walk along the road, hoping that he should soon meet some labourer going to work. Stopping by a small stream which ran across the road, he washed his head and face; as he had lain on the ground after being struck, the blood had not flowed on to his clothes.

After the wash he proceeded with a brisker step. Half an hour later he met a ploughman, riding one of his team to the fields.

"Is this the road to Lewes?" Reuben asked.

"Lewes? Noa, this baint the road to Lewes. I don't know nothing about the road to Lewes. This bee the road to Hastings, if you goes further. So they tell me; I ain't never been there."

"Is there a village anywhere about here?" Reuben asked.

"Ay, half a mile or so on."

Reuben walked on till he got to the village; and then, going to a public house, obtained some refreshment and learned, from the landlord, the direction he should take to get to the main road leading to Lewes; which was, as he expected, some twenty miles away. He found that the cart had not followed the main road towards London, but had driven by crossroads for a considerable distance, before turning north.

It was late in the afternoon before Reuben arrived at Lewes, for he had been obliged to rest often by the way, and had made but slow progress. When within a few doors of his mother's house, one of the constables of the town came up to him and touched him on the shoulder.

"I arrest you in the king's name!"

"Arrest me! What for?" Reuben exclaimed.

"For breaking into the house of Squire Ellison, of Tipping, that's what it's for."

Reuben laughed.

"You have got the wrong man this time. I have no more to do with the burglary than a child."

"It's no laughing matter," the constable said. "If you are innocent you have got to prove it; that ain't no business of mine. All I have got to do is to arrest you."

So saying, and before Reuben knew what he was about, he slipped a pair of handcuffs over his wrists. Reuben flushed up. Hitherto he had scarcely taken the matter seriously, but to be marched handcuffed through the streets of Lewes was an indignity which enraged him.

"Take these off," he said angrily. "I will go quietly with you."

"You may or you may not," the man said doggedly. "You are younger than I am, and maybe can run faster. I ain't agoing to chance it."

Reuben saw that it was of no use to argue and, silent and pale, he walked along by the side of the constable, who retained a tight hold of his collar. A little crowd gathered speedily round, for such a sight was unusual in Lewes; and Reuben felt thankful when they reached the cells, and he was sheltered from the gaze of the public. A minute later the head constable came in.

"Now, my lad, don't say anything to criminate yourself," he began; "the less you talk, the better for you. I am sorry to see you here, for I knew your father, and I have a good character of you from your employer; so I give you my advice—keep your mouth shut."

"But I am not going to keep my mouth shut," Reuben said indignantly. "Here am I, arrested in the public streets, marched handcuffed through the town upon a most monstrous charge, which has been brought against me without a shadow of evidence."

"Don't be talking, don't be talking," the constable said testily; "you will hear the evidence in time enough."

"But I will talk. I want to tell you what's happened, and you will see that I am innocent, at once."

"Very well, if you will you will; but mind, don't blame me afterwards."

Reuben told the story of his adventures from the time of leaving.

"There," he said when he finished, "isn't that enough to show that I am innocent?"

"No," the chief constable said gravely, "it's not enough to prove anything, one way or the other. I am bound to say the story looks a likely one; and if it weren't for two or three matters which I heard of, from the constable who came over from Tipping, I should have no doubt about it. However, all that is for the magistrate to decide. There will be a meeting tomorrow."

"But can't I be taken before a magistrate at once? There's Captain Fidler, within a mile."

"What would be the good?" the chief constable said. "You don't suppose anyone would let you out, only on the strength of the story you have told me. He could only remand you, and you could gain nothing by it."

"Can I see my mother?" Reuben asked next.

"Yes," the constable said, "I will send her down a message, at once."

Mrs. Whitney soon came up. A neighbour had brought her in the news when Reuben had been arrested, and she was on the point of starting to inquire about it when the message arrived. She was more indignant than grieved, when she heard the charge which had been brought against Reuben.

"The idea of such a thing!" she exclaimed. "These constables don't seem to have natural sense. The idea of charging anyone who is known as a respectable young man with such a thing as that, and shutting him up without a question. Why, there can't be any evidence against you."

"There's no saying, mother," Reuben replied. "You mustn't be too sure of that. Don't you remember that affair of the dog? Well, the same hand is at work now. Before, I only suspected who had done it; but I am sure now. However, whatever evidence they may have got, we know it isn't true. I have four years' good character here to speak for me. Still, it is hard that I should get into positions of this sort, without any fault of mine."

"It's better that it is without any fault of yours, Reuben."

"That is right enough, mother, so we will both keep up our spirits."

Chapter 4
The Trial

There were three magistrates on the bench on the following morning, when Reuben was brought up. The justice room was crowded, for the series of burglaries had caused some excitement; and the news that the house of Mr. Ellison had been broken into, and that one of the men who had been taken turned out to belong to Lewes, had created quite a sensation.

Mr. Ellison was the first to give his evidence. He testified that, on waking on the previous morning, he found that someone had been in his room during the night. He was not in the habit of locking his door, and had not been awakened. He found that a box which stood on the dressing table, containing some valuable jewelry, was gone; that his watch and that of Mrs. Ellison had been taken; that the drawers had been opened, and a case containing the more valuable jewels of his wife had also been abstracted. This was not discovered till afterwards. He first missed his watch.

He rang the servants up, for it was still early; and it was then discovered that the lower premises had been broken into, the plate chest in the butler's pantry broken open, and a large quantity of plate stolen.

"What do you estimate the value of the articles stolen, Mr. Ellison?"

"The value of my wife's jewels I should put down, roughly, at two thousand pounds; the silver plate might have been worth three hundred more; the watches and other articles, so far as I yet miss them, say another hundred."

The servants proved that they found the kitchen window open, on going downstairs. It had been opened by the catch being forced back. It was not the custom to put up shutters. The pantry door, which was a strong one, had been cut with a saw round the lock. The butler testified to the plate having been safe, the night before, and the strong chest in which it was kept having been forced open.

Directly it was discovered, the constable of the village was placed in charge of the room, with orders to admit no one; and a man on horseback was sent off to Lewes, to the chief constable. The village constable gave evidence as to the state of the place, when he was put in charge.

The constable who had been sent over from Lewes then stepped into the witness box. He testified to the marks of entry of the thieves, and said that the manner in which they had gone to work, and in which the door had been sawn through, and the chest forced open, seemed to show that it was the work of practised hands. On examining closely the butler's pantry, he found a powerful screwdriver and a heavy chisel. These corresponded to marks in the lid, and had evidently been used for the purpose of forcing it open. They had the initials "R W." burnt in the handles. The inmates of the house all denied any knowledge of these tools.

Mr. Ellison had been present when he showed them to Mrs. Ellison. On looking at them she said at once:

"R. W. Why, that must be Reuben Whitney, that wicked boy, again."

Upon making inquiries, he found that the man named worked at Mr. Penfold's, the mill wright at Lewes. He returned there at once and, going to Mr. Penfold, found the prisoner was absent from work. The men identified the brand on the tools as that of the prisoner. Another constable proved the arrest.

The chief constable then read the statement that the prisoner had made to him. The magistrates conferred together for a few minutes, in an undertone.

"Mrs. Ellison," the senior of them said, addressing that lady, who was sitting on a chair placed at the upper end of the court, "we are sorry to trouble you, but we must ask you to go into the witness box.

"I wish to ask you," he went on, when she had taken her stand in the box, "how it was you at once connected the initials with the prisoner?"

"Because he had at one time lived in the village, and was employed assisting our gardener. He was discharged on suspicion of having poisoned a watchdog which had bit him; and as the three dogs about the place had all been poisoned, on the night when the house was broken into, his name had been in my mind and, on seeing the initials, I naturally recognized them at once."

There was a deep silence in the court, when Mrs. Ellison gave her evidence. Hitherto the impression had been rather favourable to the prisoner. His story, though strange, had been by no means impossible and, if true, would have completely accounted for the finding of the tools, which were the only evidence against him. The evidence of Mrs. Ellison, however, entirely altered the complexion of the case.

Reuben had stood, quiet and composed, during the hearing. His countenance had evinced no surprise or emotion, when the tools were produced. He had, indeed, upon thinking the matter over before coming into court, come to the conclusion that the tools, which he had in a small basket at the time he was attacked, had been found in or near the house; having been left there purposely, by Tom Thorne, in order to throw suspicion upon him. Their production, therefore, was no surprise to him.

A slight shade had passed over his face when Mrs. Ellison entered the witness box. Glancing at the squire as she gave her evidence, Reuben saw that Mr. Ellison looked greatly vexed and annoyed. As before, at the conclusion of the evidence of each witness, Reuben was asked if he had any question to put. He hesitated for a moment and then, as before, replied in the negative.

Again the magistrates consulted together.

"Mr. Ellison, we shall be obliged if you will enter the witness box again. In your former evidence, Mr. Ellison, you said nothing in any way relating to the prisoner; but it now seems you had a previous acquaintance with him. Will you tell the court what it is?"

"I have not much to say," the squire said. "As a boy he lived in the village with his mother, a most respectable person; and widow of Jacob Whitney, a miller in a good way of business, who, as it may be in your memory, was found drowned in his mill pond some seven or eight years ago. The widow, being in reduced circumstances, settled in Tipping. The boy was an intelligent lad and, when the boy employed in my garden left, I gave him the place. He gave every satisfaction. One day he was severely bitten by the watchdog and, three days later, the dog was found poisoned. My gardener saw a boy running away from the spot, a quarter of an hour before the dog died. He believed it to be the prisoner, but it was too dark for him to distinguish the features.

"At the time, I certainly suspected that he had been guilty of poisoning the dog and, in spite of his denying that he had anything to do with it, as he was unable to account for where he was at the time the boy was seen, I discharged him. I wish to say publicly that I have deeply regretted having done so, ever since, and that I consider I acted hastily and wrongly in so doing. Considering his previous good character, I ought not to have assumed his guilt without more positive evidence than I had before me. I may also say that the schoolmaster of our village will give the prisoner the highest character for truthfulness, and he has known him ever since. His present employer, Mr. Penfold, is also, I believe, ready to testify to his excellent conduct during his four years of apprenticeship."

"I suppose, Mr. Ellison," the senior magistrate said, "you have not, at any time since the poisoning of the dog, obtained any actual evidence which would show that you were mistaken in your first view, and that your subsequent change of opinion was due solely to your general view of the boy's character, so far as you knew it."

"That is so," the squire assented and, no further question being asked, he resumed his seat. His evidence had caused surprise and some little amusement in court. It was clear that there was a strong difference of opinion between him and his wife on the subject; and that, while the lady had something like an animus against the prisoner, the squire was strongly impressed in his favour. After some consultation, the magistrate said:

"The case will be remanded until this day week, to see if further evidence is forthcoming; but I may say that, under the present circumstances of the case, we shall feel ourselves obliged to send it for trial. The prisoner's account of his proceedings, from the time he left Lewes on the previous evening up to that of his return and arrest here, may be true; but so far it is entirely unsupported. On the other hand, we have the evidence of the tools, admitted to belong to him, being found on the scene of the burglary. We have the further important fact that he had been formerly employed upon the place; and had, it may be supposed, some knowledge of the premises. He had been discharged upon a suspicion, rightfully or wrongly entertained, of his having poisoned a dog belonging to Mr. Ellison, and there is reason for the belief that the dogs poisoned before the burglary were got at by some one acquainted with the place."

"Will it be any use my calling evidence as to character, at the next meeting?" Reuben asked.

"No," the magistrate said. "Evidence of that kind will be useful at the trial, when the matter will be thoroughly sifted. We only have to decide that there is prima facie evidence connecting you with the offence, and of that there can be no doubt."

At the sitting a week later, no fresh evidence was produced; and Reuben was committed for trial at the next assizes. Public opinion in Lewes ran high on the subject of Reuben's guilt or innocence. The other workmen at the mill wright's were strongly in his favour—he was very popular among his fellows—and they pointed out that several hands must have been concerned in the business, that he was never seen about in public houses of an evening, or was likely to have any connection with bad characters. Was it probable, if he had gone about such a job as that, he would have taken tools marked with his own initials; or if he had, that he would have been fool enough to leave them behind?

Upon the other hand, opinion in general ran strongly against him. His story was declared to be utterly improbable, and a fellow who had once been dismissed for poisoning a dog would be likely, at any future time, to revenge himself upon the employer who turned him off. As to Mr. Ellison's declaration of his subsequent opinion that he acted hastily, little weight was attached to it. Everyone knew Squire Ellison was a kind-hearted man, and as he acknowledged himself that he had obtained no evidence which would satisfy him that he had acted wrongly in the first case, it was clear that it was from mere kindness of heart that he had changed his mind on the subject.

At Tipping the subject was never mentioned. The squire and Mrs. Ellison had, on the drive home, had the most serious quarrel which had ever taken place during their wedded life; which had ended by the former saying:

"If anyone had ever told me before, Mary, that you were a vindictive woman, I should have knocked him down. I might do so now, but I should know in my heart that he had spoken truly. For some reason or other you took a prejudice against that boy, and you never forgave his mother for standing up in his defence. I was shocked, downright shocked, when you gave your evidence in court."

Mrs. Ellison had been too much offended to reply, and the rest of the drive had been passed in silence. Upon their return home the girls were full of eager questions, but the squire said shortly:

"My dears, the less we talk about it, the better. Your mother and I differ entirely on the subject. She believes that Reuben Whitney is guilty. I am absolutely convinced he is innocent. Therefore, if you please, we will not discuss it."

The following morning Kate Ellison went down to the school house.

"Mr. Shrewsbury," she said, putting her head in at the door, "could you come out for two or three minutes? I want particularly to speak to you.

"Have you heard what took place yesterday, at Lewes?" she asked when he came out.

"Yes, Miss Ellison. I saw Jones the constable last night, and he told me all that had been said in court."

"And you think Reuben Whitney is innocent?" she asked eagerly.

"I am quite sure of it, Miss Ellison—as sure as I am of my own existence. For anyone who knows him to have a doubt is absolutely absurd. A finer young fellow than Reuben it would be hard to find."

"But what did he say? How did he account for his tools being found there?"

The schoolmaster repeated the account Reuben had given, and said:

"When the trial comes off I shall, of course, go over; and testify both as to his general conduct and to the fact that he had, as he said, promised to bring over his tools to put up some shelves in my cupboards."

"Do you think he will get off, Mr. Shrewsbury?" she asked anxiously.

"I should hope so, Miss Ellison, but I can't disguise from myself that it is by no means certain. That unfortunate old business about the dog will tell terribly against him; and though I am perfectly sure that his account of what took place is correct, there is nothing to confirm it. It is just the sort of story, they will say, that he would naturally get up to account for his absence, and for the tools being found. Of course, if the jury knew him as well as I do the result would be certain; but I have been trying to look at the facts as if he were a stranger, and I can't say what decision I should come to, in such a case. Still, of course, the high character that will be given him, and the fact that there is no evidence whatever connecting him, in any way, with bad characters, must count immensely in his favour."

The assizes were to take place only a fortnight after the date of Reuben's committal. Mrs. Whitney had engaged a lawyer in the town to defend her son and, to the surprise of this gentleman, Mr. Ellison called upon him two or three days later, and said:

"Mr. Brogden, I hear that you have been engaged by Mrs. Whitney to defend her son. I don't believe the young fellow is guilty, and therefore I authorize you to spend any sum that may be necessary in getting up his defence; and I wish you to instruct a counsel to appear for him. Of course I cannot appear openly in the matter, and my name must not be mentioned, but I will guarantee all expenses.

"It seems to me that it would be desirable to find out, if possible, the village where he says he breakfasted, and asked the way to Lewes. In his story he says he didn't know the name of the village but, as he was told it was about twenty miles from Lewes, and he can describe the road he followed, there ought to be no difficulty in finding it.

"I should advise you to have a chat with Shrewsbury, the schoolmaster at Tipping. He is a great friend of the lad's, and a very intelligent fellow. He may be able to suggest some points to be followed up. At any rate, do all you can."

Reuben had another adherent who was also acting on his behalf. The afternoon before the trial, Kate Ellison stopped before the blacksmith shop in the village and, seeing that Jacob Priestley the smith was at work, alone, she entered.

"Is it true, Jacob, that you have been summoned on the jury at Lewes tomorrow?"

"Yes, miss, it bee true, sureley. It be four years since anyone in the village was summoned, and it be mighty hard that they should have picked upon me. Still, I have never been called before, so I suppose I mustn't grumble; but it be hard to be taken away from work, to waste one's time in a court, and they say the 'sizes ull last for three days."

"Well, Jacob, you know that Reuben Whitney is going to be tried for robbery at our house."

"Yes, miss; so they says."

"Well, what do you think about it, Jacob?"

"I don't think nothing one way or the other, miss. Most folks says as how he must have done it, 'cause as how he poisoned squire's dog afore."

"He didn't do anything of the sort, Jacob; and it's very wicked of people to say so. He is innocent, quite innocent. I am sure he is, and papa is quite sure, too; and he will be terribly put out if he is found guilty. So I want you to promise me that, whatever the others think, you will hold out that he is innocent."

"Well, miss," the smith said, scratching his head, "if you be sure of it, and squire be sure, I suppose there can't be no doubt about it, for who should know better than squire; and I am sure I wouldn't go to put him about, for a better landlord than squire ain't to be found in the county. So you tell him, miss, as I will hold out."

"But papa doesn't know that I have come down here, Jacob. It wouldn't do for him to interfere, you know; especially as he is a magistrate himself. You mustn't mention to anyone that I have spoken to you about it—not to anyone, Jacob, not even to your wife—but I can tell you the squire will be heartily pleased if he is found innocent, and he will be terribly put out if he is found guilty."

"All right, miss," the smith replied. "I understand, and no one sha'n't know as you have spoken to me aboot it. It be quite enough for I to know as the squire knows as he's innocent. It ain't likely as I should stick my opinion up against his."

The day after he heard of Reuben's arrest, the schoolmaster went over to see him; and as he was the bearer of a letter from Mr. Ellison to the governor of the jail, he was able to obtain admittance.

"Was there ever such an unfortunate fellow as I am?" Reuben exclaimed, after the first hearty greeting. "Here am I for the second time accused of a crime of which I am innocent; and from which, indeed, in the present case I am a sufferer; and all this has come about, simply because I went out of my way to inquire into what seemed to me a suspicious business."

"Tell me all about it, Reuben. I have heard the statement you made to the chief constable; but tell it me again, with every detail you can think of. Some circumstance, which appears to you as trifling, may furnish a clue."

"I have seen Mr. Brogden, the lawyer. I have told him all that happened," Reuben said; "but of course, I will gladly tell you again."

And Reuben repeated the story of the adventure, with every detail that he could think of; speaking slowly, as the schoolmaster wrote it down at length.

"I will see what I can make of it, when I think it over," Mr. Shrewsbury said. "Of course, as it stands, it is so natural and probable that it would clear you at once; had it not been for that unfortunate dog business before, and the supposition, excited by it, that you had a feeling of hostility to the squire. I shall be able partly to dispose of that, for I can swear that you have frequently spoken to me of the squire in tones of respect and liking; and that, although you regretted the manner in which you left his service, you felt no ill will against him on account of it. Moreover, I shall be able to prove that the reasons you gave for having your tools with you was a true one; and although I cannot swear that I expected you specially on that evening, the fact that you were in the habit of coming over, at times, to see me, cannot but corroborate your story.

"I shall get leave for two or three days, and will hunt up the village where you breakfasted."

"Thank you very much," Reuben said, "though I have been thinking it over, and do not see that the evidence of the people at the public house would help me much. It will simply prove that I passed through there in the morning; but will not show, in any way, whether I went willingly as far as that, as one of the party who broke into the house, or whether I was taken there."

"They can probably prove that you looked pale and exhausted," the schoolmaster said.

"I fancy I should look pale, in any case," Reuben said, "if I had gone through such a night's work as that of breaking into the squire's."

"Well, keep up your courage, Reuben. You may be quite sure that your friends will do all in their power for you. I shall go now and have a chat with your mother. I am afraid that she will want comforting more than you do."

"Yes," Reuben agreed, "I am afraid so. Somehow I don't seem to take it to heart much. I shall feel it more afterwards, perhaps; but at present, the whole thing seems so extraordinary that I can't quite realize that I am in danger of being sent to Botany Bay. The worst of it is that, even if I am acquitted, lots of people will still think I am guilty. There is only one thing that can really prove my innocence, and that is the arrest of Tom Thorne, and his father."

"I hear," the schoolmaster said, "that the chief constable has written up to Bow Street, for them to put the runners on the traces of those two scoundrels. Whether they believe your story or not, it is quite evident that more than one person was concerned in the affair. Their theory, of course, is that you quarrelled with the others over the division of the spoil; and got that knock on the head, which is a very severe one. I went down yesterday with Jones, to see the spot where you said you were assaulted. There were marks where the horse stopped, and marks of feet in the field, and a patch of blood; all of which goes to prove that your story may be true, but unfortunately it doesn't prove that it was because, according to the theory against you, you might have been assaulted after the robbery, as well as before it."

"But in that case," Reuben said, "why should they have taken the trouble to carry me twenty miles away?"

"Yes, there is of course that question," the schoolmaster said thoughtfully; "but then, on the other hand, why did they take the trouble in case you were not an accomplice? In both cases the answer is the same—they did it to prevent your giving the alarm, until they had got far away from the scene. They didn't like to murder you, because of the consequences to themselves; but they would not risk your recovering consciousness and getting up an early pursuit. It cuts both ways, you see."

"So it does," Reuben assented. "It's just a question of belief; and I own, myself, that that old dog business is very much against me; and that I can't blame anyone who considers me guilty."

Reuben's was the last case taken at the assizes, and occasioned a good deal of interest in that part of Sussex, partly owing to the position of Squire Ellison, partly to the nature of the defence set up, as to which opinion was a good deal divided. The evidence for the prosecution was, to a great extent, similar to that given at the inquiry before the magistrates. Unfortunately for Reuben, the judge was notoriously a severe one; and his bias, from the first, appeared to be against the prisoner. Mr. Ellison was closely questioned by the prosecutor as to the poisoning of his dog, as this was considered to show a particular animus on the part of Reuben. He again repeated his conviction of Reuben's innocence in that affair.

"But what reason have you, Mr. Ellison," the counsel for the prosecution asked blandly, "for changing your opinion on the subject?"

This was just the question which the squire could not answer satisfactorily; and was a particularly irritating one, because it had often been triumphantly asked by his wife.

"I can really give no particular reason," he said, "except that, on reflection, the boy's previous character and antecedents convinced me that he could not have done such an act."

"In fact," the counsel said suavely, "you were influenced by your own goodness of heart, Mr. Ellison, in thus laying aside a conviction which the facts had, at the time, forced upon you."

"I don't look upon it in that light," the squire replied shortly. "I consider that in the first instance I acted hastily and unadvisedly, and on consideration I saw that I had done so."

"I am afraid, Mr. Ellison," the counsel said, "that you will not persuade the jury to agree with you."

"I have only one or two questions to ask you," the counsel for the defence said, when he rose to cross-examine, "for indeed your evidence is, as I think the jury will agree, altogether in favour of the prisoner. In the first place, was the lad, when in your employment, ever upstairs in your house?"

"Not that I know of," the squire replied. "Certainly in the course of his duties he would never be there. Indeed, it would be very seldom that he would even enter the kitchen, except to bring in vegetables. Certainly he would never pass through to go upstairs. He could not possibly have done so without exciting attention and remarks."

"He would therefore, Mr. Ellison, have no means of possessing any knowledge as to the internal arrangements of your house, beyond that possessed by the other people in the village?"

"None whatever," Mr. Ellison replied.

"Now, as to that unfortunate affair of the poisoning of your dog. Your opinion, as to the innocence of the prisoner in that matter, is not a recent one—not the outcome of his after good conduct and character?"

"Not at all," Mr. Ellison said. "I changed my opinion on the matter very shortly, indeed, after the affair."

"Within a few days, I think I may say?" the counsel asked.

"Within a very few days; I may almost say within a few hours," the squire replied. "The boy's story, told not to me but to another, that he believed the dog was poisoned by another lad in the village who owed him a grudge, and who has since turned out an exceedingly bad character, struck me as being very much more probable than that he should do it, himself."

Mrs. Ellison was next called. Her evidence as to the robbery was a mere repetition of that given by the squire. The counsel then turned to the question of the poisoning.

"I would rather say nothing about it," Mrs. Ellison said. "It is a matter which has been productive of much pain to me, and I would rather say nothing about it."

"But you must, madam," the judge said sharply. "You are here to answer any question which may enable the jury to form an opinion on this case."

"I am sorry to press you, Mrs. Ellison," the counsel continued, "but I really must do so. You took a different opinion to that held by your husband?"

"I regret to say that I did. Mr. Ellison told me the reasons he had for suspecting the boy. I thought those reasons sufficient, and have seen no cause for changing my opinion."

After the evidence for the prosecution had been given, the counsel for the defence pointed out that there was, in fact, no evidence whatever connecting Reuben with the robbery, beyond the discovery of his tools on the premises; and that, as to this trumpery story of the poisoning a dog, four years before, apparently only for the purpose of showing some sort of animus, he regarded it as altogether contemptible. When a man meant to commit a burglary in a house, he did so in order to obtain possession of the goods, and not from any spite against the owner. Had this young fellow felt any malice, for this ridiculous charge on which he had been dismissed, he would not have allied himself with burglars to rob the house; but would probably have vented his spite in the usual fashion, by setting fire to a stack or outhouse; but so far as he could see, there was no foundation for the charge brought against him, and they had already heard Mr. Ellison declare that he regretted he had suspected him, and that he believed him to be innocent.

But even had it been proved, up to the hilt, that the prisoner had poisoned the dog, he should still hold it as wholly unconnected with the present matter. If he had poisoned the dog, what then? It was not a heinous sin, nor would it affect his moral character. No boy likes having a piece taken out of his calf by a savage dog, and there would have been nothing so very dreadful had he revenged himself. It was probable that, even among the jury, there was one or more who, if he had not absolutely set poison for his neighbour's cats, for destroying his young chickens or scratching up his flower beds, had threatened to do so, and would not have regarded it as a very serious crime had he done so.

Therefore he contended that the jury should put this trumpery affair altogether out of their minds; on the double ground that, in the first place, the prisoner at the bar did not poison the dog; and that, had he done so, it would have had nothing whatever to do with the present affair.

"Why, gentlemen," he said, "it is an insult to your understanding to ask you to credit that this young fellow—whose character, which I shall presently prove to you, by unimpeachable evidence, is of the highest kind—has, for four years, cherished such malice against his employer, for dismissing him mistakenly, that he has become the consort of thieves and burglars, has stained his hands in crime, and rendered himself liable to transportation, for the purpose merely of spiting that gentleman. Such a contention would be absolutely absurd. I must beg you to dismiss it altogether from your mind, and approach it from a different standpoint, altogether. Divested of this extraneous business, the matter is a most simple one.

"The prisoner left his mother's cottage, at seven o'clock in the evening, to go over for an hour or two to his friend Mr. Shrewsbury, the schoolmaster of Tipping. He took with him a few tools, as he had promised to put some shelves in his friend's house. On the way he heard some talking down a lane, which he knew led to only a field. Thinking it strange, he went to see who it was and, some distance down, he found a horse and cart standing and, listening to the conversation of two men who were sitting under the hedge, he heard enough to inform him that a burglary was intended upon the house of Mr. Ellison. He was about to make off to give the alarm, when he was suddenly attacked by some men who had come up behind, and was felled to the ground. While lying insensible, he was bound hand and foot and left in a ditch; where he remained till the burglars returned from completing the work on hand. They then threw him into the cart, and put him down some twenty miles away. Being greatly exhausted by loss of blood, it was late in the afternoon before he arrived at Lewes, when he was at once arrested.

"This, gentlemen, is the prisoner's story, as related to the chief constable when he was taken to the lockup. Nothing can be simpler or more probable; and in some points, at least, I shall be able to confirm it by independent testimony. Mr. Shrewsbury will tell you that the prisoner had arranged to come over to see him, and bring his tools. He will also tell you that, two days after the prisoner's arrest, he went with Jones, the village constable, and found the marks where the horse and trap had stood; while, just inside the field, the grass was trampled with feet; and in the bottom of the dry ditch was a great dark patch, which he was able to ascertain to be blood. Doctor Hewitt will tell you that he was called in to strap up the prisoner's head, after his arrest; and that the cut was a very severe one, and must have been inflicted by a heavy weapon, with great force.

"I am convinced, gentlemen, that after hearing this evidence you will agree with me, not only that the prisoner is perfectly innocent of the charge, but that he is a most ill-used person; and that it is a matter of surprise and regret that the magistrates should have committed him for trial, when the only shadow of evidence against him was the discovery of these tools, a discovery which he at once explained. Of other evidence, there is not one jot or tittle. No attempt has been made to prove that the prisoner was in the habit of consorting with bad characters; no attempt has been made to show any connection, whatever, between him and the men who came in a horse and trap across the hills, for the purpose of effecting a burglary at Mr. Ellison's; and who, as we know, did effect it. No scrap of the property stolen from the house has been found upon him and, in order to account for the severe wound on his head, the counsel for the prosecution has started the hypothesis that it was given in the course of a quarrel, during the division of the plunder.

"But had that been the case, gentlemen, the prisoner would not have been standing here alone. Robbed and ill-treated by these companions of his, he would naturally have put the officers of justice on their track and, as he must have been in communication with them, and well acquainted with their ways and haunts, he could have given information which would have led to their early arrest. He could well have done this, for the crown would have made no difficulty, whatever, in promising a lad like this a free pardon, on condition of his turning evidence against these burglars; whose mode of procedure shows them to have been old hands, and who are, no doubt, the same who have committed the various robberies which have lately taken place in this part of the country.

"The prisoner is the son of highly respectable parents. His employer will come before you, and give you evidence of the extremely high character he bears. Mr. Shrewsbury will tell you that he has, for the last four years, devoted no inconsiderable portion of his leisure time to improve his education, and enable him to recover the position occupied by his father, who was a much-respected miller in this neighbourhood. I shall leave the case in your hands, gentlemen, with an absolute confidence that you will, without a moment's hesitation, find a verdict proclaiming the innocence of my client; and enable him to leave the dock, without a stain upon his character."

Chapter 5
Not Guilty!

The schoolmaster was the first witness called for the defence. After stating that, although no evening was actually settled for his coming over, he expected the prisoner one evening that week; and that he had promised to bring his tools over, to do a little job of carpentering; he also detailed his visit to the lane, and the result of his observation there; and then gave Reuben the highest character, saying that he had known him for five years, and that he had an absolute confidence in his integrity and honesty.

"He has from the first," he said, "proved a most intelligent and hard-working boy, anxious to improve himself and to get on in the world. He has learnt all that I could teach him, and more. He is one of the last persons in the world whom I should consider capable of the crime with which he is charged. As to his having any animosity to Mr. Ellison, I can swear that, on many different occasions, he has expressed his high opinion of him; and has declared that it was quite natural that, with the evidence before him, he should have thought him guilty of poisoning the dog."

The keeper of the wayside public house, where he had breakfasted, proved that he was struck with the prisoner's appearance when he entered; that he was very pale, and seemed scarcely able to walk. He had asked him the nearest way to Lewes, and had inquired whether there was any chance of getting a lift; as he was anxious to get back, as soon as possible.

Mr. Penfold was the next witness. He said that the prisoner had been apprenticed to him, four years previously; that his general conduct had been most excellent, and that he was remarkably quick and intelligent, and was an excellent workman. During the time that he had been employed, he had never lost a day.

"At the time he was apprenticed to you, Mr. Penfold," Reuben's counsel asked, "were you aware that the lad had been summarily discharged by Mr. Ellison?"

"I was aware of that fact," Mr. Penfold answered; and Reuben, with surprise, looked at his employer.

"From whom did you hear of it?"

"I heard of it from Mr. Ellison himself, who called upon me about the matter."

"How was it he came to call upon you, Mr. Penfold?"

"The prisoner's mother had applied to me about apprenticing her son. I had asked 50 pounds premium, and said that it wasn't my custom to pay any wages for the first year. She said she could only afford 20 pounds, and I thought that was an end of the matter until, a few days later, Mr. Ellison called upon me, and said that he had heard from the schoolmaster in his village, who was a friend of the boy's mother, how matters stood; and that her application had fallen through, owing to her being unable to find more than 20 pounds.

"I said that this was so. Mr. Ellison then said that he was prepared to make up the deficiency, that he had a regard for the boy's father; and that, moreover, he himself had, through a hasty misconception regarding the poisoning of the dog, discharged the lad from his service; and that he felt uneasy, in his mind, at having been guilty of a piece of injustice. Over and above the 30 pounds, he gave me six pound ten; in order that I might pay the boy half a crown a week, for the first year, which he said would be a matter of consequence to his mother. He requested me on no account to let Mrs. Whitney know that he had intervened in the matter, but to represent that I changed my mind, and was willing to take the 20 pounds she offered as a premium. He was particularly anxious on this point; because, he said, she would certainly refuse to accept assistance from him, owing to that unfortunate affair about the dog.

"I may say that, from that time to this, I have not mentioned the fact to anyone; and the sum of 20 pounds was inserted in the indenture of apprenticeship."

There was a little movement of applause in the court, as Mr. Penfold gave his evidence; and Reuben looked gratefully towards Mr. Ellison, and said heartily:

"I thank you, sir, with all my heart."

The foreman of the yard was next examined. He confirmed the high character Mr. Penfold had given Reuben, and adding that he knew the lad never entered a public house, but spent his evenings almost entirely at home studying; for that he himself had, many times, called in and had, upon every occasion, found him so employed.

The counsel for the prosecution then addressed the jury, and threw discredit upon Reuben's narrative; which, he said, was unsupported in any material particular. That he met the rest of the party in the lane was likely enough. He may have returned there with them after the burglary, and probably it was there that, in a quarrel over the spoil, he received the blow of which you have heard.

"My learned friend has told you to dismiss from your mind the question about that poisoning of the dog, four years ago; but it is impossible for you to do so. You have heard that the dog was poisoned, and that the evidence was so strong that his employer at once dismissed him. It is true that Mr. Ellison has told you that he afterwards changed his mind on the subject; but after the evidence which Mr. Penfold has given, of the kindness of that gentleman's heart, you will readily understand that no great stress can be laid upon this. The matter, so far from being trivial, as my friend represents it, is highly important; inasmuch as here we find that, again, the dogs have been poisoned just as on the first occasion. It is clear that burglars from London would be ignorant of the whereabouts of the kennels, and were not likely to have come down provided with a store of poisoned meat; had they not known, from persons well acquainted with the place, of the steps that would have to be taken before an entry could be effected into the house. You will therefore see the extreme importance of this point.

"I am perfectly ready to admit that the evidence is of a wholly circumstantial nature but, from the nature of the case, it is necessary that this should be so. Had Mrs. or Mr. Ellison awoke, when the thieves entered their room, it is probable that much more evidence would be forthcoming. It is, however, for you to weigh the probabilities of the case. You have to consider whether the theory which I have laid before you, as to the connection of the prisoner with this affair, or this wild story which he tells you, is the most probable."

The judge then summed up, with a strong bias against Reuben. He told them that evidence for character was, of course, of importance; but that it must not be relied upon too far. The prisoner appeared undoubtedly to be intelligent and well-conducted, but unfortunately his experience told him that many criminals were men of unusual intelligence. Stress had been laid, by the counsel for the defence, upon the fact that the prisoner was not known, at any time, to have consorted with suspicious characters; but this, after all, was only negative evidence. Affairs of this sort were always conducted with secrecy and, had one of these men come down from London, as was probable enough, to make inquiries as to houses which could be broken into with a prospect of good booty, he would naturally not make himself conspicuous.

They had heard the two stories, and must judge for themselves; but he agreed, with the counsel for the prosecution, that the fact that the prisoner had been discharged by Mr. Ellison for poisoning a dog, and that on the night of the robbery other dogs were found poisoned, and that probably by some one acquainted with the locality, could not but have an influence upon their minds. At the same time he would tell them that, if they had a doubt in their minds, it was their duty to give the prisoner the benefit of that doubt.

The jury consulted together for a minute or two in the jury box, and then expressed their desire to retire. A buzz of talk arose in the court, when they had left. Opinion was divided as to what the verdict would be. When the counsel for the defence sat down, the general opinion was that the prisoner would be certainly acquitted; but the speech of the counsel for the prosecution, and the summing up of the judge, had caused a reaction, and few doubted now that the verdict would be guilty.

So Reuben himself thought. It was he felt hard that, standing there to be tried for burglary, the decision should, in fact, depend upon that unjust charge which had, four years ago, been brought against him. Reuben was in the habit of what he called arguing things out by himself; and as he stood there, waiting for the verdict, he tried to put himself in the position of the jury; and he felt that, in that case, he should have difficulty in coming to a decision.

It was not until after the lamps had been lighted that the jury returned into the box. The crier shouted for order, and there was not a sound heard, as the foreman told the judge that they were not agreed upon their verdict.

"Then you must go back, gentlemen, until you are," the judge said.

"We are eleven one way, and one the other. Won't that do, my lord?"

"No, sir," the judge replied. "You must be unanimous."

The jury again retired, the judge and counsel went off to dine at the hotel, and almost all the public trooped out. Two hours later, as the jury did not return, Reuben Whitney was taken back to the jail, and the court closed. At nine o'clock in the morning, a warder entered.

"The jury have come back into the court," he said. "They are going to return a verdict."

Reuben was again placed in the dock. The seats open to the public quickly filled, as the news spread through the town. Several of the members of the bar dropped in, and then the judge came in and took his seat.

Reuben had occupied the time in trying to judge, from the faces of the jury, what their verdict was going to be. They looked sulky and tired. But as Reuben's eye rested on Jacob Priestley, whom he had at once recognized among the jury, the smith gave him an encouraging wink. At least, so

Reuben thought; but as the next moment he was looking as surly as the rest, he thought that he must have been mistaken.

"Are you agreed, gentlemen, as to the verdict you find in this case?" the judge asked.

"We are, my lord," the foreman replied.

"Do you find the prisoner guilty or not guilty?"

"Not guilty, my lord."

"Very well, gentlemen," the judge said tartly. "It is your verdict, not mine."

At the foreman's word a thrill had run through the court; for when it was known, the evening before, that eleven were one way and one the other, the belief had been general that the majority were for a conviction. Reuben himself had so understood it, and the verdict was a complete surprise to him.

The constable raised the bar for him to leave the dock, and as he moved out his friend the schoolmaster pushed forward, and shook him warmly by the hand.

"Thank God for that verdict, Reuben. I am indeed rejoiced, and I own I hardly expected it."

"I didn't expect it at all," Reuben said in a choked voice, for his sudden liberation had shaken him, more than his arrest or any of the subsequent proceedings had done.

"I congratulate you heartily, Reuben," Mr. Ellison said, putting his hand on his shoulder.

The squire had waited at Lewes until ten o'clock on the previous evening, and had driven over again the first thing in the morning, so anxious was he about the verdict.

"I didn't believe you guilty this time, my boy, from the first. I was glad indeed to hear the verdict; for after the judge's summing up, I was sorely uneasy.

"And now, Reuben, I hope," he said, as they entered the street, "that you have quite forgiven me for that old business. It has been the unfortunate cause of getting you into this affair. Had it not been for that no one would ever, for a moment, have doubted the truth of your story."

"There is nothing to forgive, squire," Reuben said. "I never blamed you for it, from the first; and even had I done so, your goodness, of which I only heard yesterday, would have made up, many times, for any mistake you may have made then."

"That is right, my lad," the squire said. "I am glad that matter is made up. And now I will not keep you, for I know you will want to be off home to your mother."

Reuben walked quietly home, so as to give the schoolmaster, who had hurried on ahead, time to break the news of his acquittal to his mother. Mrs. Whitney had remained in court during the trial, but had retired when the jury left to consider their verdict, being completely overcome with agitation and excitement. The schoolmaster had slept in the house, and had persuaded her not to go to the court in the morning; fearing as he did that the verdict would be a hostile one. She completely broke down when she was told the news, and was still sobbing when Reuben arrived.

The schoolmaster at once took his leave, leaving mother and son together; and promised them to return in a day or two. When he again came over, he saw at once that Mrs. Whitney was looking depressed and unhappy.

"What do you think, Mr. Shrewsbury? Reuben says that he shall go abroad, out to Australia. I have talked against it till I am hoarse, but it's no good. I hope you will persuade him to give up such a mad idea."

"I will hear what he has to say first, Mrs. Whitney. Reuben has generally a good deal to say for his side of a question, and I must hear his reasons before I can argue against them.

"Now, Reuben, what have you to say for yourself?"

"I made up my mind while I was in jail," Reuben replied, "that if I was acquitted, I would go right away. These things stick to a man all through his life. That first affair, four years ago, nearly got me transported now; and if a small matter like that did me such harm, what will this do? If I had been proved to be innocent, it would have been different; but as it is, I believe nine people out of ten in court thought I was guilty; and I am convinced that the jury were eleven to one against me, only the twelfth was more obstinate than they were, and so they gave in. I believe it was Jacob Priestley the blacksmith who held out, for the sake of old times.

"At any rate, a great many people will think me guilty, all their lives, unless something turns up to prove my innocence. Mother says we might settle somewhere else, where we ain't known; but I should never feel safe. Years on, someone from Lewes might see me and tell the story; or Tom Thorne might keep on my track. I won't risk it.

"I have been to Mr. Penfold, and he says if I am determined to go, he will cancel my indenture for me. I have no doubt I shall find work of some sort, out there. I am a pretty good workman now at my own craft and, if I can't get work at that, I can turn my hand to something else.

"My only trouble is about mother. I want her to go with me. I could make a living for her out there, but she won't have it. She says six months at sea will kill her, and then she has all sorts of ideas in her head about the natives. However I hope that, in two or three years' time, I shall be able to write and tell her that I have comfortably settled, and have a good home ready for her to come to; and that then she will join me."

"Never," Mrs. Whitney said, excitedly. "I was born at Lewes, and I have lived near it all my days, and I will die here. I am not going to tramp all over the world, and settle down among black people, in outlandish parts. I could not do it, Mr. Shrewsbury. It's cruel of him to ask me."

The schoolmaster was silent for a minute. He saw that Reuben's mind was firmly made up, and he could not deny the force of his reasoning. It was true that many people still considered him guilty. It was true that this story might crop up again, years on, and ruin his life. It did seem that the best thing he could do was to leave the country.

"Australia is not so bad a place as you fancy, Mrs. Whitney," he said at last. "They do have troubles with the natives, certainly, in the outlying settlements; but in the towns you have no more trouble than you have here. Besides, every year the white population is increasing, and the black diminishing. Six months' voyage is not so dreadful as it seems. And though I do think that, if Reuben goes out, it will be better for you to remain quietly here till he has a home prepared for you; I think that, when the time comes, you will change your mind about it.

"As to Reuben himself, I must own there's a good deal of force in what he says; and that until those Thornes have been sent out of the country, his story might follow him. And I have no doubt he would do well out there. He is a good workman for his age and, as he says, can turn his hand to almost anything. Labour is scarce out there and, as he has got his head screwed on the right way, I have no doubt that he will fall on his feet."

"I didn't expect this of you, Mr. Shrewsbury," Mrs. Whitney said, beginning to cry. "I thought you would have taken my part, and now you are going right against me."

"Not against you, Mrs. Whitney, for I think that Reuben's plan is best for you both. He cannot but suffer, if he remains here; and you will be unhappy in seeing him suffer. Great as the loss would be to you, I believe that you would be happier here, alone, than you would be were you to see him in constant trouble and worry. At any rate you would have the option, if you found life intolerably dull here, of joining him out there at any time.

"But how do you intend to get out, Reuben?" he asked, seeing that Mrs. Whitney made no answer, but again relapsed into tears.

"I shall work my way out," Reuben replied. "I can do any rough work as a smith or a carpenter, and I should think I ought to get my passage for my work. Anyhow, I have got twelve pounds saved up; and if I can't get out free, that and my work ought to take me."

In a short time Mrs. Whitney, finding that Reuben was not to be shaken in his determination, ceased to oppose it; and began to busy herself in preparations for his departure, which he had arranged to take place as soon as possible.

A day or two before starting, he walked over to say goodbye to Mrs. Shrewsbury. He stopped as he passed the smithy and, seeing Jacob Priestley at work alone, he went in.

"Ah, Reuben, is it you?" the smith said. "Better here than in the dock at Lewes, eh? I hears a talk of your going to foreign parts."

"Yes, I am off," Reuben said, "and I have just come over to say goodbye to Mrs. Shrewsbury; so I looked in as I passed, knowing as you were one of those who found me not guilty, and would perhaps give me a shake of the hand, before leaving."

"That will I, lad. Yes, I found you not guilty; and I jest tipped you a wink, from the box, to let you know as it were all right; but my eye! what a game we had had of it. Never had such a game, in all my born days."

And the blacksmith sat down on a stool, to indulge in a great fit of laughing.

"What was the game?" Reuben asked.

"Well, you know, Stokes he was the foreman, and a Cockney sort of chap he be. He turns round in the box and, says he:

"'In course you are all agreed.'

"'Agreed as how?' says I.

"'Why, agreed as he's guilty, in course,' says he.

"'Nothing of the sort,' says I. 'I believes he's as innocent as a child unborn.'

"Then they all comes round me and jaws; but seeing as I wasn't going to give in, Stokes he asked the judge for leave to retire.

"Well, when we retires they all pitches into me, and says as it's monstrous one man should hold out agin eleven; and that, even if I didn't feel sure myself, I ought to go as the others went. So I didn't say much, but I sits myself down and brings out a big chunk of bread and bacon, as my good woman had put into my pocket, and I begins to eat.

"'Look you here,' says I, 'I ha' got four parcels like this. Today be Friday, and I can hold on easy till Tuesday. That's how I looks at it. This young chap ain't had nothing to do with this 'ere robbery, and I ain't going to see he transported for what he never done.'

"Well, there we sits. Sometimes they would all talk at once, sometimes two or three of them would give it me. Ten o'clock comes and they got desperate like, for only one or two of them had put anything into their pockets, thinking that the matter was sure to be finished that night. When the messages were sent out again, as we couldn't agree, I sits down in a corner and, says I:

"'I ain't a selfish man, and any of you as changes your mind can have a share of what I have got.'

"I dozes off, but I hears them jawing away among themselves. It might have been two o'clock when one of them comes to me and gives me a shake and, says he:

"'Give us a cut of that bread and bacon. I am well-nigh starved. I have got a wife and children to think of, and it don't matter to me whether this chap goes to Botany Bay, or whether he don't. It didn't seem to me a certain case, all along, so I will go along with you.'

"Gradually two or three more comes, and when it got light I could see as some more was hesitating so, says I:

"'Lookee here, my friends. Those who has agreed to give this young chap another chance has lessened my stock of bread and bacon pretty considerable, and I ain't got more than enough for one more, so who's the next?'

"Four more spoke out at once. I divides the bread and bacon among them; then, as there was nine of us agin three, we goes at them and tells them how wrong it is as we was all to suffer from their obstinacy, and we works on their feelings about their wives and children; and then, says I:

"'I call it downright ridiculous, when there's a hot breakfast on twelve tables waiting for us, as three men should keep the rest from tucking in, just acause they won't give an innocent lad the benefit of the doubt.'

"Well, that finished them. The thought of the hot breakfast made the other chaps so ravenous as I believe they would have pitched into Stokes and the other two, if they hadn't have given in. So they comes round, and we sends out to say that we had agreed on the vardict. It were the best game I ever seed in my life."

"Well, Jacob, I am sure I am heartily grateful to you, and I shall not forget your kindness; though what made you so sure of my innocence, while all the others doubted it, I don't know."

"Lor', Reuben!" the smith said, "There ain't nothing to thank me about. I didn't know nowght as to whether you was innocent or guilty; and it was a good job for me as I had made up my mind about that there vardict, afore I went into court; for I should never have made head or tail of all that talk, and the fellows with white hair on the top of their heads as kept bobbing up and down, and asking all sorts of questions, was enough to turn an honest man's head. The question was settled when Miss Kate Ellison—that's the little un, you know—came in here. Says she:

"'Jacob, you are on this jury, I hear.'

"'Yes, miss,' says I.

"'Well, I hope you are going to find Reuben Whitney innocent,' says she.

"'I don't know nothing about it,' says I. 'Folks seem to think as he did it.'

"Then she went at me, and told me that she was sure you was innocent; and the squire he was sure, and he would be moighty put out if you was found guilty. So I told her natural that, the squire's being a good landlord, I wouldn't disoblige him on no account; and she might look upon it as good as settled that you should be found innocent. So she tells me not to say a word to anyone, and I ain't, not even to the ould woman; but in course, I don't consider as she meant you."

Reuben could not help laughing as he learned that he had been acquitted, not from any belief in his innocence on the part of the jury, but by the intervention on his behalf of the girl who had, before, fought his battles. Shaking hands with Jacob, he went on to the schoolmaster's.

As he was sitting there chatting with Mr. and Mrs. Shrewsbury, he saw Kate Ellison come out of her father's gate along the road with her basket, as usual. Catching up his hat, he ran out and stood bareheaded, awaiting her.

"Ah, Reuben!" she said, with a smile and a nod, "I am glad to see you before you go; for Mr. Shrewsbury told me, yesterday, you were going to leave Lewes and emigrate. I am glad,"—and she hesitated a little—"very glad that they found you innocent. I was quite sure you would not do such a thing."

"I am glad I came over today, Miss Ellison," Reuben said quietly. "Very glad that I have met you; for I have just learned, from Jacob Priestley, that it is to you I am indebted that I am not, in the present moment, a prisoner in jail, under sentence of transportation."

The girl flushed up hotly.

"Jacob Priestley is very wrong to have spoken about it. I told him he was never to mention it."

"I hope you will not blame him, Miss Ellison. He told me he had never spoken a word to anyone else, but he thought you did not mean it to apply to me. I am very glad he has spoken; for I shall carry away with me, across the sea, a deep gratitude, which will last as long as I live, for the kindness you have shown me; not only now, but always—kindness which has saved me from a terrible punishment, for an offence of which I was innocent.

"May God bless you, Miss Ellison, and render your life a happy one."

"Goodbye, Reuben," the girl said, gently. "I hope you may do well, in the new land you are going to."

So saying, she went on her errand. Reuben stood watching her, until she entered one of the cottages. Then, putting on his cap, he returned to the schoolmaster's.

A week later Reuben was wandering along the side of the London Docks, looking at the vessels lying there, and somewhat confused at the noise and bustle of loading and unloading that was going on. He had come up the night before by the carrier's waggon, and had slept at the inn where it stopped. His parting with his mother had been a very sad one, but Mrs. Whitney had so far come round as to own that she thought that his plan was perhaps the best; although she still maintained that she should never venture, herself, upon so distant a journey. He had promised that, should she not change her mind on this point, he would, whether successful or not, come home to see her.

The squire had driven over, the day before he left, to say goodbye to him. He had, through Mr. Shrewsbury, directly he heard that he was going, offered to help towards paying his passage money; but this offer Reuben had gratefully, though firmly, declined to accept.

"Well, Reuben, I wish you every good luck on your adventure," he said. "The place you are going to will be a great country, one of these days; and you are just the fellow to make your way in it. I am sorry you wouldn't let me help you; because I am in a way, you know, at the bottom of this business which has driven you from home."

"Thank you, squire, for your kind intention," Reuben answered; "but I am so much in your debt, now, that I would rather not go further into it. I am old enough now to make my own way in life. My only regret in the matter is that I cannot persuade my mother to go with me."

"I think she is right, Reuben," the squire replied. "You can transplant a young tree, easily enough; but you can't an old one. Somehow they won't take root in new soil.

"Well, lad, I wish you every success. I suppose I shall hear through Shrewsbury, from time to time, how you are going on."

As Reuben walked along the dock, he stopped to read the notices of their destination, affixed to the shrouds of most of the vessels. He had already gone on board three or four, which were loading for Australia, but in none was there a vacancy for a carpenter. He stopped before a fine-looking barque, to which no notice was attached.

"Where is she going to?" he asked a sailor, who was passing along the gangway to the shore.

"She's bound for Sydney," the sailor said. "She warps out of dock tonight, and takes on board a cargo of prisoners in the Medway."

"Do you mean men sentenced for transportation?" Reuben asked.

"Yes," the man said, "and I wish she had any other sort of cargo. I have been out with such a load before, and I would as soon go with a cargo of wild beasts."

Reuben felt a sudden chill, as he thought how narrow had been his escape of forming one of a similar party. However, he stepped on board, and went up to the mate, who was superintending the cargo.

"Do you want a carpenter for the voyage out?"

"A carpenter!" the mate repeated. "Well yes, we do want a carpenter. The man who was to have gone has been taken ill. But you are too young for the berth. Why, you don't look more than eighteen; besides, you don't look like a carpenter."

"I am a mill wright," Reuben said, "and am capable of doing any ordinary jobs, either in carpentering or smith work. I have testimonials here from my late employers."

"Well, you can see the captain, if you like," the mate said. "You will find him at Mr. Thompson's office, in Tower Street, Number 51."

Reuben at once made his way to the office. The captain refused, at first, to entertain the application on the ground of his youth; but ship's carpenters were scarce, the time was short, and there was a difficulty in obtaining men for convict ships. Therefore, after reading the very warm testimonial as to character and ability which Mr. Penfold had given Reuben, he agreed to take him, on the terms of his working his passage.

Reuben went back at once, to the inn where he had stopped, and had his chest taken down to the docks; and went on board the Paramatta which, at high water, warped out of dock into the stream.

Chapter 6
On The Voyage

The next day the Paramatta weighed anchor and proceeded down the river. Reuben had no time to look at the passing ships, for he was fully occupied with the many odd jobs which are sure to present themselves, when a ship gets under weigh. The wind was favourable, and the Paramatta ran down to the mouth of the Medway before the tide had ceased to ebb. She anchored for three hours, and then made her way up to Chatham, where she brought up close to the government yard.

It was not till late in the evening that Reuben had finished his work, and was at liberty to look round, and to take an interest in what was going on on deck.

"This is your first voyage, my lad, I reckon," an old sailor, who was standing leaning against the bulwark, smoking his pipe, remarked.

"Yes," Reuben said cheerfully, "this is my first voyage. I have shipped as carpenter, you know, to work my way out to Sydney."

"You could not have chosen a better ship than this 'ere barkee," the sailor said; "though I wish she hadn't got them convicts on board. She will sail all the faster, 'cause, you see, instead of being choked up with cargo, the deck below there has been set aside for them. That will make easy sailing and quick sailing; but I don't like them, for all that. They are a lot of trouble, and they has to be watched, night and day. There's never no saying what they might be up to; there's mostly trouble on board, with them. Then one can't help being sorry for the poor chaps, though they does look such a villainous bad lot. They are treated mostly like dogs, and I have been on board ships where the rations was not what a decent dog would look at."

"But I thought there was regular food, according to a scale," Reuben said.

"Ay, there's that," the sailor replied, "and the government officers see that the quantity's right; but, Lor' bless you! They don't trouble as to quality, and some of the owners buys up condemned stores, and such like; anything, thinks they, is good enough for a convict ship—biscuits as is dropping to pieces, salt junk as 'as been twenty years in cask, and which was mostly horse to begin with. No wonder as they grumbles and growls. A convict is a man, you see, though he be a convict; and it ain't in human nature to eat such muck as that, without growling."

"What tonnage is the vessel?" Reuben asked.

"'Leven hundred and fifty ton, and as fine and roomy a ship as there is in the trade, and well officered. I have made three v'yages with the captain and first mate, and the second mate was with us on the last v'yage."

"How many hands are there, altogether?"

"Twenty-five, counting you as one, and not a-counting the two stewards."

"We are going to take some passengers, I see," Reuben said. "I have been at work, putting up pegs and shelves for them."

"Yes, there's eight or ten passengers, I hears," the sailor said. "Passengers don't mostly like going by convict ships, but then the fares are lower than by other vessels, and that tempts a few. Besides, the Paramatta is known to be a fast ship, and the skipper has a good name; so we shall have a better class of passengers, I expect, than usually voyages with convict ships; and besides the passengers there will be the officer of the convict guard, and a surgeon, so we shall be pretty full aft."

"And what will my duties be, when we are at sea?"

"It just depends on the captain," the sailor said. "You will be put in a watch, and work with the others, except that they may not send you aloft. That depends on the terms that you shipped."

"I shipped as carpenter, and to make myself generally useful, and to obey orders. I shall be happy to do anything I can; hard work is better than doing nothing, any day."

"That's the sort, my lad," the sailor said heartily. "Now I am sail maker, but, bless your heart! Except putting a patch on a sail, now and then, there's nothing to do that way; and when not so wanted I am one of the ordinary crew. Still, if you works your passage, it ain't to be expected as they will drive you the same as a man as is paid. He's a fair man, is the skipper; and you won't find yourself put upon, on board the Paramatta."

"Can't I go up aloft now?" Reuben asked. "I would rather accustom myself to it while we are lying steady, than go up when the wind's blowing, and she is heeling over."

"Go up! To be sure you can, and I will go up with you, and tell you some of the names of the ropes, and put you up to things. There's a pleasure in helping a lad who seems in any way teachable. Some of they boys as comes on board a ship ain't worth their salt, in these days."

The sailor led the way up the shrouds. Reuben found it much more difficult than it looked. He had seen the sailors running up and down, and it looked as easy as mounting a ladder; but the slackness of the ratlines—which, as the sailor told him, was the name of the pieces of rope which answered to the rounds of a ladder—made it at first awkward. When they reached the main top the sailor told him to sit down, and look round quietly, till he became accustomed to the height.

"It looks unnatural and risky, at first," he said; "but when you get accustomed to it, you will feel just as safe, when you are astraddle the end of a yard, and the ship rolling fit to take her masts out, as if you were standing on the deck."

As Reuben had heard the sailors laughing and joking aloft, as they hauled out the earrings of the sails, he had no doubt that what the sailor said was true; but it seemed, to him, that he should never accustom himself to sit at the end of a spar, with nothing but the water at a vast depth below. It would be bad, even with the ship lying quiet, as at present. It would be terrible with the vessel in a heavy sea.

The sailor now told him the names of the masts and stays, giving him a general idea of the work aloft, and presently asked him whether he would like to return to the deck now, or to mount a bit higher. Although Reuben was now becoming accustomed to the position, he would, had he consulted his inner feelings, have rather gone down than up; but he thought it was better to put a good face on it, and to accustom himself, at once, to what he would probably have to do sooner or later.

Holding on tight then, and following the instructions of his companion, he made his way up until he was seated on the cap of the top-gallant mast, holding tight to the spar, which towered still higher above him. He was surprised at the size and strength of the spars, which had looked so light and slender, from below.

"Very well done, lad," the sailor said approvingly. "You would make a good sailor, in time, if you took to a seafaring life. There's not one in ten as would get up there, the first time of going aloft. You don't feel giddy, do you?"

"No," Reuben replied, "I don't think I feel giddy, but I feel a strange shaky feeling in my legs."

"That will soon pass off," the sailor said. "You look at them hills behind the town, and the forts and works up there. Don't think about the deck of the vessel, or anything, but just as if you were sitting in a chair, watching the hills."

Reuben did as the sailor instructed him and, as he did so, the feeling of which he was before conscious passed completely away.

"I feel all right now," he said, after sitting quietly for a few minutes.

"All right, then; down we go. Don't look below, but just keep your eyes in front of you, and never leave go of one grip till you make sure of the next."

Five minutes later he stood on the deck.

"Well done, my lad, for the first time," the first mate said, as Reuben put his foot on the deck "I have had my eye on you. I shouldn't have let you go beyond the top, at the first trial; but I didn't think you would go higher, till you were fairly up, otherwise I should have hailed you from the deck.

"You ought not to have taken him up above the top, Bill. If he had lost his head, it would have been all up with him."

"I could see he wasn't going to lose his head. Trust me for not leading a young hand into danger. He was a little flustrated, when he got into the top; but after he had sat down a bit, his breath come quiet and regular again, and I could see there was no chance of his nerve going."

The next morning, soon after daybreak, the dockyard boats began to row alongside, with grey-coated convicts. Reuben watched them as they came on board, with a sort of fascination with their closely cut hair, bullet heads, and evil faces. Although he had no doubt that the repulsive expression was due partly to the close-cut hair and shaved faces, and their hideous garb, he could scarcely repress a shudder as he looked at them. In some faces an expression of brutal ferocity was dominant. Others had a shifty, cunning look, no less repulsive.

There were a few good-humoured faces, one or two so different from the others, that Reuben wondered whether they were innocent victims of circumstances, as he had so nearly been. Not till now did he quite realize how great his escape had been. The thought that he might have had to spend the rest of his life herding with such men as these, made him feel almost sick; and he thanked God more fervently, even, than he had done when the verdict was returned which restored him to his liberty, that he had been saved from such a fate.

A hundred and eighty convicts came on board. They were in charge of ten warders, with loaded muskets, and an hour later a party of twenty marines, under the charge of an officer, also embarked. They were on their way out to join a ship in Australian waters, and were to aid the warders in keeping the convicts in good order.

The wind being favourable, no time was lost after the marines had come on board. The moorings were cast off and sails hoisted, and the Paramatta made her way against the tide to the mouth of the Medway; and there dropped her anchor to wait until the tide began to ebb, for the wind was so light that little would have been gained by an attempt to proceed at once. Sail was made again as soon as tide turned and, on turning out next morning at daylight, for he had not yet been assigned to a watch, Reuben found that the ship was lying at anchor in the Downs.

Two or three hours passed.

"What are we doing here, Bill?"

"We are waiting for the passengers. They are all coming on board here. I expect that big lugger you see, running out direct for us, 'as got them on board."

"I wonder they didn't come on board when we started," Reuben said. "I should think it would have been pleasanter than coming all the way down to Dover by coach."

"So I should think, my lad; but you see, it ain't every time as a ship has the luck we've had. It's a long job coming down to the Downs, if the wind don't serve. We might have been beating about there, at the mouth of the Thames, for a week. So you see, most of these 'longshore chaps like to send their traps on board while the vessel's in the docks, and then to come down here and stop till she comes round."

In a few minutes the lugger was alongside, the gangway was lowered, and the passengers began to come on board. They were, as the sailor had said they would be, some ten in number. There were six men, four ladies, and three children, the latter not counting as regular passengers, as they were stowed away in their parents' cabins.

The convicts who were on deck looked over the bulwarks, and cracked coarse jokes among themselves, as the passengers ascended the gangway. Reuben found that only one-third of the number were allowed on deck at once. Two soldiers paced up and down the deck, on guard of the hatchway leading below, and two sentries were posted at other points.

A number of small boxes, bags, coats and cloaks were handed up, and then the rope was cast off, and the lugger made her way back to Dover, and the Paramatta again got under sail. While they had been waiting, the chief mate had told Reuben that, according to the captain's orders, he would henceforth be in his watch.

"As you are not regularly shipped as a sailor," the mate said, "the captain does not wish you to go aloft, unless by your own desire; but there will be plenty of work for you to do on deck, hauling at the braces, scrubbing, and so on."

"I should be glad to do my work with the rest," Reuben said, "as soon as I feel I can be useful aloft. I was up two or three times yesterday, and hope in a few days to be quite accustomed to it."

"I have noticed you, my lad, and you could not be in better hands than Bill's. He is a capital sailor, and as he has taken to you, and you are willing to learn, you will be a useful hand before we get to Sydney; and even if you never go to sea again, all your life, you will find that you have learned a great deal that is useful on board the Paramatta."

The fine weather, which the Paramatta had experienced so far, speedily left her. The sky grew overcast, and the wind freshened fast, and the next morning the ship was staggering, under close-reefed canvas, in the teeth of the southwesterly gale.

For the next three days Reuben made no advance in seamanship, being prostrated with seasickness. At times he crept out from the forecastle, and tried to lend a hand whenever he saw a party of men hauling at a rope; but the motion of the ship was so great that he could scarce keep his feet on the slippery decks, and at last the mate ordered him to go back to the forecastle, and remain there until he recovered somewhat from his sickness.

"I see you are no skulker, my lad; but you will do no good on deck here, and are not unlikely to get a heavy fall, and perhaps a nasty hurt, so you had best lie off till you get over your sickness."

Reuben was already drenched to the skin by the spray, and felt so weak that he was not sorry to avail himself of the mate's orders, and to turn in again to his bunk in the forecastle.

On the morning of the fourth day he felt himself again, and turned out. The gale had almost blown itself out, but the sea was very heavy. The fresh air was delightful to Reuben, after the confinement in the forecastle; and as his watch was on deck, he at once went up to Bill and asked him what he could do.

"Glad to see you about agin, Reuben," the sailor said. "You have had a worse time of it than most. There is a lot of difference atween chaps. Some takes it bad, and some is never ill from the first. Well, there ain't nothing to do at present, but just hold on and get to feel your legs. Don't you try to go across the deck, if the hands are called, until you are accustomed to it; else you will get a fall, to a certainty."

"Is the gale nearly over, Bill?"

"Why, it's quite over. Don't you see that for yourself?"

"It seems to me to blow hard now."

"Blow hard! Why, there ain't a capful of wind. It was blowing pretty hard yesterday, if you like, but not worth calling a gale. If you are lucky, you are like to know what a gale is, when we get south of the Cape. The wind does blow there, when it has made up its mind. That's the place where they say as the helmsman has to have two men, regular, to hold on his hair."

Reuben laughed.

"I think on the whole, Bill, I would rather get to Sydney without meeting a storm like that. This has been quite enough for me. Why, some of the waves hit the vessel's bow as if they would have knocked it in."

"Wait till you have a gale in earnest, Master Reuben, and you will know about it then. Of course it seemed worse to you, because you were lying there a-doing nothing, and was weak-like with heaving yourself up. If you had been on deck, you would have seen as it was nothing worth talking about.

"Look at the ship. Everything's in its place, and ship-shape."

"Why, what has become of the tall spars aloft," Reuben said, looking up.

"Oh, they were sent down when the wind freshened," Bill said. "There ain't nothing in that."

"Where are the convicts, Bill?"

"Oh, they are all battened down below," the sailor said carelessly. "They only come up for an airing when the weather is fine. They are like the passengers only, instead of pleasing themselves, their ways are marked out for them."

"Have any of the passengers been up?"

"Two or three of the men have shown, and a gal. It ain't her first voyage, I'll bet. A pretty thing she is, and as straight as a mast. She's been on deck, off and on, ever since we started."

The next morning the sea moderated greatly and, the wind having gone round to the southeast, the Paramatta made the most of it, to get west as far as possible before turning her head to the south.

"That's a slice of luck," Bill Hardy said to Reuben; "there's nothing like getting well off, at the start. With luck, now, we oughtn't to see the land till we make the Cape."

"But I would rather see the land, Bill. When one is going half round the globe, it is pleasant to touch at ports on the way, and to get a glimpse at foreign peoples and ways."

"Ay, I like a spree on shore," Bill agreed; "but after all, it don't last long; and when you are near land, there's always the chance that the wind may shift round, and you may find yourself dead on a lee shore. The skipper gets anxious and the mates out of temper, and if it does come on to blow hard, from the wrong quarter, there's never no saying what will come of it.

"No, my lad, there's nothing like a good open sea, with no land within five hundred miles of you, at the least. The coast of Africa ain't a pleasant neighbour. What with the low shores, which you don't see till you are pretty nigh close to them; what with the currents and the changeable winds, and the precious bad lookout there is, if you do get cast ashore, I tell you the wider berth you gives it, the better."

The next morning was so fine and bright that all the passengers were on deck, and after breakfast the word was passed forward that the carpenter was wanted. Reuben found that he was wanted to nail some strips of wood on the floor of some of the cabins, to prevent the boxes from shooting out from under the berths when the vessel rolled. As he was at work at one of these, a young lady came to the door of the cabin, and uttered a little exclamation of surprise at seeing Reuben kneeling on the floor. Then, seeing what he was doing, she said:

"Oh, you are the carpenter, I suppose?"

"Yes, miss."

"I wish you would screw on some pegs I brought with me, to hang things upon. Everything does get thrown about so, when the ship's rolling. They are in that trunk, if you will not mind pulling it out."

Reuben pulled out the trunk, which the girl opened and, after some search, produced half-a-dozen iron clothes pegs. She showed him where she wished them screwed on, and stood looking on while he carried out her instructions.

"Are you the ship's carpenter?"

"Yes, miss."

"You seem very young for a carpenter, don't you?"

"I am young," Reuben replied, smiling, "and this is my first voyage. Fortunately for me, the hand who was engaged hurt himself, just as the vessel was sailing, so I obtained the berth. So far it does not appear that it is a difficult one."

The girl looked at him a little curiously. His manner of talk and conversation differed, so much, from the sailors in general.

"Are you really a carpenter?" she asked. "You don't look like a carpenter."

"Yes, I am really a carpenter," Reuben answered; "at least, I am a mill wright by trade. We are a sort of half and half between carpenter and smith.

"Is there anything else?" he asked, as he finished screwing the last screw.

"No, nothing else, thank you," the girl answered. "That will do very nicely, and I am much obliged to you."

After finishing his work in the cabins, Reuben went forward.

"Captain," the young lady said, as she went upon deck, "I have been talking to that young carpenter of yours. I am quite interested in him. Is he really a carpenter? He does not talk a bit like one."

"I believe so, Miss Hudson," the captain replied. "At least, he produced an excellent testimonial from his last employer, when I engaged him. Of course, it might not have been genuine. If there had been time, I should have made more inquiries; but he was well spoken, and had an earnest look about him. But, now you mention it, I don't know that it is very wise letting him go into all the cabins, when I know so little about him."

"Oh, I never thought of that!" the girl exclaimed. "I am sure he looks honest. It was only because he spoke so well that I mentioned it."

"He seems to be a sharp young fellow," the captain remarked, "and I see that he has taken to going aloft with the rest of the crew already. He is an emigrant rather than a sailor, for he has only shipped for a passage. I don't know whether he is going to join a man, out there; but if not, he is certainly young to go out on his own account. I do not think he's more than eighteen. He looks so young, he cannot have served all his time at his trade."

"I really feel quite interested in him, Captain Wilson," the girl said, turning to a gentleman standing by, who had been listening to the conversation. "I wish, if you get an opportunity, you would get into conversation with this carpenter of ours, and find out something about him."

"I will, if you like, Miss Hudson; but I don't suppose there's much to find out, and what there is, he's not likely to tell me. From what you say, I should guess that he had had a bad master, and had run away."

"But the captain said he had good testimonials," Miss Hudson persisted.

"As to testimonials," the gentleman said, "anyone can write a testimonial."

"How suspicious you are, Captain Wilson!" the girl laughed. "That's the worst of being a police officer, and having to do with criminals. You think whoever you come across is a rogue, until you find out he is an honest man. Now, I think everyone is honest, till I find him out to be a rogue."

"My way is the safest," the officer laughed. "At any rate, on board this ship there are five rogues to each honest man."

"Ah, but that's not a fair average," the girl objected. "Of course, in the colony one has to be careful, considering that half the shepherds and stockmen are convicts, and I must own that the natives are nearly all thieves; but how could it be otherwise, when England sends all its rogues out to us? You see, when free labour gets more abundant, and we can do without convicts, the colonists will protest against it."

"Very likely they will," the officer agreed; "but what is England to do, if she has nowhere to send her rogues?"

"That is her business," Miss Hudson said carelessly. "There is no reason why they should be shoved on to us. In the old time, when there were no colonies, England managed somehow, and I suppose she could do so again."

"She managed in a very short way," Captain Wilson said. "She hung them as fast as she caught them. It did not matter much what the offence was, whether stealing a loaf or killing a man; but she could hardly go back to that, now."

"No, she could not," Miss Hudson agreed; "but I have no doubt she can find something useful for them to do, when she has to keep them at home.

"Don't you think so, captain?"

"I daresay she could," the captain answered. "Certainly, if I were a colonist living in a lonely part of the country, I should object to transportation for, what with the natives and bush rangers and bad characters generally, no one can say their life is safe."

"Oh, it's not so bad as that, captain!" Miss Hudson said indignantly. "You are giving the place a bad character."

"I think Captain Wilson will agree it's a true one," the captain said, smiling.

"Eh, Captain Wilson?"

"I am afraid so," the latter replied. "I know they keep me pretty busy. However, after a year's holiday, I must not grumble if I find plenty to do when I get there."

The voyage down to the Cape was wholly uneventful. The Paramatta was most fortunate in her weather and, beyond trimming the sails, the crew had a very easy time of it. Captain Wilson had, as he promised Miss Hudson, taken the opportunity, when Reuben was sitting idly on deck, of having a chat with him; but he did not learn much in the course of the conversation.

"Your young carpenter puzzles me, Miss Hudson," he said to her at dinner. "He is certainly an altogether exceptionally well-spoken young fellow, for his condition of life; but I can't quite make him out. I think that he has worked as a mill wright. He spoke openly and without hesitation as to his work. But how it is he has thrown it up and emigrated, so young, I can't make out. Of course he cannot have served his time and yet, somehow, I don't think that he has run away, from the manner in which he spoke of his employer.

"He has no friends whatever in the colony, as far as I could learn. I should say he has certainly been fairly educated, and yet he seems, from his own account, to have worked three or four years at his trade.

"I certainly like the lad, though I own that, so far, I cannot altogether make him out. Perhaps I shall learn somewhat more about him, before we get to the end of the voyage, and in that case I will tell you all I know."

Miss Hudson was the daughter of a wealthy flock owner—or, as he was called, squatter—in New South Wales. Her father and mother were on board the ship with her. This was her fifth voyage. She had gone out as a baby with her parents; and had returned to England, at the age of ten, to be educated. When eighteen, she had joined her mother and father in Australia and, two years later, had come with them to Europe, and had spent some months travelling on the Continent. They were now on their way back to the colony.

The only other single lady among the passengers of the Paramatta was going out, under the charge of the captain, to fill a place as governess in a family in Sydney. Miss Furley was somewhat quiet, but a friendship had naturally sprang up between her and Miss Hudson, as the only two young women on board the ship; and the life and high spirits of the young colonist, and the musical acquirements of Miss Furley, helped to make the voyage pass pleasantly for the passengers in the Paramatta.

Captain Wilson had a good tenor voice, and sang well; and one of the other passengers was able to furnish a bass. Almost every evening, as the ship was running down the tropics before a gentle favouring breeze, the sound of solo and glee singing rose from the little party gathered on the poop; and even the convicts, on deck forward, ceased their talk and listened to the strains.

Although the passage had been a pleasant one, there was a general feeling of satisfaction when the ship dropped her anchor in Table Bay. Most of the passengers went on shore at once, to take up their quarters at the hotel till she sailed again. The captain said that it would take at least a couple of days to fill up the water tanks, and take in a supply of fresh provisions.

On the afternoon of the second day, Reuben asked permission of the first mate to go ashore for a few hours.

"Certainly, Whitney," the officer said. "You have proved a very useful hand on the way out, which is more than most do who work their passage. Nine out of ten of them are not worth their salt, to say nothing of the rest of their rations. You can stay on shore tonight, if you like; but you must come off early in the morning. We hope to get away in good time."

On landing, Reuben was much struck with the variety of the scene. In the streets of Cape Town were men of many types. Here was the English merchant and man of business, looking and dressing just as he would at home. Names over the shop doors were for the most part Dutch, as was the appearance of the majority of the white men in the streets. Dutch farmers in broad hats and homespun garments, mounted on rough ponies, clattered along through the streets. The manual work was for the most part done by swarthy natives, while among the crowd were numbers of Malays, with dark olive skins, small eyes, and jet-black hair, their women being arrayed in every shade of gaudy colour.

For some time Reuben wandered about the streets, greatly amused at all he saw. Towards evening he turned his face towards the sea, as he had no wish to avail himself of the permission given him to sleep on shore. Presently he encountered Miss Hudson and Miss Furley, walking the other way. The former nodded brightly, for she had several times spoken to Reuben, since their first acquaintanceship.

Reuben touched his hat, and proceeded on his way. He had gone but a few yards when he heard a loud cry, and everyone darted suddenly into shops or round corners.

Looking round in surprise, Reuben saw what had caused the movement. A Malay, with his long hair streaming down his shoulders, was rushing down the street, giving vent to terrible yells; in his hand he held a crease, with which, just as Reuben looked round, he cut down a native who had tried, too late, to make his escape.

The two English girls, confused and alarmed at the sudden outburst; and unable, until too late, to comprehend the cause of it, stood alone in the middle of the street and, too terrified now to move, clung to each other, regardless of the shouts to fly raised by people at the windows and doors.

The Malay, with a howl of exultation, made at them with uplifted crease. Reuben sprang forward, passed the terrified women when the Malay was within four paces of them, and threw himself with all his force upon him. The Malay, whose eyes were fixed upon the ladies, was taken by surprise by the assault; and his crease had not time to fall when Reuben sprang upon him.

The shock threw both to the ground; Reuben, as he fell, throwing both arms round his adversary. The Malay struggled furiously, and the combatants rolled over and over on the ground. Strong as Reuben was, the frenzy of the Malay gave him greater power; and the lad felt he could not long retain his grip of the arm with which the Malay strove to use his crease.

Help, however, was not long in coming. A native policeman ran up at full speed; and brought his heavy club, with his full force, down on the head of the Malay. The latter's limbs at once relaxed, and Reuben sprang to his feet; breathless, but not seriously harmed, although the blood was freely flowing from some slight wounds he had received from the Malay's sharp-edged weapon.

Chapter 7
Gratitude

Reuben looked round, upon gaining his feet. He saw Miss Hudson standing by the side of her companion; who had fallen, fainting, to the ground. Mr. Hudson and Captain Wilson, running at their full speed, were within a few paces of the girls. They had entered a shop to make a purchase, while the ladies strolled on; and although they had rushed out on hearing the alarm, they were too far off to render assistance and, impotent to help, had seen with horror the terrible death which threatened the ladies.

Frances Hudson had not uttered a word, from the moment when the Malay rushed down upon them; but as her father came up she turned round, and burst into tears as he clasped her in his arms.

As soon as it was seen that the Malay was no longer dangerous, the people poured out again from the houses and shops. It was no very unusual thing, in Cape Town, for the Malays to run amuck; and many of those in the streets hurried off, in the direction from which the man had come, to inquire how many victims had fallen to his deadly crease, and to see whether any friends were among them. On the Malay himself no one spared a moment's attention. A second tremendous blow, with the policeman's club, had dashed out his brains; for Malays running amuck were always killed upon the spot, partly in order to save further trouble with them, partly to strike terror into others.

Many of the bystanders gathered round Reuben, seized him by the hand, patting him on the shoulder, and praising him for the courage with which he had faced the maddened savage. A minute later, Mr. Hudson forced his way through the crowd. Miss Furley had already been raised, and carried into a shop.

"Go in with her, my dear," Mr. Hudson said to his daughter. "I will bring him to you directly.

"My brave fellow!" he exclaimed, as he made his way to Reuben and grasped his hand, "how can I thank you for saving my child's life? It seemed to us that she was lost, and that nothing could save her; when we saw you dash past her, and throw yourself unarmed upon the madman. It was a noble deed, indeed.

"You are not badly hurt, I hope," he added, as he saw the blood streaming down Reuben's face and arm.

"Nothing to speak of, sir," Reuben replied. "At least, I think not; but I feel rather queer from this loss of blood. I had better get myself bandaged up."

And indeed, Reuben was turning very pale, partly from the relaxation of the tension of the struggle; partly, as he said, from loss of blood.

"Stand back!" Mr. Hudson cried, "don't press upon him. The lad is nearly fainting. One of you help me get him into a shop. Where is the nearest surgeon to be found?"

It was as much as Reuben could do to walk across the street, aided by his two supporters. A strong glass of Cape smoke (as the native spirit is called) and water revived him somewhat. It was some minutes before a surgeon arrived; for five persons had been terribly wounded, and two killed by the Malay on his course, and the surgeons near were busily employed.

"Not very serious," the surgeon said, as soon as he examined Reuben's wounds. "Very different affairs from those I have just come from."

"I had hold of his hand," Reuben said, "so that he couldn't strike. They are only cuts he made in trying to get his arm free."

"That on your arm will not trouble you, though it has bled pretty freely. The one down your face is, fortunately, of no great consequence; except that it has cut down to the bone on the brow and cheek. If it had been an inch further back, it would have severed the temporal artery. You have had a narrow escape of it. As it is, you will get off with a scar, which may last for some time; but as it is an honourable one, perhaps you won't so much care. However, I will bring it together as well as I can, and stitch it up, and it may not show much."

The wound was sewn up and then bandaged, as was that on the arm. The other and slighter wounds were simply drawn together by slips of plaster. When all was done, Reuben said to Mr. Hudson:

"I shall do very well now, sir. I am sure you must wish to go to Miss Hudson. I will sit here a bit longer, and then go on board the ship."

"You will do nothing of the kind," Mr. Hudson said. "I have just sent for a vehicle, and you will come to the hotel and get into bed at once. You are not fit to stand now, but I hope a good night's rest will do you good."

Reuben would have protested, but at this moment a vehicle arrived at the door, and with it Captain Wilson entered.

"I have just taken your daughter and Miss Furley to the hotel, Hudson," he said. "They are both greatly shaken, and no wonder. So I thought it better to see them back, before coming in to shake hands with our gallant young friend here."

"He has lost a good deal of blood, Wilson; and I am just taking him off, to get him to bed in the hotel.

"So we won't do any thanking till the morning," Mr. Hudson said, seeing that Reuben's lip quivered, and he was incapable of bearing any further excitement. "Do you take one of his arms and I will take the other, and get him into that trap."

A quarter of an hour later, Reuben was in bed at the hotel. Mr. Hudson brought him up a basin of clear soup. Having drunk this, he turned over and was, in a very few minutes, asleep. The captain and most of the other passengers were at the same hotel, and there was great excitement when the news arrived of the terrible danger the two girls had run. Mrs. Hudson had, from her early life, been accustomed to emergencies; and the instant the girls arrived she took them up to the room they shared between them, and insisted upon their going at once to bed, after partaking of a cup of tea.

"What am I to do for this young fellow, Wilson?" Mr. Hudson asked as, having seen his patient comfortably in bed, he returned downstairs, and took a seat in the verandah by his fellow passenger. "I owe Frances' life to him, and there is nothing I wouldn't do for him. The question is, what? One does not like to offer money to a man, for such a service as this."

"No," Mr. Wilson agreed, "especially in his case. The young fellow appears to me very much above his condition. Your daughter first pointed it out to me, and I have since chatted with him several times, and find him a very superior young fellow. Certainly his education has been very different from that of most men in his condition of life, and I should have taken him for a gentleman, who had got into some scrape and run away, had it not been that he seems to have been regularly apprenticed to his trade. Still, there is something a little mysterious about him. I asked him casually what part of the country he came from. He hesitated a moment, and then said, 'From the south of England.' Of course, I did not ask any further questions, as it was clear he did not care about naming the precise locality, or he would not have given so vague an answer. I feel as deeply indebted to him as you do."

Mr. Hudson nodded. Only the evening before arriving at Cape Town, Captain Wilson had spoken to him on the matter of his affection for his daughter, and had asked his permission to speak to Frances. They had known each other in the colony, but had not been intimate until thrown together on board the Paramatta. Seeing that she was an only child, and that her father was considered one of the wealthiest squatters in the colony, Captain Wilson had feared that Mr. Hudson would not approve of him as a suitor; and had therefore broached the subject to him, before speaking to her. Mr. Hudson, however, had raised no objections.

"You have taken a manly and proper course, in speaking to me first," he said; "just what I should have expected from you. I own that, with the fortune the girl will have some day, I have always looked for her making what they call a good match, and settling down in the old country; but I may tell you that while she has been in Europe she has had several opportunities of so doing, if she would have taken them. She did not think fit to do so, and I have always made up my mind not to influence her in any way, providing she didn't fix her choice upon one whose character I disapproved. Certainly I have no reasons for so doing, in the present case. Your character stands high in the colony; and personally, as you are well aware, I like you exceedingly.

"What Frances' feelings in the matter are, I have no means of knowing. There is no doubt she likes you, but as to anything more, it is for you to find out. You will have plenty of time, between this and Sydney. Anyhow, you have my hearty approval of your wooing.

"I think, between ourselves you know, you must not expect, at first, any very cordial approval on the part of her mother. She had an idea, you know, that Frances would marry a duke at least, and an offer from a prince of the blood would not have surprised her. It is a great disappointment, to her, that she should have returned unmarried; and she has already been talking to me about our returning to England, in another couple of years. So she will not take quite kindly to it, at first; but you mustn't mind that. Fond of Frances as she is, she will soon come round, if she finds that the girl's happiness is really concerned in the matter.

"Take my advice, and don't push it till we get near the end of the voyage. If Frances says yes, she is the sort of girl to stick to it; and as I am with you, you may be quite sure it will come right in the long run; but we might not have a very pleasant time of it during the remainder of the voyage, you know, and as things have gone on so pleasantly, it would be a pity to spoil them."

Thus it was that Mr. Hudson nodded, when the young officer of the constabulary said that his indebtedness to Reuben was equal to his own.

"Yes," he said, "if it had been one of the sailors, I could have set the matter right by drawing a big cheque, and I shouldn't have cared how big;

but with this young fellow I do not quite see my way. However, I will shift the responsibility, by leaving the matter in Frances' hands—women are much better hands at things of this sort, that require a light touch, than we are. I do not wonder that she and Miss Furley are shaken. I feel shaken myself. I shall never forget that scene, and the two girls standing there, and that wild Malay rushing at them. My legs seemed to give way under me, and I thought I should have fallen down."

"I felt bad myself, sir," Captain Wilson said. "I have been in some tough fights, with bush rangers and natives; but I never had that sort of feeling before.

"One ran, but one felt it was no use running, as all must be over before we could get there. When it was over, I felt as weak as a child."

"Don't let us talk any more about it," Mr. Hudson said, rising. "I doubt whether I shall get a wink of sleep now; and I am sure I sha'n't, if we go on talking any more about it. Let us take a turn, and have a stiff glass of brandy and water afterwards, to settle our nerves before turning in."

The passengers by the Paramatta were up early in the morning, for the ship was to sail at nine. But early as they were, Reuben was before them; and on Mr. Hudson inquiring about him, as he turned out, he was informed that he had already gone on board the ship.

The two girls both looked pale, when they came down to their early breakfast. Both declared, however, that they had slept well.

"You must give us time, dad, to get up our roses," Frances Hudson said, in reply to her father's remarks as to their appearance. "I have no doubt a few days at sea will do it; but of course, it is only right and proper that young ladies should be pale, after going through such an adventure as we had yesterday.

"But do not let us talk about it," she said, with a shudder. "I should like not to be able to think about it, again, for six months. You used to say, dad, that I was plucky, because I wasn't afraid of wild cattle, and not very afraid of the natives or bush rangers; but I am sure I cannot lay claim to any special courage in future, for no one in the world could feel more frightened than I did, yesterday."

"Well, my dear, you were no worse than anyone else, for everyone else bolted at the first alarm. The way that street was cleared was something marvellous."

"Yes, dad; but I was too frightened to run. Not that it would have been any use if I had, for he was close to us before we knew what was the matter; and if I could have run, I don't think Emma could."

"No, indeed," Miss Furley said. "I had no idea of running and, even had there been plenty of time, I am sure I could not have got out of the way. Somehow I seemed to lose all power to move. I had just shut my eyes, and thought it was all over, when there was a shout and a rush, and I saw the Malay roll over; and then I made a snatch at Frances, and rolled over, too."

"It was a terrible moment," Mr. Hudson said. "But I agree, with Frances, that it is better for you to try and think nothing more about it, until you have perfectly recovered your health and spirits."

"I hear, dad, that the young man that saved us has gone on board ship. I asked, directly I was up, because I wanted to see him."

"And I expect, my dear, that he slipped away because he didn't want to see you. It sounds rude, doesn't it? But I can perfectly understand it."

"So can I," the girl agreed. "Did you see him this morning?"

"No, my dear. I came downstairs only a minute or two before you did, and then found that he was gone."

"Have you thought over what you are going to do, dad, for him?"

"Wilson and I have talked it over, Frances, but at present we don't see our way. It is too serious a matter to make up our minds in a hurry. Your mother is in favour of giving him a handsome present; but I don't think, myself, that that would do. Men who will do such deeds as that are not the sort of men to be paid by money."

"Oh no, dad! Surely not that. Any other possible way, but not money."

"No, my dear; so I thought. I have chatted it over with Wilson, and we have agreed that the best plan is to leave it entirely in your hands."

"I will think it over, dad," the girl said gravely. "It is a serious thing. We owe him our lives, and the least we can do is not to hurt his feelings, by the way in which we try to show our gratitude."

Reuben had slept well; and on waking, soon after daylight, jumped at once out of bed; and was glad to feel that, except for a certain amount of weakness in the legs, and stiffness in his wounds, he was all right again. He dressed quietly and, as soon as he heard persons moving about in the hotel, made his way down to the shore, and sat down there to wait for a boat from the ship; which was lying some distance out, and would, he was sure, be sending off early, as there would be many things to bring on board before she sailed.

It was not long before he saw the men descending the gangway to the boat alongside, which was soon rowing towards the shore. As she approached, Reuben saw the steward and first mate, sitting in the stern seats; and when the officer jumped ashore, his eye fell on Reuben.

"Ah, Whitney," he said, "I am glad to see you about. When the captain came off, last night, he told me all about your gallant rescue of the two ladies. I am sorry to see you bandaged up so much. The captain said you had some nasty cuts, but I didn't think they were so bad."

"They are nothing to speak about, sir," Reuben replied, "although you would think so, from seeing those bandages all over one side of the face, and my arm in a sling; but they are no great depth, and don't hurt to speak of. They were clean cuts with a sharp edge, and don't hurt half as much as many a knock I have had, with a hammer."

"Well, we all feel proud of you, my lad. It isn't everyone who would face a Malay running amuck, without weapons, I can tell you."

"I think any English sailor would do so, sir, if he saw the Malay rushing down upon two ladies. There was no time to think about danger, one way or the other. The only thing to be done was to rush at him, and so I rushed, as anyone else would have done."

"Ah, it's all very well to say so, Whitney; but I have my doubts about everyone else rushing. However, I mustn't stand talking about it now, as I have my hands full of work. The sooner you get on board the ship, the better.

"Row Whitney back to the ship, lads, and come back again in an hour's time. None of the things will be down here before that."

Reuben stepped into the boat, which at once pushed off. The men rowed easily, for they were anxious to hear the particulars of the report which had circulated through the ship. Bill Hardy was rowing the stroke oar, and did the questioning.

"You may try to make little of it," he said, "but I tell you, Reuben, it were a right down good thing—a thing any man would have right to be proud of.

"What do you say, mates?"

There was a general chorus of "Ay, ay."

"I took you in hand when you came on board, young un," Bill went on, "and I looks upon you as my chick, and I tell you I feel proud on you. I felt sure you would turn out a good un, some day, but I didn't look to see it so quick.

"In oars!"

The boat ran up alongside the gangway, and Reuben was soon upon deck. He was there met by the captain, who had just come up as the boat rowed alongside. He shook Reuben's hand heartily.

"You are a fine young fellow, Whitney; and your mother, if you have one, ought to be proud of you. I should be, if you were a son of mine. It was a lucky day for us all, when I shipped you on board the Paramatta; for it would have been a heavy day for us, if those two young ladies had been killed by that madman, yesterday.

"You look pale, lad, as much as one can see of you, and you will have to lie by for a bit. I hear you lost a great deal of blood.

"Steward, bring another cup of cocoa with mine, a large one, and put plenty of milk in."

The captain insisted on Reuben coming to his cabin to drink his cocoa.

"You had best knock off your allowance of spirits, till your wounds have healed up, lad. I will tell the second mate to serve you out port wine, instead."

Reuben now went forward, feeling very much the better for the cocoa. He again had to receive the hearty congratulations of the men; and then, rather to escape from this than because he felt he needed it, he turned into his bunk, and was soon sound asleep.

Three hours later, he was awakened by the tramp of men overhead, and knew that they were shortening the anchor chain, and preparing to be off. Going out on to the deck, he saw that the courses had been dropped, and the topsails were lying loose in their gaskets. The crew were singing merrily, as they worked the capstan. Three of the boats already hung from the davits, and two large boats were bringing off the passengers, and were already within a hundred yards of the ship; while the remaining ship's boat, with the steward, crowded with fresh stores, was but a short way behind them. As soon as the passengers were up, and the shore boats had left, she came alongside.

"Hook on the falls at once," the first mate ordered, "and run her up as she is. You can get the things out afterwards."

The anchor was, by this time, under the foot.

"Up with it, lads!" and the sailors again started, at full speed, on the capstan.

The jibs were run up, the courses and topsails shaken out and braced, and the Paramatta began to steal through the water again, for the second portion of her voyage. Mr. Hudson and his friend very soon made their way forward, and the ship was scarcely under way when Reuben, who was gazing over the bulwark at the shore, felt a hand laid on his shoulder.

"How are you today, Reuben? Better, I hope? It was too bad of you to run off in that way, this morning."

"I am all right now, thank you, sir," Reuben answered. "I felt just a little shaky at first, but the captain gave me a cup of cocoa when I came on board, and I feel now as if I were fit for duty again."

"Oh, nonsense," Mr. Hudson exclaimed, "you mustn't think of work, for days yet. No, you must come aft with me. My daughter and Miss Furley are most anxious to see you; and my wife, too, is longing to add her thanks to mine."

"You are very good, sir, but really I would rather not, if you will excuse me. It is horrid being thanked and made a fuss about, just because, on the spur of the moment, one did one's duty."

"That's all very well, Reuben; but you see, it wouldn't be fair to my daughter. If anyone did you a great service, you would want to thank them, would you not?"

"Yes, I suppose so, sir," Reuben answered reluctantly; "but really, I hate it."

"I can understand your feelings, my lad, but you must make up your mind to do it. When anyone puts others under a vast obligation to him, he must submit to be thanked, however much he may shrink from it. Come along, it will not be very dreadful."

Reuben saw that there was no getting out of it, and followed Mr. Hudson along the deck; feeling, however, more ashamed and uncomfortable even than he did when standing in the dock, as a criminal. Captain Wilson walked beside him. Hitherto he had not spoken, but he now laid his hand quietly upon Reuben's shoulder.

"My lad," he said, "I am not a man to talk much; but believe me that, henceforth, I am your friend for life."

Reuben looked up, with a little smile which showed that he understood. He had often, indeed, watched the young officer and Miss Hudson together, and had guessed that they were more than mere acquaintances.

The passengers were, with the exception of the three ladies, all gathered on the poop. But Frances had proposed to her mother that they should see Reuben in the cabin alone, as she felt that it would be a severe ordeal, to the lad, to be publicly thanked. Captain Wilson ascended to the poop and joined the others there, while Mr. Hudson went alone into the cabin.

The three ladies were awaiting him there. Frances came forward first. The tears were standing in her eyes.

"You have saved my life," she said softly, "at the risk of your own; and I thank you with all my heart, not only for my own sake, but for that of my father and mother; who would have been childless, today, had it not been for you."

"I need no thanks, Miss Hudson," Reuben said quietly.

His shyness had left him, as he entered the cabin.

"It will, all my life, be a source of pleasure and gratification to me, that I have been able to have been of service to so bright and kind a lady."

"I am not less grateful," Miss Furley said, advancing also. "I shall never forget that dreadful moment, and the feeling which darted through my mind, as you rushed past us and threw yourself upon him, and I felt that I was saved almost by a miracle."

"And you must accept my thanks also," Mrs. Hudson said; "the thanks of a mother, whose child you have saved from so dreadful a death. Believe me that there is nothing that my husband or myself would not do, to show how deeply and sincerely we are grateful to you."

Mrs. Hudson, indeed, felt rather aggrieved that she could not, at once, take some active steps towards rewarding the young man for saving her daughter's life; and she had been unable to understand the scruples of her husband and daughter on the subject. It was only, indeed, at their urgent entreaty that she had given way on this point.

"I call it monstrous, Frances," she said, almost angrily. "Of course the young man will expect something more substantial than words. It is only natural that we should reward him for preserving your life, and it would be a crime if we didn't do so. Of course, he didn't do it for money at the time, but it is absurd to suppose that a young carpenter like this, working his way out on board a ship, will object to receive a handsome present for such a service as this. Our feelings have a right to be considered, as well as his; and a nice thing it will be, for people to say that Ralph Hudson and his wife were so stingy, and ungrateful, that they did nothing for the lad who had saved their daughter's life."

"There is no fear of their saying that, mother. Everyone in the colony knows that there are no more open-handed people in New South Wales than you and my father. Besides, I do not say that we are to do nothing for him. On the contrary, I agree with you that it would be wrong, indeed, if we did not. I only say, please don't let there be a word said about reward, now. Let us thank him as one would thank a gentleman, who had done us a great service."

"Of course, I will do as your father wishes, Frances, but I call it nonsense. If he were a gentleman it would, of course, be different; but he is a young carpenter and, though you won't see it, that seems to me to make all the difference."

"From what I have seen of him, mother," Frances persisted, "I am sure that he has the feelings of a gentleman; even if he is not one by birth, about which I am not certain. Anyhow, I am much obliged to you for letting me have my own way."

"You always do have your own way, Frances," her mother laughed. "You get round your father first, and then you come to me, and what can I do against the two of you?"

Reuben briefly answered Miss Furley and Mrs. Hudson; and Mr. Hudson, feeling that the lad would rather get over the scene as soon as possible, slipped his arm though his and said:

"Now, Reuben, you must just come up for a minute on the poop. The other passengers are all waiting to shake you by the hand, and they would not forgive me if I were to let you run off, as I know you are wanting to do, without a word."

Accordingly Reuben was taken up to the poop, where the passengers all shook hands with him, and congratulated him upon his courage.

"Now, I suppose I can go, sir," he said, with a smile to Mr. Hudson, when this was over.

"Yes, you can go now," Mr. Hudson laughed. "Most young fellows at your age would be glad of an opportunity for figuring as a hero, but you talk as if it was one of the most painful businesses imaginable."

"Anyhow, I am glad it's over, Mr. Hudson, I can assure you; and now, I think I will turn in again. Considering what a night I had, I feel wonderfully sleepy."

It was not until the sun was setting that Reuben appeared again on deck. Shortly after he did so, Captain Wilson strolled up to the place where he was standing.

"I wish, Reuben," he said, after a few remarks on other subjects, "that you would tell me a little more about yourself. You understand that I do not ask from mere inquisitiveness; but after what has happened, you see, we seem to have got into close relationship with each other; and if I knew more about you, I could the easier see in what way I could most really be useful to you, out there. Are you what you appear to be?"

"I am, indeed," Reuben replied, with a smile. "My history is a very simple one. My father was a miller with a good business and, up to the age of ten, it did not appear that I should ever be working as a craftsman for my living. Unhappily, at that time my father slipped, one night, into the mill pond and was drowned; and when his affairs came to be wound up, it was found that he had speculated disastrously in wheat; and that, after paying all claims, there was nothing left.

"My mother took a little village shop, and I went to the village school. At first, I think I did not work very hard; but fortunately there was a change in masters, and the new one turned out one of the best friends a boy ever had. He pushed me on greatly and, when I was apprenticed to a mill wright, he urged me to continue my education by working of an evening. I stuck to it hard, and with his help learned, therefore, a good deal more than was usual, in my station of life. My mother was always particular about my speaking and, what with that and the books, I suppose I talk better than they generally do."

"And is your mother alive?"

"Yes, sir."

"But how came you to think of emigrating, at your age; when indeed, you cannot have served out your full time?"

"That, sir," Reuben said gravely, "I cannot tell you. Some day, perhaps, if you care to know, I may bring myself to do so. I may say that it was a serious matter, but that I was really in no way to blame, whatever people may think. My conscience is absolutely clear, and yet I would rather that the story, which I left England to escape, should not be known to anyone."

"I do not seek to know further, Reuben. I think I know enough of you to be perfectly sure that you would do nothing that was wrong, and I am perfectly willing' to take your word in the matter. However, I am glad that you have told me as much as you have. Your early rearing, your mother's care, and the education you have had, perfectly account for what seemed strange about you before. You have no objection, I hope, to my repeating your story to Mr. Hudson, who is as much interested in you as I am.

"And now another thing. I know that it is painful, to him, that one to whom he is so indebted should be forward here in the forecastle, instead of being in the cabin. He was afraid of hurting your feelings, by speaking to you about it; but I know that it would be a great relief and pleasure, to him and Mrs. Hudson, if you would allow them to make an arrangement with the captain that, for the remainder of the voyage, you should be a passenger."

"I am much obliged to them," Reuben said quietly; "but I could not think of accepting such an offer. I am working my way out independently, sir, and I owe no one anything. I am really enjoying the passage, and so far there has been no hardship worth speaking of. Even putting aside the fact that I should not like to accept an obligation which would, to most people, look like a payment for the service I was fortunate enough to be able to render to Mr. Hudson, I should feel out of my element. I am very comfortable, and get on very well with the men; while in the cabin I should feel strange, and out of place."

"I don't think you would seem out of place anywhere, Reuben. No one, from your manner and conversation, would judge you to be otherwise than a gentleman by birth; while there are several of the passengers, aft, whose talk and methods of expression are by no means up to the level of yours."

"I should feel uncomfortable myself," Reuben said, "even if I didn't make other people uncomfortable. So I think that, with all gratitude for the offer, I would very much rather remain as I am. Accustomed as I have been to hard work, during my apprenticeship, the life here appears to be exceedingly easy."

"Then we will say no more about it," Captain Wilson said. "It would have been a pleasure, both to me and the Hudsons, to have you aft, and I am sure you would be well received by all the passengers. However, as you think you would not be comfortable, we will let the matter drop.

"However, as to your work in the colony, we must have a say in that; and I hope that, when I thoroughly understand your wishes, we shall be able to help you forward there."

"For that I shall be extremely obliged, sir. It would be a great thing, indeed, for anyone on landing to have gentlemen ready to assist him, and push him forward. This is so at home, and is of course still more the case in a strange country. I am very anxious to get on, and am ready to work my hardest, to deserve any kindness that may be shown me."

"Well, we shall have plenty of time to think it over before we arrive.

"I fancy," Captain Wilson went on, looking upwards at the sky, "that our wonderful run of good luck, with regard to the weather, is likely to end shortly, and that we are in for a gale."

"Do you think so, sir?"

"I do, indeed; and if we do get a gale, it is likely to be a serious one. The Cape, you know, was much feared for its terrible storms by the Portuguese, and it has kept up its reputation ever since. I think it is going to give us a taste of its quality."

Chapter 8
A Gale

"Wilson tells me he thinks we are going to have a gale, Bill."

"Ay, ay, Reuben; anyone with half an eye could see that."

"Which way is it likely to come?"

"Most likely from the north or northwest. At least that's the quarter it's likely to settle into; but there ain't no saying which way it may take us. I thought things had been going on too smooth to last. Now you are going to see what a storm is, my lad. You thought it was blowing when we went down the Channel."

"Is it likely to be much heavier than that, Bill?"

"Heavier!" the sailor repeated scornfully. "Why, there's as much difference between a capful of wind in the Channel, and a gale off the Cape, as there is between a newborn baby and me."

"Do they last long, generally?"

"Last! Why they goes on for weeks. There ain't no end to them. I've wondered sometimes to myself where all the wind comes from, and where it goes to, onlass it works round and round."

"But it does work round and round, Bill?"

"Ay, when you are near the centre of it. Why, lad, in three hours I have gone round the compass three times, with the wind dead aft all the time; but that's only when you are near the centre. When you ain't it blows straight, and I have known vessels run for days—ay, for weeks—with the wind blowing all the time in the same quarter. Some have been blown down right to the edge of the ice, south. I have been among the icebergs myself, two or three times, and I guess that many a ship has laid her bones down in the ice fields there, and no news ever come back home as to what's come to them; and what makes it worse is as we have convicts on board."

"What difference does that make, Bill?"

"It don't make no difference, as long as all goes straight and fair. I have heard, in course, of risings; but that's only when either the guard are very careless, or the men is so bad treated that they gets desperate, and is ready to die on the off chance of getting free. So far we ain't had no trouble with them. The ship is kept liberal, and the poor wretches ain't cheated out of the rations as government allows them. The officer in charge seems a good sort, and there's no knocking of them about, needless; so there ain't no fear of trouble, as long as things go square. But when things goes wrong, and a vessel gets cast away or anything of that kind, then there's well-nigh sure to be trouble. The convicts seize their opportunity, and it ain't scarce in human nature for them not to take it, and then there ain't no saying what will happen."

"Why, what a croaker you are, Bill! I didn't expect that from you."

"I ain't no croaker, Reuben, but I knows what I knows. I have been through a job like that I am telling you of, once; and I don't want to do it again. I will tell you about it, some day. I ain't saying as I expect any such thing will happen, on board the Paramatta. God forbid. She's a tight ship, and she's got as good officers and crew as ever I sailed with. She has as good a chance as ever a ship had; but when I sees that 'ere sort of sky in these latitudes, I feels as we are in for a tough job."

The conversation was broken off, abruptly, by the call of the first mate.

"All hands aloft to shorten sail!"

"The bells is ringing up for the beginning of the performance, Reuben. Here goes aloft!"

The next minute the whole of the crew were climbing the shrouds, for the watch off duty were all on deck, and the order was expected; for the signs of the weather could, by this time, be read by every sailor on board. Above, the sky was still bright and blue; but around the whole circle of the horizon, a mist seemed to hang like a curtain.

"Smartly, lads, smartly," the captain shouted; "don't hurry over your work, but do it with a will.

"I hope we have not left it too long, Mr. James. I have held on longer than I ought, for every mile we get away from land is an advantage, and we have been running nearly due south, ever since I noticed the first falling of the glass when we got up in the morning."

"I think we shall have time, sir," the mate said. "We are going to have it, and no mistake, presently; but it don't seem to be coming up fast."

"The glass is going down rapidly," the captain said. "It's down an inch already, and is still falling.

"Mr. Mason," he went on, to the officer in command of the detachment of marines, "will you kindly place your men under the orders of Mr. James?

I am going to send down all the upper spars, and they can be useful on deck."

Never was the Paramatta stripped more rapidly of her sails, for every man was conscious of the urgency of the work. As soon as the sails were furled, the yards were sent down. The upper spars followed them and, in little over half an hour from the time the men began to ascend the shrouds, the Paramatta was metamorphosed. Her tall tapering masts and lofty spread of sail were gone. Every spar above the topmasts had been sent down to the deck; and she lay under close-reefed topsails, a stay sail, and a storm jib. The captain gave a sigh of relief, as the men began to descend the rigging.

"Thank God, that is safely accomplished. Now we are in readiness for whatever may come."

He dived into his cabin, and returned almost immediately.

"The glass has fallen another half inch, Mr. James," he said gravely. "I have never but once seen it as low.

"Ladies and gentlemen," he went on, addressing the passengers, who were gathered in a group, talking in low tones and anxiously watching the wall of vapour; which now seemed to rise from the water's edge and reach far up into the sky, the circle of view extending scarce half a mile in any direction; "I must ask you to go below, at once. The storm may strike us any moment now, and when it does come it will come heavily. I should like the deck perfectly clear, and nothing to disturb my thoughts from the working of the ship."

Reuben had not gone aloft, as he was called back, just as he began to ascend the shrouds, by the first mate, and ordered to go round the cabins and fasten the dead lights securely. When this was done, he aided the marines in nailing tarpaulins over the cabin skylights, and then went round the deck, seeing that every movable article was securely lashed. When this was done he joined Bill who, with some others, had been at work securing all the hatches. The convicts had long since been all sent below.

"Shall I send my men down, captain?" Mr. Mason asked.

"There is no occasion for it, just at present; but you had better pass the word for all of them to hold on, when the gale strikes her. That will be the critical moment. Once past that, she will be all right till the sea begins to rise. Then you had best get them below, for we shall have the water sweeping knee deep along the waist, in no time.

"I should say send them down at once; but I know many of them have been to sea before, and may be useful in cutting away, if anything goes."

"She looks snug enough, captain," the young officer said, glancing up at the diminished spread of canvas.

"She is snug enough for any ordinary gale," the captain said; "but this is not going to be an ordinary gale. When we once get her before it, it will be all right.

"Do you think we have another five minutes, Mr. James?"

"There's no saying, sir; but I should think so. What do you want, sir?"

"I want that top sail off her, altogether."

"I will do it, sir," the mate said and, calling Bill Hardy and two others of the best sailors, he led the way up the main shrouds.

Every eye on deck was fixed on the four seamen as, rapidly but steadily, they proceeded to furl and stow the sail. There was still not a breath of wind, but a low humming noise was heard.

"Quick, Mr. James, never mind the sail. All hands on deck!" the captain shouted; but the work was just done, and the sailors ran quickly down the ratlines on to the deck.

"Thank God!" the captain said reverently, "that is done."

The ship was now under the close-reefed fore-top sail, a diminutive try sail on the mizzen, and the jib. The hum had increased to a roar, but still not a breath of wind stirred the sails.

"Look up!" Bill said to Reuben; "you may be at sea fifty years, and never see that again."

Reuben looked up. Immediately overhead was a small circle of blue sky, round and round whose edge the edging of cloud seemed to be circling, with extreme velocity. The light seemed to pierce straight down onto the vessel, and she stood, pale and white, while all around her a pitchy blackness seemed to prevail.

"We are in the eye of the storm, my lad. Here it comes. Now, hold on for your life."

In another moment it seemed to Reuben that the end of all things was come. He was pinned against the bulwark, as if by a mighty invisible hand; and the vessel heeled over and over, until the deck seemed to rise in a wall above him. Then the water poured over him and, though he still held on, he thought the vessel had capsized. Then he felt her rising beneath his feet, and his head emerged from the water.

The captain, the first mate, and two seamen were at the wheel. Reuben saw the captain wave his hand, but his words were lost in the fury of the wind. The second mate, Bill Hardy, and two or three other sailors knew what was required, and hauled upon the lee brace of the fore-top-sail yard. The Paramatta was still lying nearly over on her beam ends, but gradually her head began to pay off, and she slowly righted. A minute later she was tearing directly before the gale. Scarcely had she done so, when the fore-top sail blew out of the bolt ropes, with a report that was heard even above the howl of the tempest.

"It's done its work," Bill shouted in Reuben's ear. "I thought she was gone. Just a little more, and she would have turned turtle."

The captain had used almost precisely the same words to the first officer, adding:

"She will do now, but we shall have to try to get a little more head sail on her, when the sea gets up. Call some of the hands aft, and get this try sail down. She yaws so, now the fore-top sail's gone, there is no steering her."

This was soon done and, under bare poles, the storm jib now the only sail upon her, the Paramatta tore through the water. There was little motion, for the sea had not begun to get up, seeming to be pressed flat by the force of the wind. The captain now left the helm. Two or three of the male passengers were standing at the top of the companion, peering out.

"You can come out, gentlemen, for a bit. She is running on an even keel now, though that won't last long. No one hurt below, I hope."

"Two or three of us have got bruised a little, captain; and I think we have all of us got a severe fright. We thought she was over."

"I thought so, too," the captain said. "Luckily she has got three hundred tons of iron on board, and it's all stowed at the bottom of the cargo, so that helped her up again; but it was touch and go with her, for half a minute."

"And now, gentlemen, if you will take my advice you will just look round, and then go below and turn in. Now you can do so easily. Another hour, and there will be no keeping a footing."

The captain was right. In less than the time he named, a terrific sea had got up. The Paramatta had already made more than one circuit of the compass. There was no regularity in the sea. It seemed to rise suddenly in heaps, now striking the ship on one side, now on another, and pouring sheets of water over her bulwarks. The motion of the vessel was so tremendous that even Bill Hardy and the older seamen could only move along with the greatest difficulty to carry out the orders of the captain; while Reuben clung to the shrouds, now half buried in water, now almost hanging in the air, with the sea racing along under his feet.

As yet no more sail had been put upon her, for there was no following sea. Although running almost before the gale, a slight helm was kept upon her, so as to edge her out from the centre of the storm; and the second circle of the compass took more than twice as long as the first to complete, although the vessel was proceeding with equal speed through the water.

Hour after hour the sea got up—a wild, cross, broken sea—and the motion of the vessel was so terrific as to be almost bewildering to the oldest hands. There was none of the regular rise and fall of an ordinary sea; the vessel was thrown with violent jerks, now on one side, now on the other; now plunging her bow so deeply down that she seemed about to dive, head foremost, beneath the waves; now thrown bodily upwards, as if tossed up by some giant hand beneath her. The watch off duty was sent below, for there was nothing that could be done on deck; and the water swept over her in such masses as to threaten, at times, to carry everything before it. One man had had his leg broken. Several had been seriously bruised and hurt.

"This is terrible, Bill," Reuben said, as he went below.

"Ay, lad; I have been at sea, man and boy, over forty years, and it's the worst sea I ever saw. I expect to see her masts go out of her, before long. Nothing could stand such straining as this. You had best turn in at once. Unless I am mistaken, it will be all hands to the pumps, before long. If she hadn't been one of the tightest crafts afloat, she would have been making water at every seam, by this time."

Reuben felt, the instant he lay down, that sleep was out of the question; for it needed all his strength to prevent himself from being thrown out of his bunk. The noise, too, was terrific—the rush and swell of the water overhead, the blows which made the ship shiver from stem to stern, the creaking of the masts, and howling of the wind. Night had set in, now. It was pitch dark in the forecastle, for the swinging lantern had been dashed so violently against the beams that the light was extinguished.

Half an hour after Reuben turned in, a crash was heard. A moment later the door was opened, and there was a shout:

"The mizzen has gone! All hands to cut away the wreck!"

The watch turned out and began to make their way aft, and were soon engaged with knife and hatchet in cutting away the wreck of the mizzen which, towing behind, threatened, with each heavy following sea, to plunge into the vessel's stern. A cheer broke from the men as the last rope was cut, and the wreck floated astern. The mast had gone close to the deck, smashing the bulwark as it fell over the side. The motion of the ship was easier, for its loss.

"Mr. James," the captain shouted, "we must get preventer stays, at once, upon the fore mast. The main mast may go, if it likes, and at present we shall be all the better without it, but the foremast we must keep, if we can."

"Ay, ay, sir. I will set about it, at once."

Picking out a few of the best hands, the first mate proceeded about the work.

"Go and sound the well, Reuben," the captain said.

Reuben went off at once, and returned in two or three minutes.

"There are four feet of water in it, sir."

"Four feet! Are you sure?" the captain exclaimed.

"Quite sure, sir."

The captain handed over the command of the deck to the second officer, and went below with Reuben. First wiping the rod carefully, he sounded the well.

"You are right," he said. "It is three inches over the four feet. I fear that the bumping of the mizzen, before we got rid of it, must have started a butt. She could hardly have made so much water from straining."

The captain made his way aft. The saloon was empty; the passengers, one by one, had retired to their cabins. He knocked at the doors of Mr. Mason and the chief warder.

"The ship is making water fast," he said. "We must rig the main-deck pumps. I can't spare any of the crew, their hands are full. Will you set the convicts to work?"

In a few minutes the clank of the pumps was heard. Very irregularly were they worked, for it was next to impossible for the men to stand to them, with the vessel throwing herself about so wildly.

The captain had remained on deck. He placed his hand on the shrouds of the main mast. One moment they hung loosely; and then, as the vessel rolled over, tightened themselves, with a sudden jerk, till they were as stiff as iron rods. He shook his head.

"Reuben, make your way up to the chief officer, and tell him that I am going to get rid of the main-top mast. Tell him to see that everything is cut free from the fore mast."

Reuben made his way aloft with difficulty. It needed all his strength to prevent the wind from tearing him from his grasp of the shrouds, but at length he reached the fore top, where the mate was at work. He delivered the captain's message.

"Ask the captain to wait five minutes, till I get the back stay secured. I will send a man down, as soon as I am ready."

"You take this axe," the captain said, when Reuben regained the deck, "and stand by this stay. When you see me ready to cut the other, cut at the same moment."

In a few minutes Bill came down, with a message to the captain that all was ready. The latter raised his arm to Reuben. He waited till the vessel rolled over, and then lifted his axe. The two blows fell together on the stays. A moment later the vessel began to rise again. As the jerk came there was a crash above, and the main-top mast fell over the side, clear of the deck, having snapped off at the cap like a pipe stem.

"Thank God for that," the captain said, as he cut away the connections on the other side, and the spar drifted astern, "that is off our minds."

The loss of the main-top mast and mizzen greatly relieved the strain on the ship, and she worked much easier. In half an hour, the first officer returned on deck with his party, and reported that he had done all he could to secure the fore mast.

"The sea is becoming more regular," the captain said, "now that we are getting further away from the centre of the storm. We shall soon have the waves racing behind us, like mountains, and we shall have to shake out the fore sail to keep ahead of them. Now, let us see how they are getting on below."

The well was again sounded, and it was found that the water had gained two or three inches.

"When the motion gets a little more regular, Reuben, you must take two or three hands, and work your way aft in the hold, and try and find out where the water is coming in."

"I will go at once, sir, if you like."

"No," the captain replied, "it must not be thought of. Everything will be adrift, and you would be crushed to death, to a certainty. You must wait till we are out of this tumble. If the water gains no faster than it does now, two or three hours will make no material difference, and by that time I hope we shall have got a regular sea."

Finding that there was nothing for him to do, Reuben again turned in. The motion was still tremendous, but he could feel a sensible change from what it was before. The motion of the ship was less sudden and violent and, although she rolled tremendously, she rose each time with an easier motion.

An hour later the watch turned out, and the others took their place. The wind was blowing as heavily as when the hurricane began, but the aspect of the sea had changed. It was no longer a mass of leaping, tumbling water; but was running in long waves, following each other, rising high above the vessel's stern as they overtook her. Having lashed himself to the side, he remained for an hour watching the sea. The first mate then came up to him.

"The captain thinks you might manage to get aft now. I will send Bill and Dick Whistler with you, to help you move any boxes or bales."

Reuben went back in the forecastle and got some tools, a piece of old sailcloth, and a large bundle of oakum; and then made his way with the two sailors down into the after hold. The way in which the upper tier of cargo lay heaped against the sides showed that it would, as the captain said, have been impossible to enter while the motion was at its worst. The rolling, however, had greatly diminished; the vessel rising and falling with a regular motion, as each wave passed under her. The men each carried a lantern and, with some difficulty, made their way to the stern.

"Ay, it's somewhere about here," Bill said. "I can hear the rushing of water, somewhere below. Now, the first thing is to move these bales."

They worked for a time, and then Bill returned on deck to fetch two more hands. They brought hand spikes and bars, as the bales were wedged so tightly together that it was difficult, in the extreme, to move them. It took two hours' hard work before they reached the leak. As the captain had supposed, the head of one of the planks had been started, at the stern post, by a blow from the wreck of the mizzen; and the water was rushing in with great force.

"A few hours of this would have settled her," Bill said. "All the pumps in the ship would not keep down such a leak as this."

Reuben at once set to work, cutting a deep groove in the stern post. He butted some stout pieces of wood into this, and wedged the other ends firmly against the first rib. Then he set to work to jam down sail cloth and oakum between this barrier and the plank that had started, driving it down with a marlinespike and mallet. It was a long job, but it was securely done; and at last Reuben had the satisfaction of seeing that a mere driblet of water was making its way down, behind the stuffing, into the ship.

"That's a first-rate job, lad," Bill said approvingly. "Half an hour's work once a week will keep her dry, if there is no water finds its way in anywhere else."

Reuben went aft to the well. The pump was now working steadily, the gangs of convicts relieving each other by turns. On sounding the well, he found that the water had fallen nine inches since he had last ascertained its depth. Going on deck, he found that a misty light filled the air, and that morning was breaking.

The captain had two or three times come down to the hold, to watch the progress of the work. Reuben reported to him its completion, and the fall in the water.

"Yes, it's been falling the last hour," the captain said. "She will do now. But she's making water, still. Some of the seams must have opened. I have been looking her over, and can't find out where it is; and we can do nothing until the gale has blown itself out, and we can get below and shift the cargo."

Reuben found that the fore sail had been set while he was below; and the vessel was running, some twelve knots an hour, before the wind. At one moment she was in a deep valley, then her stern mounted high on a following wave, and she seemed as if she must slide down, head foremost. Higher and higher the wave rose, sending her forward with accelerated motion; then it passed along her, and she was on a level keel on its top, and seemed to stand almost still as the wave passed from under her.

In spite of the extra lashing which had been given, the hen coops, spars, and everything loose upon the decks had been swept away; and the bulwarks had, in several places, been stove in. The galley had been carried away, but the cook had just made a shift to boil a cauldron of coffee below, and a mug of this was served out to all hands. As Reuben broke a biscuit into his portion, and sipped it, he thought he had never enjoyed a meal so much. He had now been, for eighteen hours, wet through to the skin; and the coffee sent a warm glow through him.

The captain ordered all hands, save a few absolutely required on deck, to turn in; and Reuben was soon in a glow of warmth beneath his blankets and, lulled by the now easy motion of the ship, was fast asleep in a few minutes.

After four hours' sleep, he was again on deck. The gale was blowing as strongly as ever, three men were at the helm, and the vessel was still tearing along at great speed. Several of the male passengers were on the poop, and the contrast between the appearance of the Paramatta at the same hour on the previous day, and that which she presented now, struck Reuben very strongly. Sadly, indeed, she looked with mizzen mast gone, the main mast shortened to the cap, and all the upper spars and rigging of the fore mast gone. She was, however, making good weather of it, for her hold was now so dry that the pumps were worked only on alternate hours, and the relief afforded by the loss of all her top hamper was very great.

For a week the Paramatta ran before the gale. At the end of the fourth day its force somewhat abated, but it still blew much too hard for anything to be done towards getting up fresh spars; while the lost mizzen rendered it impossible for them to bring her up into the wind.

"It's bitterly cold, Bill," Reuben said. "Its been getting colder every day, but this morning it is really bitter."

"And no wonder, lad, seeing that we have been racing south for pretty nigh a week. We have been making a little easting, but that is all, and we are getting into the region of ice. We may see some bergs any time now."

"I should like to see an iceberg," Reuben said.

"The fewer we see of them the better," Bill replied, "for they are about as nasty customers as you want to meet. I expected we should have seen them before, but this gale must have blown them south a bit. They work up with the northwesterly current, but I expect the wind will have carried them back against it. No, I don't want to see no icebergs."

"But if it were a very big one, we might get under its lee and repair damages a bit, Bill. Might we not?"

"No, my lad. The lee of an iceberg ain't a place one would choose, if one could help it. There you are becalmed under it, and the berg drifting down upon you, going perhaps four knots an hour. No, the farther you keep away from icebergs the better. But if you have got to be near one, keep to windward of it. At least, that's my 'speryence.

"They have been having some trouble with the convicts, I hears. They worked well enough at first, as long as they knew that there was a lot of water in the hold; but since then they have been a-grumbling, and last night I hear there was a rumpus, and six of them was put in irons. That's the first of it, and the sooner the gale's over, and we shapes our course in smooth water for Sydney heads, the better I shall be pleased."

An hour later, Bill pointed to the sky ahead.

"Do yer see nothing odd about that 'ere sky?"

"No," Reuben replied, "except that it's very light coloured."

"Ay, that's it, my lad. That's what they call the ice blink. You see if we ain't in the middle of bergs before night comes on. I have not been whaling for nothing."

A few minutes later, the first mate was heard to be shouting orders.

"Just as I thought," Bill said. "We are going to try to rig a jury mizzen, so as to help us claw off the ice, if need be."

A spare top mast was got up from below. Guys were fixed to one end and, with the help of the marines and a party of convicts, the spar was raised alongside the stump of the mizzen mast; and was there lashed securely, the guys being fastened as stays to the bulwarks. Blocks had been tied to the top, before it was raised; and ropes rove into them; and a try sail was brought on deck, and laid ready for hoisting.

The first mate ascended to the fore top, and at once hailed the deck that ice was visible ahead. The captain joined him, and for some minutes the two officers carefully examined the horizon. No sooner did the captain regain the deck than he ordered the try sail to be hoisted on the jury mast, and a haul to be given upon the braces of the fore sail, while the ship's course was laid a little north of east.

"It is lucky the wind has gone down as much as it has," he remarked to Mr. Hudson. "The sea is still heavy but, if that jury mizzen stands, we shall be able to claw off the ice."

"Is there much of it, captain?"

"We could see a good many bergs and, from the look of the sky, I should say there was an ice field lying beyond them. However, I think we shall do, if the wind does not freshen again. If it does, we must do our best to make a group of islands lying down to the southeast, and there refit. They are a rendezvous for whalers, in summer."

"Why not do so now, captain?"

"I would, if it were not for the convicts. But, unless as a last resource, I would not run the risk of touching at any island with them on board. As long as we are at sea they are comparatively harmless and, unless there is gross carelessness on the part of their guard, there is little fear of an outbreak. But once let them get on land, the matter is changed altogether. They are nearly three to one as against the warders, marines, and crew; and I would not run the risk, on any account, if it can be possibly avoided. No, no, Mr. Hudson, unless it be a matter of life and death, we will put in nowhere till we are in Sydney harbour."

Chapter 9
Two Offers

At nightfall the Paramatta was in the midst of the icebergs, and Reuben soon understood the antipathy which Bill had expressed for them. As a spectacle, they were no doubt grand; but as neighbours to a half-crippled ship, with half a gale blowing, their beauty was a very secondary consideration to those on board.

Additional stays were fixed to the jury mast, as it might be necessary, at any moment, to attempt to bring her up into the wind; and the word was passed that both watches must remain on deck. Fortunately the night was a light one, for the moon was up, and the sky almost cloudless. The mate stood with two of the best hands at the wheel; while the second mate took his place in the fore top, with a lantern, to signal the position of ice ahead. Fortunately there were but few small floating blocks about, and the Paramatta threaded her way through the larger bergs, without once approaching near enough to render danger imminent. It was a long and anxious night but, when morning broke, it was seen that the sea was now open ahead, and by the afternoon they had left the last berg behind.

Two days later the wind went completely down, and the crew at once set to work to repair damages. Reuben, with two men under him, filled up the breaches in the bulwarks. A respectable jury mast was rigged by the stump of the main mast; and the spar, which had done such good service among the bergs, was replaced by a longer and heavier one. All hands worked vigorously, and the sailors were assisted in the heavier work by parties of convicts.

After two days' toil all was completed. Sail was hoisted again and, under a greatly reduced spread of canvas to that which she had carried before the gale burst, the Paramatta proceeded on her way. The weather continued favourable and, without further adventure, the Paramatta arrived off Sydney heads; having made the voyage in a hundred and three days, which was, under the circumstances, a quick one.

The last evening Captain Wilson asked Reuben to go with him to the poop, as he and Mr. Hudson wanted to have a chat with him.

"Now, Reuben," Mr. Hudson said, "sit yourself down here. We must have a talk together. Now we want to know exactly what you are thinking of doing."

"I am thinking of getting work, sir," Reuben said, "at my own trade."

"Well, my lad, I don't think you will make much at that. There are mills, of course, but not a great many of them; and I fancy you would find it difficult to get anything like regular work. The distances here are tremendous, and you would spend the money you made, in one job, in looking out for another.

"That is the first view of the case. The second is, that neither Captain Wilson nor I mean to let you try it. You have saved my daughter's life, and I am not going to let the man who did that tramp about the country, looking for a day's work. Captain Wilson is going to marry my girl shortly, and of course he feels just the same about it. So the next question is, 'What is the best thing we can do for you?' Now, if you have a fancy for squatting, you can come with me up country and learn the business; and this day, twelve-month, I will hand you over the deeds of a range, with five thousand sheep upon it. Now, that's my offer.

"Now, don't you be in a hurry to refuse it, and don't let me have any nonsense about your not liking to accept it. Ten such farms would not pay the debt I owe you, and I tell you I should think it downright mean, if you were to refuse to let me pay you a part of my debt. Now you shall hear Wilson's proposal."

"My offer is not so brilliant, Reuben. Indeed, as far as making money, the pay would probably be no higher, at first, than you might earn at your trade. I am, as you know, assistant superintendent to the constabulary force of the colony. Now, if you like, I will obtain you a commission as an inspector. The pay is not high, but by good conduct you may rise to a position such as I hold. It is the position of a gentleman, and the life is full of excitement and adventure. Now, what do you say?"

Reuben was silent for a minute or two.

"I am greatly obliged to you both," he said, "more obliged than I can tell you. Your offer, Mr. Hudson, is a most generous one; but I have not been accustomed to farming, and I would rather have such a life as that which Captain Wilson offers me, although the pay may be very much smaller.

"But, sir," he said, turning to the officer of constabulary, "I fear that I cannot accept your offer, because, in the first place, you see, I am not a gentleman."

"Oh, nonsense, Reuben! Your manners and language would pass you as a gentleman, anywhere. Besides which, there are several officers in the force who have risen from the ranks, and who have had nothing like the education you have had. You can put that aside at once. Is there any other reason?"

"Yes, sir," Reuben said quietly. "I had never intended to have spoken of it, and I came out to Australia in order that I might be away from everyone who knew the story, but I couldn't accept your offer without your knowing it. I am leaving England because I have been tried for burglary."

"Nonsense!" both Reuben's listeners exclaimed, incredulously.

"If you don't mind, I will tell you the whole story," Reuben said, "and then you can judge for yourselves."

Reuben then related at length the whole circumstances, with which the reader is already acquainted.

"I remember reading your story in the papers, Reuben," Captain Wilson said. "Being in the force, you know, I take an interest in these things. I own I was puzzled at the time—because, you see, I did not know you—but how anyone who did know you, could think you guilty, passes my comprehension."

"I call it infamous," Mr. Hudson added warmly. "They must be a pack of fools, down at that place Lewes."

"Well," Captain Wilson said, "I am glad you have told me your story; for I have all along been puzzled as to what made you give up your trade, and emigrate, at your age. However, the matter is explained now; but now you have told me, I see no reason whatever why you should not accept my offer. In the first place, no one but ourselves will know your history. In the next, if they did so, that is no reason why you should not hold the appointment. No man is free from the risk of being suspected unjustly. You have been acquitted by a jury of your countrymen and, even did everyone know it, no one dare throw it in your teeth.

"No, I repeat, if you like I have no doubt that I can obtain for you an appointment as officer in the constabulary. You need not give me an answer now. Think it over for a week. You will have plenty of time, for Mr. Hudson insists upon your taking up your abode with him, when you land."

"That I do," Mr. Hudson said. "I have a place a mile out of Sydney, and there you will stop for a bit. Then I hope you will go up the country with me, for a month or two, and learn the ways of the place; till Captain Wilson has got an appointment for you—that is, if you quite decide to accept his offer, instead of mine. But remember, if ever you get tired of thief hunting, the offer will still be open to you."

Sydney was at that time but a very small place; for the great wave of emigrants had not yet begun to flow, and the colony was in its early infancy. As soon as the vessel cast anchor, Mr. Hudson and his party landed, taking Reuben with them; and an hour later he found himself installed, as a guest, at the squatter's house.

It was large and comfortable, surrounded by a broad verandah, and standing in a garden blooming with flowers, many of which were wholly unknown to Reuben. He had, of course, before landing laid aside the suit he had worn on board ship, and had dressed himself in his best; and the heartiness and cordiality of his host, his wife, and daughter soon made him feel perfectly at his ease.

"We are in the rough, you know," Mr. Hudson said to him. "Everyone is in the rough here, at present. Twenty years hence things may settle down, but now we all have to take them as we find them. The chief difficulty is servants. You see, almost every other man here is either a convict, an ex-convict, or a runaway sailor; about as bad material as you could want to see, for the formation of what they call at home a genteel establishment. The number of emigrants who come out is small. For the most part they have a little money and take up land, or at any rate, go up country and look for work there. A few, of course, who have been sent out by their friends at home to get rid of them, loaf about Sydney and spend their money, till they are driven to take the first job that offers. Well, they may do for shepherds, in places where no drink is to be had for love or money, but you would scarcely care about having them as butlers; so you see, we are driven to the three classes I spoke of. I have been exceptionally lucky. The man who carried the things upstairs just now, and who is my chief man here, is an ex-convict."

Reuben looked surprised.

"He was assigned to me when he first got his ticket of leave. I found him a good hand, and he stood by me pluckily, when my station was attacked by the blacks. So next time I came down to the town, I asked what he had been sent out here for. I found it was for having been concerned in a poaching fray, in which some of the game keepers got badly hurt. Well, that wasn't so much against him, you know, so I got talking to him one day, and found out that he came from my part of England. I found he had a wife, so I sent home money to some friends, and asked them to send her out; which they did and, finding she had, before she married him, been cook in a gentleman's family, I engaged her here, and sent up the country for Watson to come down. I had told him nothing about it; for I thought, perhaps, his wife might refuse to come out, or might have married again, or anything else.

"Well, the meeting was a happy one, as you may suppose; and I then settled him down here—at least, it wasn't here, but a smaller place I had then—and he has been with me ever since. His time was out some years ago, but that has made no difference. Nothing would induce him to leave me; and I would not part with him for any amount, for a more faithful and trusty fellow never lived, and when I go away I know everything will go along like clockwork. As for his wife, she's a treasure, and she knows how to cook a dinner, as you will acknowledge presently.

"They form the mainstay of my establishment. Besides that, there's an old chap who looks after the garden, goes down to the town, and does odd jobs. He was a sailor. He was landed here when his vessel came into port, five years ago. He had fallen off the yard on to the deck, and had broken half his ribs. He was taken to the government hospital. They did not think, at first, that he would ever get over it; but though he pulled through, it was clear he would never be fit for any hard work. So the surgeon of the hospital spoke of the case to me, and I said I thought I could find a job that would suit him, and here he has been. He is quite strong enough for all the work I want him to do, and I can trust him about the place. Of course, he breaks out and gets drunk occasionally, but one cannot expect to find a man perfect.

"Then there is a black boy—they call them all boys here—he looks after the horses, and has two black boys—they are boys—under him. I found him out on the plains. He had been shot by some bush-ranging scoundrels, out of pure mischief, I should say. He was insensible when I found him, but I saw that he was alive, and managed to get him up on my horse and took him home. We were six weeks getting him round, for the bullet had gone through his body. It would have killed a white man in an hour, but these black fellows are as hard as nails.

"My wife nursed him, for she was living up the country with me at that time; and when he got well, he declared that he would never leave us. I don't know that I was much gratified at the news, at first; but I soon found out that Sam, as I called him, was a valuable fellow about a place. He could turn his hand to everything, but I found he was specially happy when he was engaged about the horses; so at last I handed over that department to him, and when we set up this place here, I brought him down with me and made him head of the stables. It's fifteen years since I first picked him up, and I don't think I have ever had cause to find fault with him, since.

"So you see, though my establishment can't be called a genteel, it's a thoroughly good-working one, and I doubt if there's a man in the colony who is as well off as I am.

"When we go up country they all go with me except the sailor, who remains in charge. He's a great man, I can tell you, when he's left in what he calls command of the ship. He's got hold of two old muskets and a brace of pistols, and these he always loads before we start, so as to be ready to repel boarders. He looks out sharply, too, for I have never lost a thing since he came; and when you consider what a number of gentry there are, about here, with experience in housebreaking, I think that's pretty well. He is always drunk and incapable, for three or four days after our return, as a reward to himself for having kept from drink all the time we are away."

"Dinner is ready," Frances Hudson said, running into the room. "Here you are, papa, talking away as usual, whenever you get the chance. Now run upstairs quickly, both of you; for Rachel will not be pleased if you let the first dinner get cold, after she has been doing her best to turn out something special, in honour of the occasion, ever since she heard the Paramatta was in port."

"I won't be a minute, Frances.

"Ah, here comes Wilson. I was wondering what had become of him. He promised to come on, as soon as he had seen his chief."

The dinner was an excellent one, and fully bore out Mr. Hudson's assertion with respect to his cook. All were in high spirits, with the exception of Mrs. Hudson, who was cool in her manners to the young officer, and was evidently desirous of showing her disapproval of his engagement to her daughter, which had only taken place two days before.

"I have news for you, Reuben," Captain Wilson said, in the first pause of conversation. "I saw the chief, and told him I wanted an appointment for a young friend of mine, who had come out in the Paramatta, and who had shown great pluck and presence of mind in an affair at the Cape, which I described to him. He said that he could appoint you at once, as young Houghton, a district superintendent, was killed three weeks ago, in an affair with the bush rangers up country. He said he was very glad to hear of someone likely to make a good officer, to fill his place. So if you make up your mind to be a constable, the place is ready for you."

"Thank you very much, sir," Reuben said, "I was thinking the matter over last night, and quite made up my mind to accept the place you were kind enough to offer me, if you think me fit to fill it."

"I have no fear on that score, Reuben. I am sure you will do credit to my recommendation. So then, we may consider that as settled."

"There," grumbled Mr. Hudson, "that's just like you, Wilson; you upset all my plans. It was arranged he was to come up to my station, and there, before you are on shore two hours, you arrange the whole business; and I suppose you will be wanting him to get into his uniform, and be off before a week's out."

"I daresay we can manage a fortnight," Captain Wilson laughed, "and I have no doubt he will have plenty of opportunities for visiting you, later on. Indeed, I don't know why he should not be able to look you up, as soon as you get there. He will, of course, be placed under an old hand for six months, to learn his duties and get to speak a little of the native lingo.

"Hartwell, who has your district, is as good a man as he can be put with. He is a careful officer, though perhaps a little slow; but he will be a good man for Reuben to serve under, and I know the chief will put him with him if I ask him, as it can't make any difference where he goes first."

"Well, if you can arrange that, Wilson, I will forgive you. And now, where are you going to?"

"For the time, I am not going anywhere in particular," Captain Wilson replied. "The chief says he thinks that things have got rather slack, since I have been away. There are several bands of bush rangers, who have been doing a deal of mischief up country; so to begin with, he wishes me to make a tour of inspection, and to report generally. After that, I think I shall be settled here for a time. At any rate, it will be my headquarters. I think it probable the chief himself will be going home on leave, before very long."

"The sooner you are settled here, the better," Mr. Hudson said; "for I know I shall get no peace, now, till Frances is settled, too. Ever since she was a child, when she once made up her mind that she wanted a new toy, she worried me till I got it for her; and you are the last new toy."

"Oh, papa, how can you say so!" Frances said, laughing and colouring. "As far as I am concerned, it may be months and months."

"Oh, that is all very well," Mr. Hudson broke in. "I know what you want. You want Wilson here to be always, neglecting his duty, and galloping over from the other end of the colony to see you. No, no, my dear, if Wilson is a wise fellow, he will bring you to book, as soon as I can either build, or get hold of, a place fit for you. We shall be having no peace, now. Every time he is off on duty, you will be picturing him as engaged in some dreadful struggle with bush rangers and blacks; and if letters don't come as often as you expect them, you will be fretting yourself into a fever."

"What nonsense, papa! I know, of course, George will have to do his duty. I don't suppose he's always going to be tied to my apron string."

"You take my advice, Reuben," Mr. Hudson said, "don't you go and lose your heart; for if you once do, there's a police officer spoiled. It don't so much matter with Wilson, because he has done his share of dangerous work, and is pretty well up at the top of the tree; but a man that has to tackle bush rangers and blacks, ought not to have a woman at home thinking of him."

"There is no fear of that, for a good many years to come," Reuben laughed. "Are these blacks really formidable fellows, Captain Wilson?"

"Formidable to the settlers," Captain Wilson said, "but not to us. They drive off cattle and sheep, and sometimes attack solitary stations, and murder every soul there; but they seldom stand up in fair fight, when we come down upon them; but they fight hard, sometimes, when they are acting with bush rangers."

"Bush rangers are mostly escaped convicts, are they not?"

"Almost always," Captain Wilson replied, "except that, of course, they have among them a few men such as runaway sailors, and ne'er-do-wells who get sick of shepherding and take to the bush; but the great proportion are convicts. It is not to be wondered at, when you look at the life many of these men have led at home, and the monotony and hardship of their lives in many of the up-country stations, allotted to men as ignorant, and sometimes almost as brutal as themselves.

"Some of them, too, escape from the road gangs, and these are generally the worst; for as often as not, they may have killed a warder in making their escape, and know that it will go hard with them if they are caught.

"It may be said that there are two sorts of bush rangers. The one are men who have taken to the bush, simply from a desire of regaining their liberty. Sometimes they join parties of blacks, and live with them. Sometimes two or three get together, and all the harm they do is to carry off an occasional sheep, for food. And the other kind are desperadoes—men who were a scourge in England, and are a scourge here, who attack lonely stations, and are not content with robbing, but murder those who fall into their hands.

"They are in fact wild beasts, to whom no mercy is to be extended; and who, knowing it, will fight to the last. They are not easy to hunt down, their instinct having made them wary; and being generally in league with the blacks, who are as cunning as foxes, and can run pretty nearly as fast as a horse can gallop, they are kept very well informed as to our movements and, the country being so immense, we should never run them down, were it not for our native trackers.

"These fellows are to the full as sharp as the Red Indians of North America. They seem, in fact, to have the instinct of dogs, and can follow a track when the keenest white's eye cannot detect the smallest trace of a footprint. It is something marvellous what some of them will do."

"Have you many of these trackers in your employment?"

"There are one or two attached to every up-country station. They are, in fact, our bloodhounds; and although some of our men pick up a little of their craft, we should do nothing without them."

The next morning, Reuben met Captain Wilson down in Sydney, and was taken by him to the chief of the constabulary, who at once made out his appointment. On his return, Mr. Hudson again started with him for the town, and insisted upon ordering his equipment. As Reuben saw that he would be hurt by any shadow of denial, he accepted Mr. Hudson's kind offer; although he had intended to ask Captain Wilson to make an advance of pay, in order that he might get what was necessary. He could not, however, have purchased such an outfit as Mr. Hudson insisted on getting for him; the latter ordering not only uniforms but suits of plain clothes, together with saddlery, holsters, a sword, and a brace of excellent double-barrelled pistols. He did not need to buy a horse, having in his stables one in every way suitable, being at once quiet and fast—it was, indeed, one of the most valuable animals in the colony.

"You will have to keep your eyes open, Reuben," he said, as he gave him the horse, "or he will be stolen from you. These bush ranger fellows are always well mounted, and anyone at an up-country station, who has an animal at all out of the ordinary way, has to keep his stable door locked and sleep with one eye open; and even then, the chances are strongly in favour of his losing his horse, before long. These fellows know that their lives often depend upon the speed of their horse and, naturally, spare no pains to get hold of a good one.

"Ah, I have a good idea.

"Jim," he shouted to one of the black boys, "come here."

The lad, who was about eighteen years of age, trotted up.

"Jim, this gentleman is going to be a police officer, and he's going to take the bay with him; now he wants a good servant. Will you go with him?"

The lad looked longingly at the horse, which he had groomed and was very fond of; but he shook his head.

"I no leave Massa Hudson."

"Yes, but I wish you to go, Jim. This gentleman is a great friend of mine, and when bad black man attacked young Missy, he saved her life. So I want him to be taken good care of; and the horse, too, and to see no one steals it. So someone I can trust must go with him. If you don't like him for a master, after you have tried him, Jim, you can come back to me again. You have been a good boy, and I have no wish to get rid of you; but this gentleman don't know the ways of the country, and I want to be sure he has someone with him he can trust."

The lad looked at Reuben gravely, with his small eyes deeply sunken under the projecting eyebrows.

"Jim will go," he said. "He look after white man and Tartar, to please Massa Hudson and young Missy."

"That's right, Jim," his employer said.

"That's a good stroke of business," he went on, as he turned away with Reuben; "if you treat these black fellows well, and they get attached to you, they are faithful to death."

"You will see that fellow will never let your horse out of his sight. If you ride twenty miles across country, there he will be by your side as you dismount, ready to take it, and looking as fresh as paint. At night he will sleep in the stable, and will be ready, at all times and places, to make a fire, and cook a damper or a bit of meat, if you are lucky enough to have one by you. All the people about the place would do anything, I believe, for Frances; and the fact that you have saved her life will bind this boy to you, at first. Afterwards he will get to care for you, for yourself."

A fortnight later Reuben, in his uniform as an officer of the constabulary, rode out of Sydney. His baggage had been sent on, three days before, by a waggon returning up country. Jim trotted, with an easy stride, behind him. Reuben at first was inclined to ride slowly, in order to give his attendant time to keep up with him; but he soon found that, whatever pace he went, the lad kept the same distance behind, without any apparent exertion; and he was, therefore, able to choose his own pace, without reference to Jim's comfort.

Four years passed. Reuben Whitney gave every satisfaction to his superiors, and was considered a zealous and effective young officer. So far he had not been placed in a position of great responsibility; for although for the last two years he had been in charge of a district, it was not far from Sydney, and his duties consisted principally in hunting for convicts who had made their escape, in looking after refractory ticket-of-leave men, and in ordinary constabulary work. He had learned in that time to become a first-rate rider, and a good shot with a pistol, accomplishments which would be of vital service when he was ordered to an up-country station. For his pistols he had as yet, however, had no actual use, as neither bush rangers nor natives penetrated so far into the settlement.

At the end of the four years' service, he received a letter from Captain Wilson, who had just succeeded to the chief command of the constabulary, ordering him to hand over charge of the district to the young officer who was the bearer of the letter, and to report himself at headquarters.

Reuben was now nearly three-and-twenty, and had grown into a very powerful young man. A life spent for the most part on horseback had hardened his muscles, and filled out his frame. He stood about five feet nine, but looked shorter, owing to his great width of shoulders. He was still quiet in manner, but he had the same bright and pleasant expression which had characterized him as a boy; and his visits to Sydney, where he was introduced by Captain Wilson and Mr. Hudson into the best society, had given him ease and self possession.

The native, Jim, was still with him. He had become greatly attached to his master, and his fidelity and devotion had been of the greatest service to him and, go where he would, the black was always at his heels.

On his presenting himself at Sydney, Captain Wilson said, after the first greetings:

"I know you have been a little disappointed, Reuben, because hitherto you have been at stations where you have had but little opportunity of distinguishing yourself. However, I thought better to keep you at quiet work, until you were thoroughly master of your duties; and had, moreover, got your full strength. I don't know whether you have quite arrived at that yet, but I think you will do, anyhow," and he smiled as he looked at Reuben's shoulders.

"I think I am as strong as most of them," Reuben said, smiling too. "Four years' mill-wright's work, and four years on horseback in this bracing air, ought to make one strong, if there's anything in one to begin with. I think I shall do, in that respect."

"I think so, Reuben. I don't think there are many men in the force who could hold their own with you, in a grapple.

"And now to business. You have heard of that affair of Inspector Thomas, in the Goora district—it was a bad business. He and two of his men were out, after some natives who had driven off cattle; and he was set upon by a party of bush rangers, and he and his men killed."

"So I heard, sir," Reuben said quietly.

"Well, I have decided in sending you up in his place. It is a bad district—the worst we have, at present—and it needs a man of great resolution, and intelligence. I am sure that you have plenty of both, and that I cannot make a better choice than in sending you there. Your age is the only thing against you—not with me, you know, but others may think that I have done wrong, in selecting so young an officer—but you see, I know my man. I know, too, that several of the inspectors are getting too old for this sort of work. I do not mean too old, perhaps, in point of years, but they are married men with families, and for desperate work I prefer men without encumbrances.

"The post should be held by an inspector, but I cannot promote you, at present. It would be putting you over the heads of too many. But you will have a good chance of earning early promotion, and I know that is what you like."

"Thank you very much, Captain Wilson. I will do my best to show myself worthy of your confidence."

"You will have all your work cut out for you, Reuben. The district has, all along, been a most troublesome one. The number of settlers, at present, is small. There is a good deal of higher bush than usual about it, which makes it very difficult to run these fellows down; and the natives are specially troublesome. Besides which, at present there are two or three of the worst gangs of bush rangers in the colony, somewhere in that country. You will have to be cautious as well as bold, Reuben. It is a dangerous service I am sending you on; still, the more danger, the more credit to you."

"You could not have given me a station I should have liked better; and I hope, ere long, I may be able to give you a good account of the bush rangers."

"And now, Reuben, if you will call again in an hour, I shall be free, and then I will drive you home. You need not start for a day or two; and you will, of course, stay with me till you do."

Chapter 10
An Up-Country District

Mrs. Wilson received Reuben, as usual, with the greatest cordiality; but she exclaimed loudly, when she heard that he was going to the Goora district.

"You don't mean it, George. You can't mean that you are going to send Reuben to that dreadful place. Why, we are always hearing of murders and robberies there; and you know the last inspector was killed; and the one before recalled, because you said he had lost his nerve; and now you are sending Reuben there!"

"But I look upon it as the greatest honour, Mrs. Wilson, being chosen for such a station; and you see, there will be capital chances of distinguishing myself, and getting promoted."

"And capital chances of being killed," Mrs. Wilson said, in a vexed tone. "I do call it too bad, George."

"But, my dear, we want a man of pluck and energy. Besides, you know, we have been getting into hot water over that district. The press have been saying very severe things, about our incompetence to protect the outlying settlements, and I was obliged to choose a man who will give satisfaction; and you will agree with me that Reuben will do that."

"Of course he will," Mrs. Wilson agreed. "I shouldn't be alive now, if he hadn't had plenty of pluck and energy; but for that very reason, you ought not to send him to such a dangerous post."

"But I wish to give him an opportunity for distinguishing himself. He wants to get on, and I want to push him on; but you see, I can't promote him over the heads of some eight or ten men, senior to him, unless he does something a little out of the way."

"Well, I don't like it, George, I tell you frankly. I always thought he was wrong, to go into the constabulary at all, instead of accepting papa's offer. I can't think why you men are so fond of fighting, when you could choose a quiet and comfortable life."

"But it is not always so quiet and comfortable, Frances, as a good many have found, in the district he is going to; and after all, it is less dangerous fighting bush rangers and natives when you are prepared for it, than to be woke up of a night with a band of them thundering at your door, and with no assistance within twenty miles."

As Frances Wilson remembered how, in her childish days, her father's place had been, for three days, beset with blacks, she had no answer ready for the argument.

"Well, I do hope, Reuben," she said, "if you do go to this horrid place, you will take care of yourself, and not be rash."

"He's going to take care of others, Frances. You know, if he had taken care of himself and hadn't been rash, you would not have come so well out of that Malay business. I am sure he looks as if he could take care of himself, doesn't he?"

"Yes, he is big enough and strong enough," Mrs. Wilson agreed, "but that's no good against spears or boomerangs, to say nothing of rifles and pistols."

"Why, Frances, you are not generally a croaker," her husband said lightly, "but for once, you seem to be determined to do your best to frighten Reuben, before he starts."

Mrs. Wilson laughed.

"No, I don't want to frighten him, George. I only want to make him careful."

"I will be as careful as I can, Mrs. Wilson. That boy Jim is a treasure. I will warrant, if there are any black fellows about, he will sniff them out somehow. That fellow has a nose like a hound. He has always been most useful to me, but he will be invaluable at Goora."

Two days afterwards, Reuben left for his new command. It took him eight days to reach it. His headquarters were at Goora, a settlement of some twenty houses; besides the barracks in which the constabulary force, consisting of a sergeant, eighteen constables, and two native trackers, were quartered. The sergeant, a north-country Irishman named O'Connor, was somewhat surprised when Reuben rode up to the station; for the officers previously in command had been much older men.

Reuben's own quarters were in a cottage, close to the main building, and he asked the sergeant to come, in the evening.

"Now, sergeant," he said, after a little preliminary talk, "I have been sent up by Captain Wilson, with instructions to root out these bands of bush rangers."

The sergeant smiled grimly.

"We have been doing our best for the last three years, sir, but we have not made much of a hand at it."

"No," Reuben agreed, "and I don't suppose, of course, that I am going to succeed all at once. In the first place, tell me frankly, what sort of men have we got?"

"The men are good enough, sir, but they have certainly got disheartened, lately. One way and another, we have lost something like ten men in the last two years; and of course, that last affair with poor Mr. Thomas was a bad one."

"I understand," Reuben said quietly, "some of them are not quite so eager to meet the bush rangers as they used to be."

"Well, that is perhaps about it, sir; but I must say the men have been tremendously hardly worked—pretty nigh night and day in the saddle, often called out by false news to one end of the district; and then to find, when they return, that those scoundrels have been down playing their games at some station at the other end. It's enough to dishearten a man."

"So it is, sergeant. I was speaking to Captain Wilson about it, and saying that if we are to succeed we ought to have some fresh hands, who will take up the work with new spirit. We are seven below our force, at present; and he has promised to send me up fifteen new hands, so there will be eight to be relieved. I will leave it to you to pick out the men to go. Mind, put it to them that they are to be relieved simply because Captain Wilson thinks they have had their share of hard work, and should therefore be sent to a quiet station, for a time. Just pick out the men whom you think would be most pleased to go."

"Very well, sir. I am glad to hear the news, for to tell you the truth, I do think we want a little fresh blood amongst us."

Three days later the new detachment arrived, and Reuben saw, at once, that Captain Wilson had chosen a picked set of young men. About half of them were freshly enlisted in the force. The others had all been employed at up-country stations, and were well acquainted with the nature of the work before them. The same afternoon, the eight men picked out by Sergeant O'Connor as being the least useful on the station started for Sydney, most of them well pleased at being relieved from their arduous duties.

Reuben found that there were, in the office, a great many letters from settlers, asking for protection. It was impossible to comply with all these but, after consultation with O'Connor, he sent five parties, of three men each, to as many exposed stations; keeping ten in hand, to move as required.

Taking Jim, and two of the constables who had been longest on the station, he spent two months in traversing his district, from end to end, and making himself thoroughly acquainted with its geographical features; for he felt that, until he had mastered these, he should only be working in the dark. For a time the outrages had ceased, the bush rangers having shifted their quarters, and the natives withdrawn after the murder of the late inspector. This was a great relief to Reuben, as it permitted him to gain an insight into the country before setting to work in earnest.

Upon his tour, he and his followers were everywhere most hospitably received at the stations at which they halted. Everywhere he heard the same tale of sheep killed, cattle and horses driven off, and the insolent demeanour of the natives.

"I was thinking of giving it up, and moving back into the more populated districts," one of the settlers said to Reuben; "but now you have come, I will hold on for a bit longer, and see how it turns out. You look to me the right sort of fellow for the post; but the difficulty is, with such a large scattered district as yours, to be everywhere at once. What I have often thought of, is that it would be a good thing if the whole district were to turn out, and go right into the heart of the black country, and give them a lesson."

"From what I hear," Reuben said, "it will be next to impossible for us to find them. The country is so vast, and covered with bush, that there would be no searching it. They have no fixed villages, and the want of water would render it impossible for us to go very far. But the worst point would be that they all seem to be well informed as to what is going on. I suppose they get warnings from the native herdsmen and servants, and if we were all together to enter their country, we must leave the stations unprotected, and we should find them in ashes, on our return."

"Yes, that is true," the settler said. "I suppose it couldn't be done. But it's anxious work sleeping here, night after night, with one's rifle by one's bedside, never certain at what hour one may be woke by the yelling of the blacks. But they are not as bad as the bush rangers. If the blacks can but drive off your cattle, they are contented. You have got nothing else that is much use to them. The bush rangers don't want your cattle, beyond a head or two for present use; but they want everything else you've got, and whether you like it or not is quite immaterial to them. Thank God I have got no money in the place, and I and my three men can make a pretty good fight of it. But I pity the men with wives and daughters."

"Well, I hope we shall soon put a stop to it," Reuben said cheerfully. "We will give them a lesson if we catch them, you may be quite sure."

"I hope so," the settler said. "But you folks have been mighty unlucky, lately. Never seem to have been at the right place at the right time. Not that I am surprised at that, in such a district; but somehow they never come up with the fellows, afterwards."

"No, they seem to have had bad luck," Reuben agreed. "I hope we shall do better now."

Three days after his return from his last visit of inspection of his district, a settler rode, at full speed, up to the station.

"Captain," he said—for although Reuben had no right to that title, he was always so called by the settlers—"the blacks have been down at my place. They have killed my two shepherds, and driven off the sheep."

"Sergeant O'Connor, turn out the men at once," Reuben shouted. "See that their ammunition is all right, and let each man take a water skin and four days' provisions in his haversack.

"When was it?" he asked, turning to the settler again.

"Some time yesterday afternoon—at least, I judge so. One of the men was to have come in for supplies, and when night came and he hadn't come in, I began to be afraid something was wrong, for I knew that they were getting short. So this morning, at daybreak, I rode out with the hands I have about the house. We could see nothing of the sheep, so we rode straight to the men's hut. There, lying some twenty yards away, was the body of one of the men, riddled with spear holes. He had evidently been running to the hut for shelter, when he was overtaken. I did not stop to look for the other, for no doubt he had been killed, too."

"Well, we will do what we can for you," Reuben said. "I will be ready in five minutes."

He ran into the house, buckled on his sword, put some cold meat and a small bag of flour into his haversack, together with some dampers Jim had just cooked, and then went out again. Jim had already brought his horse round to the door. Before mounting he took the pistols out of the holsters, and examined them carefully.

By this time the sergeant and ten men were in the saddle, and placing himself at their head, with the settler, whose name was Blount, he rode off at full speed; followed by his men, the two native trackers, and Jim. Reuben soon reined his horse in.

"It will not do to push them too hard, at first. There is no saying how far we shall have to go."

"Do you mean to follow them into their own country?" Mr. Blount asked.

"I do," Reuben said. "I will follow them till I catch them, if I have to go across Australia."

"That's the sort," Mr. Blount said. "I expect you will find half-a-dozen other fellows at my station, by the time you get there. I sent my hand off on horseback to the stations near, to tell them what had taken place, and that I had ridden off to you, and asking them to come round."

"How far is it?" Reuben asked.

"About forty miles."

"But your horse will never be able to do it," Reuben said.

"I got a fresh horse at a friend's, four miles from your station, so I am all right."

"They will have more than a day's start of us," Reuben remarked presently.

"Yes; thirty-six hours, for you will have to stop at my place tonight. But they can't travel very fast with sheep, you know."

"No," Reuben agreed. "If they had had cattle, it would have been useless following them; but with sheep we may come up to them, especially if they don't think they will be followed far."

"No; that's my hope. They will know I had forty miles to ride to your station. Besides, had it not been that I was expecting the shepherd in for supplies, I might not have found it out for two or three days. So I expect they will think that they are pretty safe from pursuit. They have never been followed far into the bush. It's nasty work, you see."

"It's got to be done," Reuben said. "It is impossible to keep guard everywhere, and the only way to put a stop to these outrages is to teach the blacks that punishment will follow, wherever they go."

It was late in the afternoon before they arrived at Mr. Blount's station. They found fourteen or fifteen of the neighbouring settlers gathered there. They came out as the sound of the trampling of the horses was heard. Several of them were known to Reuben, from his having stopped at their stations.

"Glad to see you, captain, but I am afraid you are too late," said Dick Caister, a young settler whose station lay about twelve miles away.

"That remains to be proved," Reuben replied, as he dismounted.

"Oh, they have got twenty-four hours' start, and it's too late to do anything tonight. They must be thirty miles away in the bush, already."

"If they were a hundred, I would follow them," Reuben said.

There was an exclamation of surprise, and something like a cheer, on the part of some of the younger men.

"The difficulties are very great," one of the elder settlers said. "There is neither food nor water to be found in the bush."

"I know it's not an easy business," Reuben said quietly. "But as to food, we can carry it with us; as to water, there must be water in places, for the natives can no more go without drinking than we can. There must be streams and water holes, here and there. But however difficult it is, I mean to attempt it. It is the only way of bringing the blacks to book; there can never be safety among the outlying settlements, unless the fellows are taught a lesson.

"And now, gentlemen, before we go further, I want to say this: I know that you are all ready to help, that you are all thirsting to wipe out old scores with the blacks; but at the same time I would point out to you that it is likely enough that the bush rangers, who certainly work with the blacks, will follow up this stroke. Therefore, it will not do to leave the stations defenceless. I do not want a large force with me. If we once overtake the blacks, I have no fear whatever of being able to give a good account of them. Therefore I would urge, upon all of you who are married men, that it is of the first importance that you should stay at home, in case the bush rangers take the opportunity of our being away to pay you a visit. That is the first thing to be thought of. If any of the others like to go with us, I shall be very glad of their assistance. We may be away for a week or more, for ought I know."

"That is certainly the best plan, captain," Dick Caister said. "As you say, let the married men stop at home and guard their stations. I think the rest of us will all go with you."

There was a chorus of approval. Eight of those present were married men and, though reluctant to give up the thought of punishing the blacks, they were yet glad that they were not called upon to leave their wives and families. With many good wishes for the success of the expedition, they at once mounted, and rode off to their respective stations, some of which were more than twenty miles away.

"Now for ways and means," Reuben said. "What spare horses have you, Mr. Blount?"

"I have only two, besides the one I am riding."

"I should like to take at least six. We must carry a good store of provisions."

"I don't think you need trouble about that," Mr. Blount said. "We must take a supply of flour with us, and of course tea and sugar; and a few bottles of rum will not be amiss. All these I can furnish. But as to meat, I do not think we need trouble. Going as fast as the blacks will travel, there are sure to be lots of the sheep fall by the way. The blacks will eat as many as they can, but even a black cannot stuff himself beyond a certain extent, and there will be plenty for us."

"Yes, I did not think of that," Reuben replied; "in that case two spare horses will be enough."

"It would be a good thing to have a few with us, though," one of the young men said. "My place is only six miles off. I will ride over and bring back three with me; they are all good ones, and I should be sorry to find they were gone when I get back. I can lead one, my black boy can ride another and lead the third. It is likely enough some of the horses may give out, or get speared if the blacks make a fight of it, and half a dozen spare horses would come in very handy."

Reuben thought the plan was a good one, whereupon two of the others also volunteered to ride over and fetch—the one three and the other two—horses.

"That will make ten altogether, with Blount's two. We shall travel all the faster, because we can ride the spare horses by turns."

The three settlers rode off at once, and returned late at night with the spare horses. They had not been idle at Mr. Blount's. A bullock had been killed and cut up, and a considerable portion cooked, so that each of the twenty men going on the expedition would start with ten pounds of cooked meat, in order to save the time that would be spent in halting to cook the carcass of any sheep they might come upon. The question of weight was immaterial, as the meat could be packed on the spare horses.

As soon as day broke, the party were in their saddles. Mr. Blount led them first to the hut near which he had found his shepherd killed. The native trackers now took up the search. The body of the other shepherd was found half a mile away. It was in a sitting position by a tree; the skull was completely smashed in by the blow of a waddy, and it was evident that a native had crept up behind him, and killed him before he was conscious that any danger was at hand. The trackers were not long in finding the place where the sheep had been collected together and driven off, and a broad track of trampled grass showed, clearly enough, the direction which had been taken.

"How many of the black fellows do you think there were?" Reuben asked one of the trackers.

"Great many black fellow, captain," he replied.

"What do you call a great many?" Reuben asked.

"Twenty, thirty, captain; can't say how many. No use, captain, look for dem, gone right away into de bush, never find them."

"I am going to try, anyhow," Reuben said. "Now, do you lead the way."

"I tink dere are more dan thirty black fellow," Jim said to Reuben, as they started; "quite a crowd of dem. Me no much like those two black fellow," and he nodded towards the trackers, who were running on ahead. "No good, those fellows."

"What makes you think that, Jim?"

"Two days ago, Jim saw dem talking wid black fellow, half a mile from the station. Not know Jim saw dem. Secret sort of talk. Why dey never find de tracks before black fellows and bush rangers always get away? Jim tink those fellows no good."

Reuben himself had often thought it singular that such continued bad luck should have attended the efforts of his predecessor to hunt down the bush rangers, but the thought that they had been put off their scent by the trackers had not occurred to him. He had the greatest faith in Jim's sagacity and, now that the idea was presented to him, it seemed plausible enough.

"Very good, Jim, you keep your eye on those fellows. I will do the same. We shall soon find out if they are up to any tricks."

Jim had been running by his master's stirrup, while this conversation had been going on; and he now dropped into his usual place at the rear of the party. For some miles the trail was followed at a hand gallop, for the grass was several inches in height, and the trail could be followed as easily as a road. The country then began to change. The ground was poorer and more arid, and clumps of low brush grew here and there. Still, there was no check in the speed. The marks made by the frightened flock were plain enough, even to the horsemen; and bits of wool, left behind on the bushes, afforded an unmistakable testimony to their passage.

"They were not going so fast, here," Mr. Blount said, after dismounting and examining. "The footprints do not go in pairs, as they did at first. The flock has broken into a trot. Ah! There is the first, ahead."

In a hundred yards they came upon the skin and head of a sheep. Nothing else remained. Unable to keep up with the flock, it had been speared, cut up, and eaten raw by the blacks. In the next mile they came upon the remains of two more; then the track widened out, and the footprints were scattered and confused. The horses were reined up, and Jim and the trackers examined the ground. Jim returned in a minute or two.

"Black fellows give em a rest here. Could no go any furder. Lie down and pant."

One of the trackers then came up.

"They stop here, captain, five six hours till moon rise. Make fire, kill sheep, and have feast."

Reuben and some of the settlers rode over to the spot to which the tracker pointed.

"Confound them!" Blount exclaimed. "Look there! There are at least twenty heads."

"So there are," Reuben said. "There must have been a lot of natives."

"Yes, there must have been a good many," the settler agreed, "but not so many, perhaps, as you would think. Nobody has ever found out, yet, how much these blacks can eat when they make up their mind to it; but two could certainly devour a sheep. They will eat till they can't sit upright."

"They would hardly eat as much as that, with a long journey before them," Reuben said; "but allow only three to a sheep, there must be sixty of them. My man said there were a good many more than the trackers put it down at."

"So much the better. I only hope they will show fight."

After five minutes halt, the ride was continued for the next three hours. Then three dead sheep were passed. This time the flesh had not been devoured, but the poor beasts had, in every case, been speared.

"Savage brutes!" Reuben exclaimed. "They might at least have given the sheep a chance of life, when they could go no further, instead of wantonly slaughtering them."

"That's their way, always," Mr. Blount said. "They kill from pure mischief and love of slaughter, even when they don't want the meat. But I don't suppose it makes much difference. I expect the sheep have dropped as much from thirst as from fatigue, and they would probably have never been got up again, after they once fell. I fancy we shall come upon a stream, before long. I have never been out as far as this before, but I know that there is a branch of the Nammo crosses the bush here, somewhere."

Another five miles, and they came upon the river. The wet season was only just over, and the river was full from bank to bank. It was some thirty yards wide, and from two to three feet deep. A score of sheep lay dead in the water. They had apparently rushed headlong in, to quench their thirst; and had either drunk till they fell, or had been trampled under water, by their companions pressing upon them from behind.

For the next ten miles the track was plain enough, then they came to a series of downs, covered with a short grass. At the foot of these another long halt had been made by the blacks.

"We must have come twenty-five miles," Reuben said.

"Quite that, captain. The flock must have been dead beat, by the time they got here. I should think they must have stopped here, last night. We will soon see—there is one of their fireplaces."

The settler dismounted, and put his hand into the ashes.

"Yes," he said, "they are warm still. They must have camped here last night. They started when the moon rose, no doubt. Thus they have eight or nine hours' start of us, only; and as they can't travel fast, after such a journey as they had yesterday, we ought to be able to catch them long before night."

"They will go better today than they did yesterday," Mr. Blount said. "They were over-driven to start with, and that was what knocked them up; but the blacks will begin to feel themselves safe today, and will let them go their own pace. Sheep can do twenty miles in a day, if not hurried."

"Well, at any rate," Reuben said, "we will give our horses a couple of hours' rest. It is just eleven o'clock now, and I should think everyone is ready for a meal."

There was a chorus of assent. The troop dismounted at once. The girths were loosened, the bits taken from the horses' mouths, and they were turned loose to graze in the long grass at the foot of the hill. There was no fear of their attempting to stray, after their journey of the morning. Some of the men set to to cut brush, and in a few minutes a fire was lighted. One of the sheep, of which there were several lying about, was skinned and cut up; and slices, on skewers of green wood, were soon frizzling over the fire.

Twenty minutes later, the water in a large pot hanging over the fire was boiling. Three or four handfuls of tea were thrown in; and with the fried mutton, cold damper, and tea a hearty meal was made. Then pipes were produced and lighted; while several of the men, lying down and shading their faces with their broad hats, indulged in a doze.

"One o'clock," Reuben said at last, looking at his watch. "It is time to be moving again."

The horses were fetched in, the bridles replaced, and the girths tightened.

"Now, which way?" Reuben asked the trackers.

"Along here, captain, by de foot of de hill, de trail is plain enough."

It was so. A track of some width was trampled in the grass.

Reuben was about to give the order to proceed, when he caught Jim's eye, and saw that the black wished to speak to him privately.

"What is it, Jim?" he asked, going apart from the rest.

"That not de way, captain. A hundred, two hundred sheep gone that way, wid four or five black fellow. De rest have all gone over de hill."

"Are you sure, Jim?"

"Me quite sure, sar. De ground very hard; but while de captain smoke him pipe, Jim went over de hill, saw plenty sign of sheep. Went straight uphill, and then turned away to de left. Dis little party here hab only gone to frow white man off de trail."

"The trackers ought to have seen that as well as you, Jim," Reuben said angrily.

"Dey see, sar, sure enough. Could no help seeing, wid half an eye. You see, sar, dose fellows up to no good. Lead party wrong if dey can. Don't say, sar, Jim told you. If you say dat, put 'em on their guard. Massa ride along the trail for a bit, just as if talk wid Jim about odder affair; den after little way, begin to talk about trail being too small, den turn and come back here, and go over de hill."

"A very good idea, Jim. I will do as you say."

Chapter 11
The Black Fellows

A few minutes after his conversation with Jim the party started, following the broad track through the grass along the foot of the hill. Reuben informed Mr. Blount of what Jim had told him.

"By Jove, I think he is right," the settler said. "The track is as broad as it was, but it is nothing like so much trampled down; but if your fellow says the main body have gone over the hill, why are you following this track?"

Reuben gave his reasons, and said that his man had, before, had suspicions that the trackers were in communication with the wild blacks.

"He thinks that's why it is that they have so frequently failed, here, to catch any of these fellows."

"I shouldn't be at all surprised," Mr. Blount said savagely. "The best thing would be to put a bullet into each of the rascals' heads."

"I think Jim's idea is best," Reuben said. "Now that we have once got our eyes open, they won't be able to do us any more harm; and my black fellow will see we follow the trail right. I don't want them to see we have any suspicions of them, as that would put them on their guard; and by keeping our eye upon them, we may be able to turn the tables."

"That is so," Mr. Blount agreed. "What are you going to do, then?"

"I will call to them, in a minute or two, and tell them that it is your opinion that only a small portion of the flock have come this way. Then we will have a consultation and, no doubt, some of your friends will notice that the ground is not much trampled. Then we will decide to ride back to the point from which we started, and will follow the other trail."

"Yes, that will do very well," the settler agreed.

Reuben at once called to the trackers, who were trotting on ahead, and then ordered a halt. The two blacks came back.

"Joe," Reuben said, "Mr. Blount thinks that the main body of the flock have not come this way. He says he thinks only a hundred or two have come. The ground does not look to me anything like so much trampled as it was before we halted."

"I tink most of dem hab come along here," the tracker said sullenly.

"What do you think?" Reuben asked the other settlers, who had gathered round.

"I did not notice it before," Dick Caister said; "but now Blount has pointed it out, I agree with him entirely. There are nothing like the full number of sheep have passed along here. I should say that they have not gone along more than two or three deep."

There was a general chorus of assent.

"You can't have been keeping your eyes open," Reuben said to the trackers, sharply. "If you don't look sharp in future, we shall quarrel.

"Come, gentlemen, let us ride back to the halting place, and see if we cannot find out which way the main body have gone."

Ten minutes' riding took them back to their starting place.

"They must have gone over the hill," Reuben said. "They certainly have not kept along at the foot, or we should see their tracks in this long grass."

The trackers had exchanged a few words in a low tone, and they now moved up the hill, and began to examine the ground carefully.

"Some of dem have gone this way, captain."

"Of course they have," Mr. Blount said. "A blind man might see that."

The marks of the sheep were indeed plain enough to all, when their attention had once been drawn to the subject. On getting beyond the crest the trackers turned to the left, and Reuben saw that they felt it would be hopeless to attempt, further, to mislead a party containing several settlers who were perfectly capable of following the trail.

Jim had, since speaking to his master, remained in the rear of the troop. After three miles' riding across the downs, they again came down upon a flat country, thickly covered with brush. Here and there pieces of wool sticking to thorns were visible, and the trackers went steadily on for some little time. Then their pace became slower, and finally they stopped.

"Trail ended, captain."

"What do you mean by the trail ended?" Reuben asked angrily. "Why, I can see a piece of wool, on there ahead."

"Dat so, captain; but only a few sheep hab passed here."

Some of the settlers dismounted and, having examined the ground carefully, declared that they were of the same opinion as the trackers.

"Very well," Reuben said; "then in that case, we must go back again to the foot of the hill. They were all together there, and we must take up the trail afresh."

On reaching the foot of the hill, Jim and some of the settlers joined the trackers, and penetrated the bush in all directions. Each returned bringing in pieces of wool.

"It is plain enough," Reuben said, "what they have done. They have broken up into small parties, and have scattered. The question is, 'What are we to do now?'"

"What do you think, Mr. Blount? You have had more experience than anyone here, and you are the most interested in our overtaking these rascals. What do you recommend?"

"I don't know what to recommend," the settler said. "They have no doubt done it to confuse us, in case we should follow so far, and avoid being thrown off the scent the other side of the hill. The band may really have scattered, and gone off in small parties to different parts of the bush; or again, they may have scattered with the understanding that they will meet again, at some given spot, which may be ten and may be fifty miles ahead."

"The worst of it is," Reuben said, "I fear now that there is an end of all chance of coming up with them, today; and now the question of water comes in. If we could have caught them before nightfall, the horses, having had a good drink at that stream, could have done very well till we'd gone another thirty miles; but as that seems hopeless, now, we must consider seriously what we had best do, before we go any further. Does anyone here know anything of the country ahead?"

There was a general silence.

"The horses can do very well, tomorrow, without water," Mr. Blount said. "They will chew the leaves of this scrub; and can, if pressed, hold on for even two or three days upon it."

"In that case," Reuben said, "let us go on. We will break up into three parties. One shall go straight forward, the other two moving to the right and left, each following the tracks as well as they can. We will not go much beyond a walk. We have five more hours of daylight yet, and the horses can manage another fifteen miles. I will halt, an hour before it gets dark, and light a fire. The smoke will be a guide to the other two parties, who should not be more than a couple of miles to the right and left, and they will then close in.

"If you can suggest any better plan than that, Mr. Blount, please do so. Of course, I see the objection that the blacks may make out the smoke, and will know that they are being followed."

"Yes, that is an objection," Mr. Blount said; "but the chances are that they will know it without your telling them. It is more than probable that some of them have remained behind, on the watch; and that they will have signalled our coming, long ago."

"Dey have done that, sar," Jim, who was standing close to Reuben's elbow, put in. "Jim saw smoke curl up from the top of de hill, just when we turned, when we lost the trail."

"Why didn't you tell me before, Jim?" Reuben asked.

"De captain didn't ask Jim any question. Jim thought de captain see it for sure."

"I didn't see it, Jim. I don't think any of us saw it. We were all too much occupied looking for the trail. Another time, you tell me what you see without my asking.

"Well in that case, Mr. Blount, there can be no harm in my making a smoke, as they know already that they are pursued. Will you take charge of the right hand party? Sergeant O'Connor will take command of the left. Do you each take a tracker with you. I will take my boy. Three constables will go with each of your parties, and four with me.

"Will you gentlemen please to divide up, so as to make seven altogether in each party, without the natives?"

"I need not tell you to keep a sharp lookout, Captain Whitney. We know the blacks are a very strong party and, now they know that they are pursued they may, as likely as not, make a stand."

"Yes, that is quite possible," Reuben agreed. "Will you please be careful that neither of your parties get more than two miles, at the outside, away from mine? We can hear the sound of rifles, at that distance. If either party fires, the others will of course hurry to their assistance. Now, let us move forward."

With Jim in advance, Reuben's party moved on, the black carefully examining the ground and bushes as he went; and occasionally, somewhat to Reuben's surprise, rising from the stooping position in which he was walking, and looking back over his shoulder. The motive was explained when Jim exclaimed:

"Dere, captain, dere are de signals again."

Reuben turned in the saddle. On the crest of the hill behind him were three columns of smoke. Scarcely had he looked at them when the smoke ceased to ascend, as if the fires had been suddenly put out.

"That's to tell them that we have divided in three parties?" Reuben asked the black.

Jim nodded, and proceeded on his way again.

"That's awkward," Reuben said, "I must warn the other two parties."

So saying, he at once ordered two of the constables to ride right and left and warn the others, who were not as yet more than a quarter of a mile on either hand, that the natives were aware that they had broken up, and that the greatest caution must, therefore, be observed. In ten minutes the two constables returned, having performed their mission.

Although he had no reason to believe that the blacks were within ten miles of him, Reuben now took the precaution of sending one constable out on each flank, to a distance of fifty yards. A third was directed to keep with Jim, fifty yards ahead of the main body; consisting of Reuben himself, a constable, and two colonists. Occasionally Reuben rode forward to question Jim.

"How many sheep do you think have gone along the track you are following?"

"About thirty sheep, and three black fellow."

"How do you know there are three black fellows, Jim? I can see marks, sometimes, of the sheep's feet; but I have not seen a man's footprint at all."

"Jim see 'em, captain, plain enough. When dey all follow sheep, not very plain to see; but sometimes, when de sheep want to scatter, Jim see one footmark on one hand and one on the other, and sure to be one man behind."

"How far are the sheep ahead, Jim, have you any idea?"

"Six, eight hours, sar, when dey pass here; but dere's no saying how far they are, now. May be long way on, may be only little way. Me tink dat they hab not gone so berry far; dat smoke berry thin, not see him more than ten miles."

"I wish you had said that before, Jim," Reuben said. "We would have kept together and have galloped on, and taken our chance of finding them."

"Might have found four or five of dem," Jim replied, "but de others all scattered. No good to find dem, till dey come together again."

"No, you are right there, Jim. We must catch them all together, if we can. There are some twelve hundred sheep, somewhere ahead. Mr. Blount said there were about fifteen hundred driven off. We have come upon a hundred dead ones, and two or three hundred may have taken that turn to the right. As you say, it would be no good coming upon thirty."

For four hours the party continued their journey.

"It is six o'clock," Reuben said, looking at his watch. "We will halt, now, and light that fire."

Two of the constables were told off to keep watch, some fifty yards in front; and the others dismounted, and gathered together materials for a fire. This was soon done, and the smoke mounted straight and clear, a signal to the other two parties to close in.

Suddenly a cry was heard from one of the sentries. The men stooping round the fire leaped to their feet, just in time to see one of the constables struck from his horse by a boomerang, while a dozen spears whizzed through the air at the other. He fell forward on his horse, which carried him up to the fire; as he fell from the saddle, as it stopped, he was caught by two of the others. Three spears had pierced him.

"Stand to your arms. Steady, for your lives," Reuben shouted.

"Jim, throw the horses at once, and fasten their legs.

"We must defend ourselves here," he continued, turning to the others, "until help comes."

Not a moment was lost. The little party threw themselves down in a circle, each taking shelter behind a bush; and Jim speedily got the eight horses down in the centre, for each party had with it three of the spare animals. The whole time, from the first alarm until all was ready to receive the natives, did not occupy two minutes.

The horses of the sentries had galloped wildly on, both having been struck by spears; and Jim had no difficulty with the remainder, which were all standing in a group when the alarm was given, the owners not yet having removed their saddles.

All was done without flurry or excitement, although the yells of the natives rose from the bush all round them. The bush was fortunately not very thick at the point where they had halted, Reuben having selected it for that very reason; but the bushes were sufficiently near to each other to enable an enemy to creep up, within thirty yards or so, without being seen.

"Don't throw away a shot," Reuben called out; "but pick off the blacks, as they stand up to throw their spears.

"Ah!"

The exclamation was accompanied by a shot from his rifle, as a native rose suddenly from the bush and hurled his spear. It missed Reuben by an inch or two only; but, as his rifle flashed out, the black threw up his hands and fell back in the bush.

"Here, sah, dis make good shelter;" and Jim propped up his saddle, almost in front of him.

"That's a good idea, Jim; help the others in the same way."

The five men were all engaged now. The spears whizzed fast over and among them, but most of them were thrown almost at random; for the blacks soon learned that to raise themselves above the bushes, to take aim, was to court sudden death. Jim, after distributing the saddles to their owners, had lain down by the side of his master; and loaded his rifle as fast as he discharged it, Reuben using his pistols as effectually as the rifle, in the intervals.

Fortunately all the party were provided with these weapons. Had it not been so, each man would have been liable to be rushed by the blacks every time he discharged his rifle. As far as possible they fired by turns; so that each man, while loading, was covered by the fire of those on his right and left.

For half an hour the fight continued. Many of the blacks had fallen, but they continued the assault as vigorously as before, and all the defenders had received more or less serious wounds from the spears.

"The others ought to have been here, long before this," Reuben said, "if they had followed my instructions. I only hope they have not been attacked, too; but as we don't hear any firing, that can hardly be so."

"I hope they will be up before dusk," Dick Caister said. "It will be dark in another half an hour. These fellows are only waiting for that to make a rush. If they do, it is all up with us."

"They will find it a tough job, even then," Reuben said; "but the others must be here long before that. I told them to keep within two miles of us. They have had time to ride double that distance, since we made the smoke for them."

Another ten minutes elapsed.

"Hurrah!" Reuben exclaimed, "I can hear the trampling of horse's hoofs. The moment they arrive, make a rush for your horses and charge."

"I am afraid the horses are killed," Dick said ruefully.

"In that case," Reuben said, "we must get to our feet, and pick off the blacks as they run. They will get up like a covey of partridge, as the horsemen come among them."

A loud cheer was heard, and the little party, with an answering shout, sprang to their feet and, rifle to shoulder, stood expecting the blacks to rise; but the ears of the natives were sharper than those of the whites, and they had begun to crawl away before the latter heard the approaching horsemen.

Finding this to be the case, the party ran to their horses. Four exclamations of wrath and grief were heard, for seven of the horses were completely riddled with spears.

Tartar, however, at his master's voice, struggled to rise to his feet. Reuben, aided by Jim, quickly threw off the hobbles; and leaped on to its back as it rose to its feet, just as Mr. Blount, with his party, rode up.

"Keep close together," Reuben exclaimed, as he dashed forward, "we may find some of the scoundrels."

But the chase was in vain. It was already growing dusk, and there was no saying in which direction the natives had crawled away in the bush. After riding for a mile, Reuben reined in his horse.

"It is no use," he said; "we may as well get back to the fire.

"What made you so late, Mr. Blount? We were fighting for three quarters of an hour, before you came up."

"I am very sorry," Mr. Blount replied; "somehow or other, we went wrong altogether. There is nothing to guide one in this flat bush, and the tracker who was leading the way said he was certain he was going as you ordered him. Just before six o'clock we halted, and looked in the direction in which we expected to see your smoke, but there were no signs of it. Presently one of the constables exclaimed:

"'There's the smoke, sir, right behind us.'

"I looked around and, sure enough, there was a column of smoke, and a long way off it was.

"'What have you been doing, you rascal?' I said to the black. 'There's the smoke right behind us. You have been leading us wrong, altogether.'

"The black insisted that he was right, and that the fire must have been made by the black fellows. I didn't know what to make of it. It was two or three minutes past six; and I noticed, when we halted before, that your watch was exactly with mine. So I said to the men:

"'We will wait five minutes longer and, if we see no other smoke, you may be sure that that is made by Captain Whitney.'

"We waited the five minutes, and then I gave the word to start, when one of the men exclaimed:

"'The black fellow's gone.'

"Sure enough, he had slipped away without being noticed, while we were looking for the smoke. I felt sure, now, that something must be wrong; and we galloped towards your smoke, as fast as the horses could lay their feet to the ground. When we were about half way, we heard the sound of firing, and I can tell you that we didn't lose a moment on the way, after that. Have you had any losses?"

"Two of the constables are killed," Reuben said, "and we have all got some more or less ugly scratches. My left arm is useless for a time, I am afraid. A spear went right through it. I fear some of the others have worse hurts."

"What can have become of the sergeant's party?" Mr. Blount said.

"They must have gone the wrong way, too," Reuben replied. "I told you I suspected those trackers of being in league with the blacks, and I have no doubt your fellow led you purposely astray, in order to give them an opportunity of cutting us off before you could arrive to our assistance. I suppose the other party has been misled in the same way. It is fortunate, indeed, that you made up your mind to ride for our smoke when you did. A quarter of an hour later, and you would have found only our bodies, and would probably have been ambushed in turn."

"Yes, it has been a close thing, indeed," Mr. Blount said. "I was wrong, after what you told me, to trust that black scoundrel so entirely; but I own it never entered my mind that he was leading us astray."

By this time they had reached the fire, which was blazing high.

"How are you all?" Reuben asked. "Nobody badly hurt, I hope?"

"Nothing very bad, captain," Dick Caister replied cheerfully. "We have all had our skin ripped up a bit, but nothing very deep. That dodge of the saddles, of your black fellow, saved us. Mine was knocked over half a dozen times by spears, each of which would have done its business, if it hadn't been for it. I owe him my life so completely, that I forgive him for making our horses a barricade, to save yours."

Reuben laughed. He had noticed, when he ran for his horse, that Jim had thrown him in the centre of the others: and their bodies completely sheltered him from the spears of the natives.

"It was not fair, perhaps," he said; "but my horse would have been killed, as well as yours, had he not done so; and Jim loves him almost as well as he does me. He has watched over and guarded him for the last three years."

"I am not angry with him," Dick said. "Nothing could have saved our horses from being killed, and if one was to be saved, it is as well it should be Tartar, and not one of the others, as yours was far the most valuable of the five."

"Pile on the bushes," Reuben said to one of the constables. "Make as big a blaze as you can. It will act as a beacon to the sergeant and his party."

Half an hour later the trampling of horses' hoofs was heard and, a few minutes later, the sergeant and his party rode up.

"I am sorry I am so late, sir," the sergeant said. "Somehow or other we went wrong altogether, and saw nothing of your smoke. I was afraid something was wrong, but did not know what to do; so we halted till it came on dark, and presently made out a fire; but it was miles away, and right in the direction from which we had come. I did not think it could be you but, whether it was you or the blacks, that was the place to ride to."

"Have you got the tracker with you, sergeant?"

"Yes, sir; at least, I saw him trotting ahead, ten minutes ago. Why, where has he got to?"

The tracker was not to be seen.

"He has made off to join the blacks, I expect," Reuben said. "You have been led astray purposely. We have been attacked, and Brown and Simpson are killed."

An exclamation of rage broke from the men, who were in the act of dismounting.

"I expect," Reuben said, turning to Mr. Blount, "that the fellows noticed the talk I had with Jim, before we turned back from the false trail, and concluded that we had some suspicion that they were in league with the blacks; and so, when the party separated, they determined to lead the two flanking columns astray, so as to give their friends a chance of attacking us, and then to bolt."

"I expect that is it," Mr. Blount agreed. "And now, the first thing is to get something to eat. When that is done, we will have a consultation."

While the meat was cooking over the fire, Reuben told off a party of eight men to bury the bodies of the two constables who had fallen. The task was speedily completed, two holes being easily scraped in the light, sandy soil.

After supper was over, the settlers gathered round Reuben.

"Now, captain, what do you mean to do?" Mr. Blount asked. "I have given up all hope of seeing my sheep again, so don't let them influence you, but just do as you think best. The blacks are in strong force, that is evident; and it will be a serious business pursuing them any further, in their own country."

"I am going to pursue them till I catch them," Reuben said; "that is to say, as long as there is a sheep track to serve as a guide. I don't ask you, gentlemen, to go further, for I know it is a serious risk; but it is my duty to hunt those fellows down, and give them a lesson, and I mean to do it. We shall never have safety in the settlements, until those fellows come to understand that, whenever they attack us, they will be hunted down."

"I think you are right," Dick Caister said, "and as long as you go on, I go with you for one, whatever comes of it. But how I am to go without my horse, I don't know."

"There are the spare horses," Reuben said; "Fortunately we have still got six of them."

"So we have," Dick exclaimed joyfully. "I had forgotten all about them. What luck, our bringing them with us!"

The other settlers all announced their intention of continuing the chase, as long as Reuben was willing to push on.

"I will tell you what my idea is," Reuben said. "The horses are already worn out and, by the end of another day, they will be half mad with thirst. I propose that we take two days' supply for ourselves, in our water bottles;

and that we push forward on foot, sending two of the constables back to the stream, with our horses. I propose that we should push forward tonight. I expect the track we are following is the true one, and the stars will do as a guide.

"At daybreak we will lie down in the bushes. The blacks will probably leave some fellows behind, as scouts. They, seeing nothing of us, will suppose we have given it up and gone home, and they will make but a short journey. At night we will go on again, and the chances are that, before morning, we shall catch sight of their fires, and will fall upon them at daylight. What do you think of the plan?"

"I think it is a good one," Mr. Blount said, warmly. "A capital plan. Of course we don't much like leaving our horses, for in this country one almost lives on horseback. Still, it will be the best plan, certainly; for as you say, the poor brutes will be half mad, by tomorrow night, with thirst."

"It will be a long tramp back again," a settler said dismally.

"We won't tramp all the way," Reuben said with a smile. "Directly we have overtaken the blacks, and given them a lesson, I will send Jim back again for the horses. He can cover the ground at a wonderful pace, and coming back he will ride one of them, and help the two constables to keep them together. They will have had two days' rest, and plenty of food and water, and will meet us before we get halfway back. There will be no fear of the blacks attacking them."

All agreed that the plan was excellent, and half an hour later the whole party—with the exception of the two constables, who were to start at daybreak with the horses, for the river—set out on their march. The sky was cloudless, and the stars would have been a sufficient guide, even had they not had Jim with them. The black, however, took his place at the head of the party, and strode along as unhesitating as if it had been broad daylight.

Chapter 12
The Bush Rangers

Scarce a word was spoken as the little party marched along. It was possible, although very improbable, that the natives, on scattering before the charge of Mr. Blount and his companions, might have left some of their number behind, to watch the movements of their pursuers. They would, however, certainly not anticipate the whites pushing forward that night. The fire had been piled high, the last thing before leaving, and the two men left there were told to keep it burning brightly till morning, and to start before anyone watching in the distance would be able to see whether the horses were mounted, or not. Should any natives approach the fire, after they had gone, they would take it for granted that the whole party had ridden back to the settlement.

All night, Reuben and his companions marched steadily forward; and were glad to throw themselves down on the ground, at the first appearance of daybreak. Four sentries were placed, with strict orders to keep a bright lookout through the bushes, but on no account to raise their heads above their level; and, arrangements having been made for their relief, every two hours, the rest of the party were soon sound asleep.

Except to relieve the sentries, there was no stir among them until late in the afternoon. Then there was a general movement, and soon all were sitting up, and appeasing their appetite upon the cold meat and dampers they had brought with them.

"There is no harm in a pipe, I suppose, captain?" Dick Caister said laughingly.

"No, I think we can risk that," Reuben replied. "The eyes of the savages may be wonderfully keen, but they would be a great deal sharper than I can give them credit for, were they to notice the smoke of a dozen pipes, curling up among the bushes."

"I suppose, Mr. Blount," Reuben said as, after the meal was finished, the party lighted their pipes and drew closely round the fire, "you have heard of a good many bad businesses, with the blacks and bush rangers, in your time?"

"I have, indeed," Mr. Blount replied. "In the early days, the settlers had a hard time of it with the blacks; who were, of course, stronger than they are now and, after they had got over their first fear of firearms, more fearless of the whites. The bush rangers too were, when first they began to send convicts here, more numerous than at present. I do not know that they were as desperate as they are now—not so ready to take life, without provocation. You see, there was a very much larger run of country open to them; and many convicts who escaped, and took to the bush, were content to have gained their freedom. Some of them took black gins, and never troubled the colonists again; beyond, perhaps, coming down to a station and carrying off a sheep or two, or a bullock, when they got sick of kangaroo meat and wanted a change.

"You see, the first settlers were generally poor and hard-working men. Young men with a little capital had not as yet been attracted here, so there was but little inducement for the escaped convicts to meddle with them. There were, of course, some notorious scoundrels, who seemed to murder for the pure love of the thing. The worst of them, I think, was a fellow who went by the name of Cockeye. What his real name was, I never heard.

"That man was a perfect devil; and was, for a long time, the terror of the settlers. He never worked with other white men, but lived among the blacks. Of course, in those days the police system was in its infancy, and we had to rely upon ourselves. I had a narrow escape, once, of losing my life, from him and his blacks.

"When I was about seventeen, I lived with my father and mother in a station about fifty miles from Sydney, or as it was called then Port Jackson. It was at that time quite an outlying station. We had two convicts allotted to us, both of them honest fellows enough, who had been transported for poaching or something of that kind—anyhow, they were not old hands, and gave no trouble. My father was a kind master, and we always felt that, in case of need, we could rely upon them just as upon ourselves. In those days it was next to impossible to get hired hands for, as there was plenty of land for anyone to squat upon, comparatively close to the port, the men who came out generally set up for themselves, at once.

"One day I had been out on horseback, to look for a couple of bullocks which had strayed away; and was on my way back when, ahead of me, I heard the cooey of the blacks. I didn't think much of it, because they were common enough at that time, and a party had made a sort of encampment at a stream, about a mile from the house; but when, a minute later, I heard a gun fired, I guessed that there was mischief.

"The sound seemed to come from away towards the right, where I knew that one of our men was out, herding the bullocks; so I clapped spurs to my horse, and rode in that direction. When I got near, I saw the cattle running wildly about, and a mob of black fellows among them. I could see no signs of our man, and guessed that he must have gone down; and that I had best ride and warn them, at the house.

"The blacks saw me, and started at a run in my direction, but I soon left them behind. I was within a quarter of a mile of the house, when a native yell burst out ahead of me, followed by two shots. I rode on and, when I got near the house, saw a lot of black fellows round it.

"Then came a flash from one of the upper windows, and I saw one of them roll over. That was a satisfaction, for I knew they hadn't caught my father asleep. I knew the doors and shutters were strong, and that he could make a good fight of it. Still, there was only him and my mother at home, for both the men had gone out before I left in the morning; and one man hasn't much chance of holding a house, attacked on all sides. So I made up my mind to try to dash through them, when the shutter opened a little, and my father shouted out:

"'Ride for help, Bill. I will keep them off, till you get back.'

"So I turned; but when I had gone a few yards I looked over my shoulder, and I saw a man dash out from behind the house on horseback, and start at a gallop after me. It was a bay with a white leg, and I knew that Cockeye used to ride such a horse, and that there wasn't a better in the colony. Almost at the same moment I heard a shot again, but I didn't look round.

"I can tell you I felt pretty badly frightened, for there was no mercy to be expected from that scoundrel, and I knew that he was a good deal better mounted than I was. The next station was about four miles off, and I had about two hundred yards start, but before I had gone half a mile, he was within fifty yards of me. I could hear him, cursing and swearing and shouting to me to stop, but I had made up my mind I would not do that.

"I had got a brace of pistols with me, but I wasn't much of a shot. I had, soon after I started, pulled them out of the holsters and shoved them into my belt in front of me; so that, as he came up, he shouldn't see my hand go down for them. My hope was that he would ride straight up to the side of me, not knowing that I was armed; and that would give me a chance of suddenly letting fly at him.

"You would think the chance was a poor one; and that he would, to a certainty, shoot me down before he got up. I did not much think he would do that, for I guessed that the scoundrel would do with me as he had in some other cases; namely, take me and carry me back to the house, and there either threaten to shoot me, or hang me up over a fire, or some such devilry, to make those inside give in. I was determined this shouldn't be, and that if I could not shoot him I would be shot myself; for otherwise he would have got my father and mother, and it would have been three lives instead of one.

"Presently—crack!—came the sound of a pistol, and I heard the bullet whiz close by. I expect that it was only to frighten me into stopping; but in a second or two he fired again, and the shot just grazed my shoulder, so he was in earnest that time.

"I bent low on my saddle, got a pistol out of my belt, and prepared. There was another shot, the horse gave a spring and I knew he was hit, but for a time he went faster than ever; still, the last shot wasn't from more than twenty yards behind; and I expected, every minute, to see his horse's head coming up beside me. Then I heard a curse and a sudden fall and, looking round, saw his horse was down.

"Cockeye was on his feet in a moment, and drew another pistol from his holster; so I concluded to keep on as hard as I could go, without waiting to make inquiries. I guessed pretty well what had happened. The shot I had heard my father fire, as he started after me, had hit the horse; and the poor brute had kept on until he dropped. I understood the fellow's firing, now. He felt his horse was failing under him, and his only chance was to stop me.

"I kept on till I got safe to the station. The three men there started in different directions, to fetch assistance, and by the evening we had a score of men assembled there, and started back to our station. We heard a cooey when we were within a mile of the place, and guessed it was a fellow on the watch. By the time we got there they had all cleared off, but it was a close thing.

"My mother was a courageous woman, and had defended the back of the house, and my father the front. The blacks had made several attempts to burn the place down; but the roof, like the walls, was made of solid timber; which is the only safe way to build a house, when you are exposed to attacks of the blacks.

"As long as daylight lasted the old people had done very well, and had kept the blacks at a distance; and we saw, by the marks of blood in the morning, that they must have killed or wounded eight or ten of them; but if we hadn't come up before the blacks had darkness to cover them, it would have gone hard with them. Of course we knew that, and calculated so as to get there before nightfall."

"What became of the bush ranger?" Reuben asked.

"Well, curiously enough, that was the last time he ever troubled the settlements. We never knew exactly what became of him, but it was said that the blacks killed and eat him. I know that was very often the end of those fellows. As long as all went on well, the blacks were friendly enough with them, and were glad to follow their lead; but after a repulse like that they got at our station, or perhaps as a result of some quarrel about the division of the plunder, or their gins, or something of that sort, they would fall suddenly on their white friends, and make cooked meat of them."

"I suppose the blacks seldom spare any whites who fall into their hands?" Reuben asked.

"Scarcely ever," Mr. Blount replied. "That was why they were more dreaded than the bush rangers. The latter would kill, if they were in the humour for it; but if there was no serious resistance, and none of their number got hurt, more often than not they contented themselves by leaving everyone tied, hand and foot, till somebody came to unloose them.

"I remember one horrible case, in which they so tied up three white men at a lonely station, and nobody happened to go near it for three weeks afterwards. It struck someone that none of them had been seen, for some time; and a couple of men rode over and, to their horror, found the three men dead of hunger and thirst.

"Now the black fellows don't do that sort of thing. When they do attack a station and take it, they kill every soul; man, woman, and child."

"I suppose, in that affair you were telling us of," Reuben asked, "both of your ticket-of-leave men were killed?"

"Yes. One seemed to have been surprised and speared at once. The other had made a stout fight of it, for the bodies of three natives were found near him."

"I remember one case," one of the others said, "in which the blacks did spare one of the party, in a station which they attacked. It was a little girl of about three years old. Why they did so I don't know; perhaps the chief took a fancy to her. Maybe he had lost a child of the same age, and thought his gin would take to the little one. Anyhow, he carried her off.

"The father happened to be away at the time. He had gone down to Sydney with a waggon, for stores; and when he got back he found the house burned, and the bodies of his wife, two boys, and two men, but there was no trace of that of the child.

"He was nearly out of his mind, poor fellow. The neighbours all thought that the body must have been burned with the house; but he would have it that there would have been some sign of her. No one else thought so; and besides, it wasn't the custom of the blacks to carry off anyone. The father got a party to try and follow the blacks, but of course it was no use. They had pretty near two days' start.

"The father never took to his farm again, but hung about the out stations, doing a job here and there for his grub. Sometimes he would be away for a bit, and when he came back, though he never talked about it, everyone knew he had been out hunting the blacks.

"I do not know how many of them he killed, but I know he never spared one, when he got him outside the settlement. After a time the blacks never troubled that part. So many of them had been killed that they got a superstitious fear of the man, and believed he was possessed of an evil spirit; and I don't believe twenty of them, together, would have dared to attack him.

"At last, from some of the half-tamed blacks in the settlement, he got to hear some sort of rumour that there was a white girl, living with one of the tribes far out in their country, and he set out. He was away four months, and he never said what he had been doing all the time. In fact, he started almost directly for the port, and went home by the next ship.

"However, he brought his child back with him. It was four years since she had been carried off, and she was a regular little savage, when she arrived in the settlement with him. Of course she could not speak a word of English, and was as fierce as a little wildcat. I expect she got all right, after a bit.

"I didn't see the man, but I heard he was worn to a shadow, when he got back. He must have had an awful time of it, in the bush. What with hunger and thirst, and dodging the blacks, I don't know how he lived through it; but he looked contented and happy, in spite of his starvation, and they say it was wonderful to see how patient he was with the child.

"They got up a subscription, at Sydney, to send them both home. I heard that the captain of the ship he went in said, when he came back the next voyage, that the child had taken to him, and had got civilized and like other children before they got to England."

"Of course, such fellows as Cockeye and Fothergill are the exceptions, and not the rule," Mr. Blount said. "Were there many of such scoundrels about, we should have to abandon our settlements and make war upon them; for there would be no living in the colony till they were exterminated.

Most of these fellows are the colonial version of the highwaymen, at home. It is just 'Stand and deliver.' They content themselves with taking what they can find in a traveller's pockets, or can obtain by a flying visit to his station."

"Yes, I had several of those in my last district," Reuben said. "They were just mounted robbers, and gave us a good deal of trouble in hunting them down. But none of them had shed blood during their career, and they did not even draw a pistol when we captured them. That style of bush ranger is a nuisance, but no more. Men seldom carry much money about with them here, and no great harm was done."

"You see," Dick Caister said, "these fellows have a remarkable objection to putting their necks in the way of a noose; so that although they may lug out a pistol and shout 'Bail up!' they will very seldom draw a trigger, if you show fight. So long as they do not take life they know that, if they are caught, all they have to expect is to be kept at hard work during the rest of their sentence, and perhaps for a bit longer. They don't mind the risk of that. They have had their outing, sometimes a long one; but if they once take life, they know its hanging when they are caught; and are therefore careful not to press too hard upon their triggers.

"But once they have killed a man, they don't generally care how many more lives they take. They are desperate, then, and seem to exult in devilry of all kinds. As to being stuck up by an ordinary bush ranger, one would think no more of it than of having one's pockets picked, in England.

"It's lucky for us, on the whole, that the black fellows have such a hatred of the white men. Were it not for that, a good many of these fellows would go all lengths, relying on taking to the bush when they had made the colony too hot to hold them. But there are only a few of them that have ever got on well with the blacks, and many a man who has gone out into the bush has found his end there. You see, there's no explaining to a dozen natives, who jump up and begin to throw spears and boomerangs at you, that you are a bad white fellow, and not a colonist on the search for fresh runs.

"No, the bush rangers on the whole are not such a bad lot of fellows. I suppose there is not one of us, here, who hasn't had men ride up and ask for food; who were, he knew pretty well, bush rangers. Of course they got their food, as anyone else would who rode up to a station and asked for it.

"Once, only, I was told to hand over any money I had in the house. As, fortunately, I had only a few pounds I gave it up without making a fight for it. It's no use risking one's life, unless for something worth fighting for. I suppose most of us here have had similar experiences."

There was a general chorus of assent among the settlers.

"Many of them are poor-spirited wretches. Two of them bailed up a waggoner of mine, coming out with a load from the port. He pretended to give in and, as they were opening some of the boxes, he knocked one over with the butt end of his whip. The other fired a hasty shot, and then jumped on to his horse and galloped off again; and my man brought in the fellow he had stunned."

"Did you hand him over to the police?" Reuben asked.

"Not I," the settler laughed. "I thought he had got what he deserved, so I bandaged up his head and let him go. Those poor beggars of convicts have a dreadful hard time of it, and I don't think there are many settlers who would hand over any man who had escaped, and taken to the bush, even if he had occasionally bailed up a waggoner or so. We know what a flogging the poor wretch would get and, as long as it's only an occasional robbery, to keep themselves from starving, we don't feel any great animosity against them. It's different, altogether, when they take to murder. Then, of course, they must be hunted down like wild beasts.

"And now I vote that we have a nap. My pipe's out, and I suppose we shall be on the tramp again, as soon as it is dark."

Chapter 13
Bush Rangers

As soon as it became dark, the journey was renewed.

"Now, Jim, you must keep your eyes well open," Reuben said. "There is no saying when we may come upon them, now."

"I tink dey not berry far off, sah. Dose sheep too tired to go far. Black fellow glad to stop and rest, when he see no one coming after him.

"De ground more up and down here. Must no make noise. May come upon dem sudden."

It was nearly midnight when Jim suddenly halted.

"What is it, Jim?" Reuben asked, in a low voice.

Jim stood sniffing the air.

"Me smell fire, captain."

Reuben sniffed the air, but shook his head.

"I don't smell anything, Jim."

"I smell him, sah, sure enough; not very close, perhaps, but in de air."

"What is it, Captain Whitney?" Mr. Blount asked, as he came forward and joined them.

"Jim says he smells fire, but I can't smell it."

"Oh, you can trust Jim's nose," the settler said. "It is wonderful how keen is the scent of these natives. They are like dogs in that respect; and can perceive the smell of a fire, when the wind brings it down to them, miles away."

"Dis way now, sah," Jim said, turning off to the left, at right angles to the course which they had been pursuing. "Smell come down the wind, dat's sartin. We follow him far enough, we sure to catch dem."

For fully two miles, Reuben followed the black without speaking. Then he said:

"I don't smell any smoke, Jim. Are you quite sure you are right about it?"

"Quite sure, sah. De smoke much stronger than he was. Some of dese bushes make very sharp smell; can smell him very far away."

"That's all right, Jim, on we go then. I must take your word for it."

After another half-an-hour's walking, Reuben thought that he too could smell an odour of burning wood and, soon afterwards, he became convinced that it was so. The ground on which they were crossing was slightly undulated and, on nearing the crest of one of the slight rises, Jim said:

"De smoke am getting strong now, sah; and Jim can hear de bleating of de sheep. If de captain will wait here, Jim will go on ahead, and find out where dey lie."

"But perhaps you won't be able to find us again."

"Der no fear of dat, sah. But if I not come straight back, I give a little whistle-like this—when I get on to a rise; and if the captain answer in just the same way, then I come straight back to him."

So saying, Jim glided away in the darkness; while Reuben gave the word for the men to halt, and lie down till his return. There was, however, no occasion for a signal for, in little over half an hour from the time of Jim's leaving, he rejoined them again; his coming being unnoticed until he stood among them, so noiseless were his footsteps.

"We hab dem dis time, sure enough, captain."

"Why, is that you, Jim? You quite startled me. Well, what is your news?"

"De black fellows and de sheep are a little over a mile away, sah. Dey got a big fire down in a bottom. Some of dem eating still, but most of dem fast asleep round de fire."

"How many are there of them?"

"About fifty, sah—at least, dat about the number Jim saw. I expect I was right when I tell you dat there was well nigh a hundred, at fust. Some ob them go off wid de sheep, de odder way, and we kill over twenty in dat fight."

"Do you think we killed so many as that, Jim?"

"I went round, sah, and counted sixteen of dem; and some sure to have crawl away and die in de bush. Dere were over twenty killed altogether, for sure; and I specks dat some more hab left de party today, and gone off wid dere share of de sheep to der people."

"Well, what do you think, Mr. Blount—shall we attack them tonight, or wait till morning?"

"I should say wait till morning, certainly," the settler said. "We might shoot a few if we attack them now, but the rest would be all off, at the first flash of our gun; and we should never get another shot. I think our best plan would be to remain where we are, for another couple of hours—it is two o'clock now—then Jim will guide us to the place, and we can take up our position as close as we can get, and wait for daylight."

"There is no fear of their making a move before it is light, Jim?"

"No, sah. Dey tink dey am safe now, and eat one big feast. Dey not move till light, sartain."

"Very well, Mr. Blount, then we will do as you say. When we get near them we will divide into four parties. You, with four men, shall move up close to the sheep, Sergeant O'Connor, with four others, shall work up from the other end of the bottom. Five others shall make a detour, and get right on the other side of their fire; and I, with the other three and Jim, who you see has got one of the constables' rifles and ammunition, will come down on them from this side.

"Jim will place all the parties, taking them by turns, as near the fire as he thinks safe; and will then return to me. Only, as we shall attack them from four sides, let everyone be careful about his shooting; otherwise we shall have casualties from our own shots.

"All will remain quiet until I fire. Then a general volley must be poured in, with bullet and buckshot; and when the rifles and guns are empty, go right at them with pistol and sword."

The plan was carried out as arranged and, before daybreak, the four parties were lying in the positions allotted to them, within forty yards of the blacks. A few of these were seen sitting by the fire, the rest were all asleep.

Gradually the light began to creep over the sky and, as it became lighter, there was a movement among the blacks. As soon as he could see perfectly, Reuben was about to fire in the air; for he did not like to fire at unsuspecting men, in spite of the deeds of blood and rapine they had performed in the settlement.

Presently, however, his eye fell upon one of the treacherous trackers, who had so nearly brought destruction upon them. He levelled his rifle and fired, and the man fell dead in his tracks.

As the rest of the blacks leapt to their feet, a volley from nineteen guns was poured into them—followed by seven or eight more, as most of the settlers were armed with double-barrelled guns; a few buckshot being dropped into each barrel, over the bullets. Then came the sharp cracks of the pistols, as the whites rushed down to the assault.

The natives attempted no resistance. Panic stricken at the sudden appearance of the foe, whom they imagined by this time far back on their way to the settlements; and paralysed by the slaughter made by the first volley, they thought only of flight. A few caught up their spears and waddies, as they made a dash for the bushes, and strove to effect their escape between the parties advancing on each side of them; but the latter were now close at hand and, for a minute or two, a fight took place between the whites, with their clubbed muskets, and the natives with their spears and waddies. But it was soon over, for the natives only fought to escape and, as soon as they saw an opening, bounded away into the bushes.

Only one of the assailants was killed, but several were more or less severely wounded by the spears; while no less than thirty-four of the blacks were killed. The victors made no attempt at pursuit but, as soon as the last of the natives had escaped, they gathered to ascertain what loss had taken place, on their side.

"Poor Phillips is killed," Mr. Blount said, as he examined the body. "The spear has gone right through his throat. Fortunately he was a single man. He has only been out here a few months, and was staying down at Dick Caister's."

"Poor Tom," Dick said, in feeling tones. "He was a capital young fellow, and I am deeply sorry. Fortunately he has left no one behind to grieve more than I do for him, for he lost his father and mother shortly before he came out, and was alone in the world."

"I am thankful it's no worse," Mr. Blount said. "We have given the blacks a terrible lesson. I think, as far as they are concerned, we can sleep in peace for a long time. Of course we have not done with them, for they are very revengeful; but a blow like this will render them careful, for a long time, how they attack us.

"How many of them have fallen?"

"Thirty-four," Reuben said. "Jim has just been counting them up.

"Now, Mr. Blount, we will have another of your sheep for breakfast, and then we'll be off."

The sheep had scattered somewhat, at the alarm of the fire, but were soon driven together again. One was caught and killed, and slices of the meat were stuck up on ramrods, and were soon frizzling before the fire.

"Well, Mr. Blount, how many sheep do you think there are here?"

"I have just been looking them over," the settler replied, "and I should say there must be nearly twelve hundred; so that, allowing for two hundred driven off in the other direction, and a hundred dropped by the way, the whole flock are accounted for. I am indeed obliged to you, and to my friends here. I never expected to see a tail of them again, when I found they were off."

"I am very glad you have recovered so many of them," Reuben said, "and still more, that we have given the blacks such a lesson. We will, as soon as we have finished, be on the march. Jim will go on ahead at once, as we agreed; and he tells me will get to the stream where the horses are before night, and will start out with them at once, so that we may be able to meet them tomorrow, early. I fancy our water bottles are all getting very low, but we can hold on for today."

As soon as he had finished eating, Jim started off at a run, which Reuben knew he would keep up for hours. The body of young Phillips was buried; and then, collecting the flock and driving it before them, the rest started upon their return. The sheep could not travel fast, for many of them were footsore with their hurried journey; but they had found plenty of nourishment in the grass at the bottoms, and in the foliage of the bushes and, being so supplied, had suffered little from thirst.

Jim, before starting, had pointed out the exact line they were to follow, and this they kept by compass. With only one or two short halts, they kept on until nightfall and, leaving the sheep in a grassy bottom, lit their fire on the crest above it, in order that its flame might serve as a guide to Jim, should he get back with the horses before daylight.

There was but little talking, before each stretched himself at length before the fire. They had been twenty-four hours without sleep, and all were now suffering severely from thirst. The last drops in the water bottles had been emptied, early in the day; and they were parched not only by the heat of the sun, but by the stifling dust raised by the flock as they travelled.

There had been but little supper eaten. Indeed, most of them contented themselves with chewing pieces of raw meat, to satisfy their thirst rather than their hunger. Although they had no fear of the return of the natives, Reuben thought it only prudent to keep watch, and each of the party had half an hour on sentry duty.

The day was just beginning to break, when the man on guard exclaimed:

"I can hear the trampling of horses!"

The news brought everyone to their feet, and in a few minutes the two constables and Jim rode up, driving before them the horses of the rest of the party.

"Well done, Jim!" Reuben exclaimed. "Now, the first thing, get one of the water skins off."

One of the skins was unfastened in a minute and, after copious draughts, everyone felt refreshed and ready for work again.

"We cannot start for a few hours," Reuben said. "The horses must have come over forty miles, and won't be fit to travel till the afternoon; fortunately there is plenty of grass for them in the bottom. And now that my thirst is allayed, I begin to discover that I am hungry."

There was a general chorus of assent. The fire was made up again. The men went down to the bottom, and killed and brought up a sheep; and all were soon engaged in making up for their twenty-four hours' fast.

In the afternoon a start was made; but although they travelled all night, they did not reach the stream until the following afternoon, as they were obliged to accommodate their pace to that of the sheep. The following morning Reuben rode forward to the settlements, leaving Mr. Blount, with two of his friends, to come on with the flock at his leisure.

At the first farm he reached Reuben heard that, as he feared, the bush rangers had taken advantage of so many of the settlers being away to recommence their attacks. At the first two houses they visited, they had found the inmates on the watch, and had moved off without making any attack. At the third they had surprised and killed a settler, his wife, and two hired men, and had sacked and burned the house. Reuben learned that some of the police had gone off in pursuit.

Leaving his horse to the care of the settler, Reuben borrowed a fresh animal and rode off to the scene of the outrage, which was some thirty miles distant. Just as he arrived there he met the party of eight police, who had been in pursuit of the bush rangers, and they reported that they had lost all trace of them.

For the next two or three weeks Reuben did not return to his headquarters, spending the time in riding from station to station, with a small party of police, and urging upon the settlers the necessity not only of strongly barricading their houses, but of keeping a watch by turns; as the bush rangers seldom attack a place, unless they can gain the advantage of a surprise.

As nothing had been heard of the bush rangers, Reuben determined to return to his barrack. He was spending the last night at Dick Caister's when, just as they were about to turn in, the sound of a horse's hoofs, at full gallop, was heard.

"Something is the matter," Dick said. "Men don't ride like that, at night, for nothing."

He went to the door and opened it, just as the horseman stopped in front.

"Quick, Caister!" the man said as he leaped down, "the bush rangers are not fifty yards behind."

And indeed, the sound of the trampling of other horses sounded close behind.

"Come in, come in!" Dick cried. "Ah! Is it you, Shillito? Never mind the horse, he must look after himself. Luckily the captain's here, and we will give it them hot. Just run round and see that all the shutters are fastened."

As Dick spoke he was barring the door, and he now shouted at the top of his voice to the two hired men, who were in bed upstairs; but before any answer could be returned, there was a thundering knocking at the door.

"What is it?" Dick shouted.

"Open the door, and be quick about it, or it will be worse for you. We want that chap that's just ridden up, and we mean to have him, so he had best come out at once. If you don't open the door at once, we will cut the throats of every soul in the house."

"You have got to get at our throats first, my fine fellow," Dick said jeeringly.

The knocking was at once renewed, but with greater violence.

"The door's a strong one," Dick said to Reuben, "and it will stand a good deal of that sort of thing; but we may as well move the table and benches up against it, then we can see how things stand."

Reuben had been busy taking down the guns, which hung over the fireplace; dropping a ramrod into them to see that they were charged, and putting fresh caps on to the nipples. His own rifle stood in the corner; and was, he knew, ready for service.

"What arms have you altogether, Caister?"

"I have that rifle and double-barrel gun. Both my hands have got muskets; I got them up from Sydney, a few months back."

The two men now came running down from above, each with his musket.

"Where is Jim?" Reuben said, looking round.

"He went out about ten minutes ago," Dick said. "I fancy he went to look after your horse. He takes as much care of that animal as if it were a child."

"I hope they won't find him in the stable, and cut his throat," Reuben said. "He is wonderfully faithful and attached to me. I would not have harm come to him, for anything.

"Now, I will go upstairs and reconnoitre. Now those fellows have left off knocking at the door, they are a good deal more dangerous than when they were kicking up all the row."

"Mind how you show yourself, captain, as likely enough one of them is on the watch, expecting that we should be sure, sooner or later, to take a look out of that window. So keep well back. The night is pretty light, so I expect you will be able to make them out."

"Can we get a view of the stable from that window?"

"Yes," Dick replied, "I rather had that in my mind's eye, when I put the stable up. It's always a good thing, men knowing that their master can have an eye upon them, when they least expect it. Why do you ask?"

"Because if the window commands the stable door, we can prevent them getting the horses out."

"Yes," Dick said, "after losing two in that last affair, it would be a serious matter to have the rest of them carried off."

Reuben went up the stairs and made his way towards the window, standing a short distance back. He could see no one moving about in the yard, and he was about to move close to it, when a tremendous crash took place below, followed by loud shouts. He ran downstairs again.

The bush rangers had moved round to the back of the house and, there picking up a young tree which had been brought in, to saw up into billets for firewood, they used it as a battering ram against one of the shutters; and at the very first blow broke it off its hinges, and then made a rush at the window. Two shots rang out almost together; and then, firing a hasty volley into the window, the bush rangers began to climb in. But by this time Reuben had arrived, and the sharp cracks of his pistols rang out.

"They have got the police here!" one of the men exclaimed, as he caught a sight of Reuben's uniform.

"Draw off, lads, I expect it's that accursed captain," another voice exclaimed. "He's always riding about, with nobody but that black fellow with him. He has got to go down, that fellow has, or he will give us no end of trouble; but draw off from that window, for a moment."

"What will they do next, I wonder?" Dick Caister said as, leaving the two hands to guard the window, he returned into the other room with Reuben.

"I rather expect they are going to try to burn us out. We must keep them from that, if we can.

"Mr. Shillito, will you go up to the upper room, and keep an eye on the stables? Shoot down anyone who may pass your line of sight.

"Haven't you got any loopholes, Caister?"

"Yes, of course I have," Dick replied. "I had forgotten all about them. Yes, there are two loopholes in the logs in each side of the house, upstairs. They have been shut up by wisps of straw, ever since the house was built."

Giving strict orders, to the two men, to shout instantly if anyone moved near the window, the two young men went upstairs.

"Have you seen anything, Shillito?"

"Not a thing. One would almost think that they have bolted."

"They will hardly do that, I fancy," Reuben said. "There are ten or twelve of them, but I think one or two must have got a bullet in them."

"I wish they would come on," Dick said, as he pulled out the straw from the loopholes.

Reuben went to them all in succession, and looked out, but nothing could be seen of their assailants. Presently, however, a number of dark figures appeared, each bearing a burden.

"They have been cutting brush wood!" Reuben exclaimed. "I was right, you see. They are going to try to smoke or burn us out. Now I think it's time to give them a lesson."

"Look, look!"

The exclamation was excited by a sudden glare of light, on the other side of the stables.

"The scoundrels have set fire to the stables!" Shillito said.

"What shall we do—make a sally?" Caister asked. "I am ready for it, if you think right."

"No," Reuben said, "they would only shoot us down as we come out. They must guess that some of us are up at this window, or they would try to carry the horses off, instead of destroying them.

"I only wish we were on the poor beasts' backs. We would go for them, though they were twice as many.

"I don't see the others now—they must have gone round to the other side of the house."

Scarcely had Reuben taken up his station, at one of the loopholes behind, than he again saw the dark figures. He took steady aim and fired. There was a sharp cry, and one of the fellows fell to the ground. The others at once threw down their burdens, and fled. Three minutes later there was a shout.

"Look here, you policeman, and you, Caister, you shall pay dearly for this night's work. I swear it, and Bill Fothergill never forgets his word in that way. It's your turn, this time. It will be mine the next, and when it is, take care."

The only reply was a shot from Reuben, aimed in the direction from which the voice came. A minute later there was a trampling of horses.

"They are gone!" Shillito exclaimed.

"Perhaps it is only a trick, to draw us out," Dick suggested.

"No, I don't think it's that," Reuben said. "They are not strong enough to send a party off, and to attack us with the rest. No, I think they have gone. They know that we can't follow them.

"They have taken good care of that," he added bitterly, as he glanced at the stables, which were now a sheet of flame. "However, we will look round and see."

The three men descended to the room below and, being joined by the two hands, removed the furniture piled against the door, and threw it open.

"We mustn't go round to that side of the house, so as to get into the glare of the fire, till we have looked round," Reuben said. "I believe they are all gone; but they may have left a couple of them lurking, somewhere about, to pick us off when we show in the light.

"I will take one of your hands, Caister, and scout round on one side. Do you three go the other side."

A quarter of an hour later the two parties met near the stables, where the fire was now burning low. The roof had fallen in, and only some of the uprights were erect, with flicking flames licking them as they stood glowing above the mass of still blazing debris.

"I wonder whether that poor fellow is under that?" Reuben said.

"I hope not, indeed. I fancy he must have got away. He might have slipped off when they first rode up. He may be hiding somewhere round, afraid to come near till he knows how matters have turned out."

So saying, he gave a loud cooey. They stood silent for a minute, but no answer came back.

"There is nothing to be done, till morning," Dick said, "and it's no use hanging about here. Before it gets light I will start for Watson's. There are two of your men there; and they, with the two Watsons and ourselves, can set out after these fellows, if you are agreeable. That is, as soon as we get hold of some horses."

"I hardly think I shall be justified in taking you," Reuben said, as he walked back towards the house. "These scoundrels are all armed to the teeth, and they are first-rate shots. They know every foot of the country, and against anything like equal numbers they would make a desperate fight of it, even if they did not thrash us. Of course, in anything like an equal number of my own men I should not hesitate, but I don't think it will be fair for you settlers to undertake such a service as that."

"Listen!" Shillito exclaimed, "they are coming back again."

Surely enough, on the night air the sound of horses, galloping at full speed, could be heard.

"I don't think it can be them," Reuben said. "They would have no motive in coming back, after they once rode off. They would know we should be ready for them."

"I don't see who else it can be. At any rate, all our guns are loaded; and if it is them, all the better."

Suddenly a loud cooey was heard.

"That's Jim!" Reuben exclaimed. "I should know his call among a thousand. He must have made off to get help at once, but I don't know how he can have done it in time."

"Why, it's the Watsons and my men!" he exclaimed, as the party rode up into the light.

"All safe?" one of the settlers cried, as he jumped from his horse.

"All safe, thank God," Reuben replied. "Did Jim bring you news that we were attacked?"

"Yes; fortunately we were sitting up late, talking, when he rode up; so there was not a minute lost."

"Rode up!" Reuben repeated, in surprise; "why, where did you get a horse, Jim?"

"Rode master's horse," Jim said.

"What!" Reuben exclaimed in delight, "what, is Tartar safe? I was afraid his body was under those ruins. Why, how did you get him out?"

"Jim was in de stable, sah, when bush ranger ride up. De horses was stamping, and I not hear dem till dey come quite close, den it was too late to run out.

"De moment dat dey began to make bobbery at door, I opened stable door and bring out de three horses."

"What! Did you get mine out, too?" Dick shouted. "Jim, you are a trump, and no mistake."

"Den," Jim went on, paying no attention to the interruption, "me led de other two hosses little way, and let them go loose, sure not go far from home; and I jump on Tartar, and ride like de debel to Watson's for de police."

"Well done, Jim. You have done capitally. Now let us talk over what we had better do."

The party re-entered the house. Fresh wood was thrown on to the fire, and one of Dick's hands proceeded to put food on the table, and prepare tea, while the others consulted what course should be pursued.

It was agreed, at once, that more aid would be necessary, before they could think of attacking the bush rangers; but all were ready to join in the hunt for them. Therefore it was decided that Dick Shillito and the two Watsons should each ride, at once, to neighbouring stations to bring aid. At one of the stations two more policemen would be found, and as in the pursuit they should probably pass near other stations, their numbers would swell as they went. When this was settled, the party sat down to the meal.

"How did you come upon them, Shillito?" Caister asked.

"I had been spending the day with the Wilkinsons. I did not start to ride home till it was rather late, and I was riding fast when, about a quarter of a mile before I got to my place, I rode right into the middle of a lot of men on horseback. They evidently hadn't heard me coming, and were as much surprised as I was.

"There was a general shout of 'Bail up!' and I saw at once what sort of gentry they were. However, I didn't stop, but in the confusion dashed through.

"A few shots were fired at me. I suppose they were too surprised to aim straight. Then they started off after me. I knew it was no use making for home, for there was only one man there; so I swept round and made for your place. My horse is a good one, you know, and I gained on them all except one man, who must have been capitally mounted, for he gradually crept up to me. He wasn't twenty yards behind me when he shouted:

"'Stop, or I fire!'

"I pulled straight up and, as he came up to me, let fly at him. He tumbled off his horse, and I galloped off till I got here."

"What has become of your horse, I wonder?"

"I gave him a cut with my whip, as I jumped off. He cantered away. Of course they may have caught him, but I don't think it's likely."

"You will find him somewhere about at daylight, I expect. I will ride Caister's spare horse, now."

For Jim, with one of the hands, had gone out to fetch in the two horses from the spot where they had been turned loose.

Chapter 14
An Unexpected Meeting

As soon as it was light the party were assembled and started, Jim leading the way, at a swinging pace which kept the horses going at a hand canter. The marks were, for a time, perfectly easy to follow. Five miles on the tracks led to a shepherd's hut. At their call, the man came out.

"You had a visit from bush rangers last night?"

"What if I did?" the man replied gruffly. "I can't help where the bush rangers pay their visits. Yes, they came in here and said they wanted some supper; and you may guess I did not keep them waiting long, for they were not in a particularly good temper. From what they said, three of their men had been killed."

This was already known to the party, as Jim had found three bodies at a short distance from the house. Two of these had evidently been carried there from the back window, where they had been killed in trying to effect the entry. The other had been shot when approaching to fire the house.

"The captain of the gang was terrible put out, and was a-cussing and swearing as to what he would do to those as did it. I wouldn't be in their shoes, if they were to fall into his hands."

"They didn't say anything which would give you an idea as to the direction they were taking?"

"Not they," the man replied. "You don't suppose they would be such fools as that and, if they had, you don't suppose as I should be such a fool to split on 'em. Not likely. I ain't no desire to wake up, one night, and find the door fastened outside and the thatch on fire."

"We may as well ride on," Reuben said. "We shall learn nothing here. The fellow is a ticket-of-leave man, and as likely as not in league with these scoundrels.

"I wonder what they came here for," he added, as they started again.

"I tell you, sah," Jim said. "Dat fellow has driven his herd ober their trail—all stamped out—no saying where they hab gone to."

"We must follow the herd, then," Reuben said. "If we look sharp, we ought to be able to see the traces where they left them."

Jim shook his head.

"No find," he said decidedly. "Plenty places where de ground am berry hard, and horse feet no show. Dey choose some place like dat and turn off; perhaps put rug under horses' feet, so as to make no mark. Me sarch, sah. Jim look him eyes very hard, but tink no find."

And so, to their great disappointment, it turned out. They followed the tracks of the herd three miles, until they came upon them, quietly grazing; but nowhere could they see any trace of a party of horsemen turning off. All the party were greatly vexed at the ill success of their expedition; for all had hoped that they were, at last, going to overtake the gang who had done such mischief in the colony.

Reuben was especially disgusted. He had, only the day before, received a letter from his chief acknowledging the receipt of his report describing the pursuit of the blacks, and congratulating him warmly upon his success. The letter ended:

"If you can but give as good an account of the bush rangers, we shall be indeed grateful to you. As it is, you have more than justified my selection of you for the post."

Leaving two constables as guards, at Dick Caister's station, in case, as was probable enough, the bush rangers should return to take revenge for the repulse they had experienced there, Reuben rode back to his headquarters, from which he had now been absent some time. The evening after his return, he called Jim into his room.

"Jim," he said, "I want your advice as to the best way of finding out where these bush rangers are quartered. How do you think we had better set about it? Would it be of any use, do you think, for you to go among the natives and try and find out? There is no doubt they know, for they have often acted with the bush rangers. Do you think you could pass among them?"

"No, sah," Jim said at once. "Me no speak deir way. Me understand black fellow, me talk dar language, but not same way. They find out difference directly and kill me. De wild black fellows hate those who hab lived wid de white men. We hate dem just de same way. We say dem bad black fellow, dey say we no good."

"But those rascally trackers who led us wrong, that day of the fight, they were friendly with them."

"Yes, sah, but dey not so very long away from the bush, and always keep friends wid the others. Meet dem and talk to dem, and tell dem dey set the white men on wrong tracks."

"Well, Jim, but could not you do the same?"

"No good, sah. Me brought up among de whites, eber since me little boy. Dey not believe me if I go and say dat to dem. Jim ready to get killed, if de captain want him; but no good at all him getting killed in dat way."

"I don't want you to get killed in any way, Jim, and if that's your opinion about it, we will give up the plan at once. Can you think of any other way?"

"Me tink a lot about him. Me know de captain want very much to catch dose fellows, but Jim no see how dat can be done, for sure. But de best plan me can see is for Jim to go out by himself, and search de country outside white man's bounds. If he find de track of horses, he follow dem up. Me know about de way dey ride off after dey be killing people at de stations. If Jim look, and look, and look berry sharp he find dar track for sure; and once he find dem, he follow dem up. Must be water, for sure, where dey live. Dat good guide to begin with.

"But captain must not hurry; Jim may be long time before he find dem, dar no saying how long. Captain wish Jim to go?"

"Well, Jim, I don't want you to go; that is to say, I should miss you very much; but if you could find out the haunts of these scoundrels, you would be doing me a very great service, as well as the people of all the stations."

"Jim no care about oder people," the black said. "He care for de captain, and will go out and try and find tracks."

"Be careful, Jim, and don't get into trouble with them. If you were to fall into their hands, and they were to find out you were connected with the police, they would shoot you like a dog."

"Dey won't find out. White man not understand. Black fellow all one to him. You hab no fear for Jim. Who look after hoss, while Jim away?"

"I shall appoint one of the policemen as my orderly, Jim, and he will look after him."

Jim made a contemptuous gesture, to signify that he had little confidence in the power of any white man to look after Tartar. For the rest of the evening Jim was occupied in cooking, and in the morning he was gone.

A week later, Reuben was among the outlying stations again. He had heard nothing of the bush rangers, and no fresh attacks had been made by them, since that upon Dick Caister's station.

One evening, just as he had gone up to bed, he was roused by a sharp knocking at the door of the house in which he was stopping. The settlers had grown cautious now, and an upper window was opened, and Reuben heard the questions, "Who is there?" and "What is it?"

"Is Captain Whitney here?"

"Yes, do you want him?"

"Yes, I want to see him directly."

In a minute, Reuben had opened the door.

"I am Captain Whitney," he said. "What is it?"

"I am glad I have found you, sir. They told me at the next station you were here yesterday, but they did not know whether you were here now.

"Well, sir, I am shepherding some twenty miles away; and this afternoon, just as I had got back to my hut, in runs a black fellow. It is a lonely spot, and I reached for my gun, thinking there was more of them, when he said:

"'No shoot, me friend. Me sarve Captain Whitney of de police. You know him?'

"I said I had heard your name.

"'You know where he is?' the black asked.

"I said I did not know for certain; but that when my mate went in for grub, two days before, he had heard say that you had been along there that morning.

"The black said: 'Good. You run and find him.'

"'Thank you,' says I. 'What for?'

"'I find out about the bush rangers,' he said. 'You go and tell captain dat, tomorrow morning before de day begins, dey attack the station of Donald's.'

"'Are you quite sure?' says I.

"'Quite sure,' says the black. 'Me heard dem say so.'

"So as I hates the bush rangers like poison, I saddles up and rides into the station; and when I had told the boss, he said I better ride and find you, if I could. You would be at one of the stations this way. I stopped at three of them, and at the last they told me you was here."

"Thank you greatly, my good fellow. Donald's! I don't know the name. Where do they live?"

"They have only been here a couple of months," Reuben's host, who was standing beside him, replied. "They bought that station of Anderson's. He was a chicken-hearted young fellow, and sold out because of the bush rangers. There is a man, his wife, and her sister, I believe. I fancy they have got a pretty fair capital. They took Anderson's stock, and have been buying a lot more. That's why the bush rangers are going to attack them."

"I thought," Reuben said, "that Anderson's was not one of the most exposed stations."

"No, that was what everyone told him, before he sold it."

"How far would you say it was from here?"

"Thirty-five miles," the settler said. "It's ten miles from Barker's, and I reckon that's twenty-five from here."

"Well, of course I shall ride at once; as there are women there, it makes the case all the more urgent. I have got my orderly, and there are two more men at the station, this side of Barker's."

"I will go, of course," Reuben's host said, "and will bring two men with me.

"You had best stop here for the night," he added, turning to the shepherd. "You have ridden pretty well thirty miles already, and that at the end of your day's work."

"Not I," the man replied. "Jim Walsh is not going to be lying in bed, with the thought of two women in the hands of them murderous bush rangers. You might lend me a fresh horse, if you have got one. If not, I must try and pick one up at one of the stations, as we go along."

"I have plenty of horses in the yard," the settler said.

"Well, let us be off as soon as possible," Reuben put in. "It's past twelve o'clock now, and we have thirty-five miles to ride, and to stop at two or three places, so we haven't a minute to lose."

In a few minutes the horses were saddled, and the six men dashed off at full gallop. At three stations, which they passed on the way to Barker's, they picked up seven more. There was but little delay as, the instant the news was told, the men hurried up, saddled their horses, and rode after the party, who pushed straight on when they had told their story. At Barker's they were joined by Barker himself, and two men. Two constables had also been picked up on the way.

The others overtook them here, and the party now numbered twenty men. There was a pause to allow all to come up, and to give the horses breathing time, for they had traversed twenty-five miles at a rapid pace, with scarce a halt.

Mrs. Barker herself prepared a meal, to which, while the horses got their breath, their riders did justice. Then they mounted again, and rode for Donald's.

"It all depends," Reuben said, "as to our being there in time, whether the man keeps a careful watch. If he does they may not attack till the doors are opened, and then make a sudden rush and catch them unawares. If, when they arrive there, they find the whole house is asleep, they may burst in at once."

"I think they will be careful," Mr. Barker said. "I know Donald is very anxious; and no wonder, with two women with him, both young and pretty—quite out of the way, indeed. In fact, he told me the first day I rode over, he had no idea of the unsettled state of the district, and wouldn't have taken the place if he had, not even if Anderson had given it as a gift; and he wrote down at once to some agent, and told him to sell the place again, for whatever he can get for it; but I expect there will be some trouble in finding a purchaser. The district here has had a bad name for some time and, if Donald had not arrived fresh from England, he must have heard of it."

"Listen! I thought I heard the sound of firing."

There was a momentary pause, but no one could hear anything. Nevertheless, they went on at redoubled speed. They were now within three miles of the station.

Suddenly, on coming over a crest, a faint light was seen ahead. It increased rapidly, and a tongue of flame leapt up.

"Come on, lads!" Reuben exclaimed. "The scoundrels are at their work."

At a hard gallop they crossed the intervening ground, until they were within half a mile of the station, from which a broad sheet of flame was leaping up. Then Reuben drew rein, for he had outridden the rest of his party, and it was important that all should ride together.

"Now," he said, when they were gathered; "let us keep in a close body.

"If they ride off as we arrive there, do you, Jones and Wilkins, stop at the station and see if you can render any help. If not, follow us at once.

"Let the rest keep on with me, straight after the bush rangers. There is already a faint light in the east. In half an hour it will be broad day so, even if they have got a start, we shall be able to follow them. Now, come on."

At the head of his party, Reuben rode at full speed down to the station. As he neared it he saw, to his satisfaction, that the flames arose from some of the outbuildings, and that the house itself was still intact; but as no firing had been heard, he hoped that it still resisted.

There was a shrill whistle, when the party approached within a hundred yards. Men were seen to dash out of the house, and to leap upon their horses.

With a shout, Reuben rode down. He did not pause for a moment, but dashed past the house in the direction in which the bush rangers had fled. They were, he knew, but a hundred yards ahead; but it was not light enough for him to see them, especially after riding through the glare of the fire. The sound of the horses' feet, however, afforded an indication; but as there was no saying in which direction they might turn, he was forced to halt, every two or three minutes, to listen.

To his mortification he found that, each time, the sound was getting more indistinct; for the speed at which they had travelled had taken so much out of the horses, that they were unable to compete with the fresher animals ridden by the bush rangers, who were all well mounted, many of the best horses in the district having been stolen by them. At last the sound could be heard no longer, and Reuben was reluctantly obliged to give the order to halt; for he feared he might override the trail.

"It is no use," he said, as he reined in his horse. "They will know as well as we do that they are out of hearing now, and might turn off anywhere. It is terribly annoying. We are too late to save the station, and the bush rangers have escaped.

"However, we will take up their trail as soon as it is daylight. Indeed, I am expecting every moment to be joined by Jim, who is sure to be somewhere near, and can perhaps guide us direct to their hiding place."

Deeply disappointed, the party dismounted from their horses.

"The scoundrels must have had someone on the watch," Reuben said, "or they would never have taken the alarm so soon. I am sorry, now, that we did not send a party round to the other side before we charged down upon them; but my blood was on fire at the sight of the burning station, and at the thought of the women in the hands of those scoundrels."

A minute later, a man rode up at full speed from behind.

"Is that you, Jones?" Reuben said, stepping forward.

"Yes, sir," the man replied, reining in his horse. "I left Wilkins behind, and rode on to tell you what had happened."

"What has happened, Jones?"

"It's a bad business, sir, a shocking bad business; but it might have been worse. It seems they broke in about half an hour before we got there. One of the hands was supposed to be on watch in the stockyard; but either he was asleep, or they crept up to him and killed him before he could give the alarm. Then they got up to the house and burst in the door, before the others were fairly awake.

"They shot the two hands at once; but I suppose, as their blood wasn't up, and no resistance was offered, they thought they had plenty of time for fooling; for they must have reckoned that no force they need be afraid of could be got together, for three or four hours. So they made Donald and his wife and sister get breakfast for them. The women, it seemed had got pistols, and both swore they would blow out their brains if any man laid a hand on them. However, the bush rangers did not touch them, though they told them they would have to go off with them.

"They made Donald sit down at one end of the table, while their captain took the other; and the two women, half dressed as they were, waited on them. It was lucky for them that we were so close when the alarm was given, for all made a rush to get to their horses; only the captain stopping a moment, to let fly at Donald."

"Did he kill him?" Reuben asked.

"No, sir, the bullet hit him in the body, and the ladies were crying over him when I went in, thinking he was dead. I thought so, too, but I found he was breathing. They poured some brandy down his throat, and presently he opened his eyes; then, as there was nothing for me to do, I thought I had best gallop on and give you the news, for I knew that you would be anxious to know what had taken place."

"Thank you, Jones, you did quite right. What an escape those poor ladies have had! Another quarter of an hour, we might have been too late, for those villains would not have kept up the farce long."

"No, sir, especially as they were drinking wine. The table was all covered with bottles."

"You did not see anything of Jim, did you?" Reuben inquired.

"No, sir, I did not see or hear anyone stirring about the place."

Reuben gave a loud cooey.

"That will bring him, if he is anywhere within hearing."

But no answering call came back.

"I hope nothing has happened to the poor fellow," Reuben said, after a pause.

"He could not possibly be here by this time," Mr. Barker said. "The place where he warned the shepherd must be sixty miles from here."

"Yes, quite that; but he can run nearly as fast as a horse can go, and he would be ten miles nearer here, in a straight line, than the way the man went round to fetch me."

As soon as it became light they followed the track, which was plainly visible; but when they had gone half a mile further, there was a general cry of dismay—the ground was trampled in every direction.

"Confound it," Mr. Barker said, "they have done us! Do you see, they have ridden right into the middle of a large herd of cattle, and have driven them off in every direction; and have, no doubt, themselves scattered among the cattle. They may go like that for three or four miles, and then draw off from the cattle at any spot where the ground is hard, and no tracks will be left; to meet again at some appointed place, maybe fifty miles away."

"Then you don't think it's any use in pursuing them?" Reuben asked, in a tone of deep disappointment.

"Not a bit in the world," Mr. Barker replied decisively. "If we had a native tracker with us, he might possibly follow one horse's track among those of all the cattle, discover where he separates from them, and take up his trail; but I doubt, even then, if he would be successful. These fellows know that a strong party is in pursuit of them, and each of them will do everything they can to throw us off the scent. They are sure not to go straight to their place of meeting, but each will take circuitous routes, and will make for thick bush, where it will be next to impossible for even a native to follow them. No, they have done us, this time."

"Well, gentlemen, I hope you will all wait as long as you can at the station here. If my boy has not been shot by those scoundrels, he is sure to find his way here; and will be able, in all probability, to set us on the right track.

"At any rate, though the bush rangers have given us the slip, we may congratulate ourselves on our morning's work. We have at least saved those poor ladies."

So saying, Reuben turned and, with the party, rode slowly back to the station. On arriving there, they dismounted and unsaddled their horses, and turned them into a paddock close to the house, to feed. Reuben and Mr.

Barker then went up to the house. The constable who had been left behind came out.

"Well, Wilkins, how is Mr. Donald, and how are the ladies?"

"He is sensible now, sir; but I don't think there's much chance for him."

"We ought to get a surgeon, at once," Reuben said. "Who is the nearest, Mr. Barker?"

"The nearest is Ruskin."

"Is there no one nearer than that?" Reuben asked. "Why, he lives about halfway between where I was sleeping last night, and my own place. It must be seventy miles away."

"He's the nearest," Mr. Barker said; "take my word for it."

"I'll tell you what will be the best plan," Reuben's host of the night before said. "I will ride at once to Mr. Barker's and, if he will let me get a fresh horse there, I will gallop straight back to my place, and will send a man off the moment I arrive there to fetch Ruskin.

"It is only eight o'clock now. I can be home before noon, and my man will do the next stage in a little over four hours. If he finds Ruskin in, he can get to my place by ten o'clock at night, and can start again at daybreak; so by eleven o'clock tomorrow he can be here. If he isn't here by that time, it will be because he was out when my man got there. At any rate, he is sure to start directly he gets the message."

"That will be the best plan," Reuben agreed; "and I am sure the ladies will be greatly obliged to you, when I tell them what you have undertaken."

"Oh, that's nothing," the settler said. "We don't think much of a seventy miles' ride, here."

Without any further delay, the settler saddled his horse and went off at a gallop towards Mr. Barker's, where he was to get a fresh mount.

"And now, how are the ladies, Wilkins?"

"They are keeping up bravely, sir. I think, as far as they are concerned, Donald's being hit has done them good. It has given them something to do, and they have not had time to think about what they have gone through, and what a narrow escape they have had."

"Which room are they in, Wilkins?"

"In there to the left, sir."

"As you have seen them, Wilkins, you had better go in and tell them that we have sent off, at once, to fetch a surgeon; and that they may rely upon his being here some time tomorrow, we hope before noon. Ask if there is anything that we can do for them, or for Mr. Donald."

The policeman went in, and Reuben called one of his other men.

"Perkins, do you, Jones, and Rider go in and fetch out the bodies of the men who have been killed. Don't make more noise than you can help about it. Carry them out to that shed there, and then get a bucket and wash down the floors, wherever there are bloodstains about. I want to have the place straight, so that those poor ladies may avoid seeing anything to recall the scene they have passed through. Of course, you won't go into the room where they are now."

Three or four of the settlers at once volunteered to set to work to dig a grave.

"Choose a place a bit away from the house," one of them said. "The farther, the better; it will remind them of this affair, whenever they see it."

While Reuben was arranging this point, the constable had come out and told Mr. Barker the ladies would be glad to see him.

"It's a terrible business," the settler said to Reuben, as he turned to go into the house. "I feel downright afraid of facing them. To think how bright and pretty they looked, when I rode over here ten days ago; and now there they are, broken hearted."

He returned in a few minutes.

"How is Donald?" was the general question.

"He is hard hit," the settler said, "just under the ribs on the right-hand side. I expect the fellow aimed at his head, but he was starting from his seat at the moment. He isn't in much pain. I have told them they must keep him perfectly quiet, and not let him move till the surgeon comes.

"They have asked me to see about everything. It's better we should not be going in and out of the house, as he must be kept perfectly quiet; so I think we had better establish ourselves under that big tree over there. There are some sheep half a mile over that rise, if two of you will go over, kill one and fetch it in. If you will light a fire under that tree, I will hand out from the house flour, tea, sugar, and some cooking things."

There was a general murmur of approval, for all felt silent and awed at being so close to the house of death and sorrow. Two men got their horses, and rode off to fetch the sheep. The others carried the various articles requisite up to the place fixed for the bivouac, while Wilkins was installed in the house, to assist in anything that might be required there.

"The poor things told me to tell you, captain, how grateful they felt to you for the exertions you have made. I told them how it was we came to be here; and how you had ridden, when you got the news, to be here in time. Mrs. Donald did not say much, poor thing, she seemed half dazed; but her sister, who seems wonderfully cool and collected, quite realized what they had escaped; and there's many a young fellow who would give a good deal, to win that look of gratitude she gave me when she said:

"'I shall never forget what I owe you all.'

"I am just going to send off one of my men, to fetch my wife over here. It will be a comfort to the two girls, for they are little more, to have a woman with them."

"There's nothing to be done for Donald, I suppose?" Reuben asked.

"Nothing. The wound is hardly bleeding at all. I told them that, as far as I knew, the best thing was to keep on it a flannel dipped in warm water, and wrung out; and that they should give him a little broth, or weak brandy and water, whenever he seemed faint. My surgery does not go beyond that. If it had been a smashed finger, or a cut with an axe, or even a broken limb, I might have been some good; for I have seen plenty of accidents of all kinds, since I came out twenty years ago, but a bullet wound in the body is beyond me, altogether."

After the meal was cooked and eaten, there was a consultation as to what had best be done next. Two or three of the settlers who were married men said that they would go home, as their wives would be anxious about them. The rest agreed to stop for, at any rate, another day.

Mr. Barker had found out from Mrs. Donald's sister the direction in which the sheep and cattle were grazing, and two or three of the party rode off to tell the shepherds and herdsmen—for there were three men on the farm, in addition to those who had been killed—what had happened; and to tell them that they had better bring the sheep and cattle up to within a mile or so of the house, and come in themselves for their stores, when required.

A grave was now dug, and the three men buried. In the afternoon Mrs. Barker arrived, and at once took charge of the affairs of the house. In the evening Mr. Barker came up to the fire round which the men were sitting.

"Will you come down to the house, Captain Whitney? The ladies have expressed a wish to see you. They want to thank you for what you have done."

"There is nothing to thank about," Reuben said. "I only did my duty as a police officer, and am disgusted at those scoundrels having got away.

I have done all I could, since I arrived; but I can't help feeling, being in command of the force here, that we are to some extent to blame for these fellows carrying on, as they have done for months, without being caught."

"I think you had better come down, Whitney," Mr. Barker said. "There is something bright and hopeful about you, and I think that a talk with you might cheer the poor things up a bit. When people are in the state they are, they seem to turn to everyone for a gleam of hope, and comfort."

"Oh, if you think I can do any good, of course I will go; though I would rather stop here, by a good way."

So saying, Reuben went down with Mr. Barker to the house. A lady met them at the door.

"Arthur has just dozed off," she whispered. "Mrs. Barker is sitting by him. She insisted on our coming out. Will you come in here?"

As silently as possible, the two men followed her into the kitchen, and closed the door after them. The fire was blazing brightly, Wilkins having piled on some fresh logs before going out to smoke a pipe. Mrs. Donald was sitting in a dejected attitude, by its right, when her sister entered with Mr. Barker and Reuben. She rose and, coming towards Reuben, said:

"How can we thank you, sir, for the exertions you have made, and for having saved us from I dare not think what fate? As long as we live, my sister and I will bless you."

"I can assure you, Mrs. Donald," Reuben said, "that I have done nothing but my duty, and I only regret that we did not arrive half an hour earlier."

"Ah, if you had!" Mrs. Donald said. "But there—we must not repine— even in my sorrow, I feel how much we have to be thankful for."

"Yes, indeed," her sister said, "we have truly reason to be grateful."

As she spoke, Reuben looked at her more and more intently. He had started when she first spoke, outside the house.

"Good heavens!" he exclaimed, "is it possible, or am I dreaming? Surely you are Miss Kate Ellison?"

"Certainly I am," she said in surprise, at his tone; "but I don't think—I don't remember—why, surely it is not Reuben Whitney?"

Chapter 15
At Donald's

It is difficult to say whether Kate Ellison, or Reuben Whitney was the most surprised at this unexpected meeting. The former, indeed, was aware that Reuben had come out to Australia; but that the boy, whose cause she had championed, should now stand before her as the officer, to whose energy and activity she and her sister owed so much, seemed almost incredible.

But the surprise of Reuben was at least equal to that which she felt. He could scarcely credit the evidence of his senses, at seeing before him the young lady whom he had believed to be thousands of miles away, in England. As is usual in these cases, the girl was the first to recover from her surprise.

"And it is to you we owe so much!" she said, holding out her hand. "Mr. Barker spoke of our preserver as Captain Whitney; but somehow it never, for a moment, occurred to me to connect the name with you.

"Is it not extraordinary, Alice?" she said, turning to her sister.

"The surprise to me is even greater than to you, Miss Ellison," Reuben said. "Mr. Barker always spoke of Mrs. Donald and her sister, and I had not the least idea that you were in the colony. My mother wrote to me, a year ago, telling me of the changes which have taken place; but although she said that you had left Tipping, she said nothing about your coming out here."

Reuben had, in fact, been much disturbed in his mind, a year previously, by hearing from his mother that Mr. Ellison had died suddenly. He had, it seemed, lost a large sum of money, from the failure of a bank in which he was a shareholder, and the blow had killed him. The estate was, when Mrs. Whitney wrote, for sale.

Reuben had written back, begging his mother to send him all particulars that she could gather; but communication between Australia and England was in those days very slow, and no answer had yet been received. Another letter had, indeed, told him that the estate had been sold. Mrs. Ellison, he knew, had died a few weeks after he had left England.

"It is very simple," Kate Ellison said quietly; "although of course it seems so strange to you, our being here. My sister was engaged to Mr.

Donald before papa's death and, as you know, almost everything went owing to that bank; and as I had no reason for staying in England, I came out here with them."

Reuben subsequently learned that Mr. Ellison had disapproved of the engagement of his daughter with Mr. Donald, who was the younger son of a neighbouring squire. When, after his death, Mr. Ellison's affairs were wound up, it was found that there remained only the six thousand pounds, which his wife had brought him, to be divided between her daughters. Mr. Donald possessed no capital, and had no prospects at home. He and Alice were quietly married, three months after her father's death, and had sailed a week later for New South Wales; where, as land could be taken up at a nominal price, it was thought that her little fortune would be ample to start them comfortably. All this, however, Reuben did not learn until some time later.

After chatting for a short time, he returned to the camp fire.

"This is very awkward, Mr. Barker," Mrs. Donald said; "do you know that Captain Whitney was, at one time, gardener's boy to our father?"

"Oh, Alice!" her sister exclaimed, "what difference can that make?"

"It seems to me," Mrs. Donald said, "that it makes a very great difference. You know mamma never thought well of him, and it is very awkward, now, finding him here in such a position; especially as he has laid us under an obligation to him.

"Do you not think so, Mr. Barker?"

"I do not pretend to know anything about such matters, Mrs. Donald," Mr. Barker said bluntly; "and I shouldn't have thought it could have made any difference to you, what the man was who had saved you from such a fate as would have befallen you, had it not been for his energy. I can only say that Captain Whitney is a gentleman with whom anyone here, or in the old country, would be glad to associate. I may say that when he came here, three or four months ago, my friend Mr. Hudson—one of the leading men in the colony—wrote to me, saying that Captain Whitney was one of his most intimate friends, that he was in every respect a good fellow, and that he himself was under a lifelong obligation to him; for he had, at the risk of his life, when on the way out, saved that of his daughter when she was attacked by a mad Malay at the Cape.

"More than that, I did not inquire. It was nothing to me whether he was born a prince, or a peasant."

Mrs. Donald coloured hotly, at the implied reproof of Mr. Barker's words. She had always shared her mother's prejudices against Reuben Whitney, and she had not been long enough, in the colony, to become accustomed to the changes of position which are there so frequent.

"You do not understand, Mr. Barker," she said pettishly. "It was not only that he was a boy employed in the family. There were other circumstances—"

"Oh, Alice!" Kate broke out, "how can you speak of such things? Here are we at present, owing more than our lives to this man, and you are going now to damage him by raking up that miserable old story.

"Mr. Barker," she said impulsively, "my father, one of the most just, as well as one of the most kind of men, had the highest opinion of Reuben Whitney; believe me, there was nothing in the circumstances to which Alice alludes which could cast the slightest slur upon his character."

"I feel certain of that, my dear young lady," Mr. Barker said, "even without your assurance. Your sister is shaken by the events of the day, and no wonder; and I am quite sure that when she thinks this matter over she will see that, whatever her preconceived ideas may be, it would be most ungrateful and ungenerous to breathe a single word in disparagement of Captain Whitney."

So saying, he turned on his heel and left the room; and Kate, wishing to avoid further words on the matter with her sister, followed his example.

Mrs. Donald's reflections were not pleasant. She felt that Mr. Barker's reproof was well deserved, and that she had acted ungratefully and ungenerously. As a rule, Mr. Ellison's elder daughter was by no means of an unkind disposition; but she was essentially her mother's child.

The question of Reuben Whitney had been one which had caused more serious dissension, between her father and mother, than any she ever remembered. She had taken her mother's view of the case, while Kate had agreed with her father; and although the subject had been dropped, by mutual consent, it had been a very sore one; and at the sight of Reuben, the remembrance of the old unpleasantness had caused her to play a part which she could not but feel was mean and unworthy. She felt angry at herself— angry with Mr. Barker, with her sister, and with Reuben.

She was standing there, with her lips pressed together as she thought over the matter, when Mrs. Barker came into the room.

"He is awake now, my dear. Perhaps you had better go in to him."

Then she dismissed from her mind the events of the last few minutes, and went in to take her place by the side of her husband. But as, during the long hours of the night, she sat there and thought over what had passed since the preceding evening, the thought of how much she owed to Reuben Whitney was uppermost in her mind; and when in the morning Mrs. Barker relieved her, she went into the other room, where Mr. Barker and Kate were about to sit down to breakfast, and said:

"Mr. Barker, I thank you for what you said to me last night. You were right and I was wrong. I was ungrateful, and ungenerous. I can only say that it was a very sore subject, and that in my surprise I thought of the past, and not the present. Believe me, I am very sorry for what I said."

"That is quite enough, Mrs. Donald," Mr. Barker said heartily. "I am very glad you have said what you have. I was sure that you would, upon reflection, feel that whatever the old grievance might have been, it could not weigh an instant against what you owe to that young fellow now. Let us say no more on the subject. You were shaken and not yourself, and I was wrong in taking you up so sharply, under the circumstances."

Kate said nothing, but her face showed that she was greatly pleased at her sister's change of tone.

"What is going to be done, Mr. Barker?" Mrs. Donald asked. "Of course, the friends who came to our rescue cannot stay here; and there is no chance of my husband being moved, for a long time."

"I am afraid not, indeed," Mr. Barker said. "Most of them will leave this afternoon, in time to get back to their stations tonight.

"I have been speaking with Captain Whitney, and he says that he with his men will certainly stay here, for the present.. He sent off a messenger, last night, for six more of his men to join him here; for he still hopes to get news from his native boy, which may set him on the tracks of the bush rangers. You need, however, be under no alarm; for I think there is no chance, whatever, of the bush rangers returning.

"By the way, Whitney would like to speak to you, after breakfast. He wants you to give him as minute a description as you can of the fellows you saw. We have already descriptions of four or five of them, given by men whom they have stuck up; but the band must have increased lately, and any particulars might be useful."

Reuben came round in a quarter of an hour later. Mr. Barker fetched him into the room where Mrs. Barker and Kate were sitting.

"Mr. Donald is no worse, I am glad to hear," he said, as he shook hands with the two ladies.

"I see no change whatever," Mrs. Barker said. "He is conscious, but does not speak much. He asked me, this morning, to tell you and all your friends how deeply he feels indebted to you."

"His thanks are due to the settlers, rather than to me, Mrs. Barker. They were volunteers, you know, while I was simply on duty. We had, however, one common interest—to get here in time to save the station and, above all, to catch and break up this gang of scoundrels.

"And now, Miss Ellison, if you feel equal to it, would you kindly give us an account of what happened? Mr. Barker said that he would not ask you, yesterday; but something, perhaps, let drop by chance, might serve as an indication to us as to the direction in which these fellows have gone."

"I will tell you, certainly," the girl said, her face paling a little; "although it is dreadful, even now, to think of. We of course had no idea of attack, and had gone to bed as usual. One of the men was always on guard, on the outside of the house; for these attacks made Mr. Donald nervous for the safety of my sister, and myself. Simpson was on guard that night. Whether he went to sleep or not, I cannot say."

"He did, Miss Ellison," Reuben interrupted. "We found his body round by the end of the house. He had evidently been sitting down on a log, against the house; and had been killed by a crushing blow with some heavy instrument, probably one of the tools they used for breaking in."

"The first we knew about it," Kate went on, "was a tremendous crash downstairs, which was followed by a continuous thundering noise. I think they must have burst the door in with crowbars, or something—that was the first noise we heard—but a strong wooden bar, inside, kept the door in its place till they battered it down with a log.

"I hurried on some things. Just as I had done—it was not a minute, I think, from the time I woke—Alice ran in, partly dressed, too. I had heard Mr. Donald shout to the men, then there was another great crash as the bar gave way, and then some shots were fired.

"Mr. Donald had been standing just behind the door, and had fired through it the moment before it gave way. He had not time to step back, and was knocked down by the door. It was fortunate for him, for the bush rangers rushed in and shot down the two men, instantly.

"Alice would have run down to see what had happened to her husband, but I would not let her out of my room. She could have done no good, and might have been shot. Then we heard them moving about the house, swearing and using all sorts of horrible language. Then they shouted up to us to come down, or else they would come and fetch us; so we opened the door, and came down at once.

"Alice gave a little cry of joy, as she entered the room and saw her husband standing unhurt, though still looking dazed and confused from his blow.

"The leader of the band—I suppose you have not seen him, Captain Whitney?"

"No, indeed," Reuben said. "I would give a good deal to catch sight of him."

"What do you know about him?"

"I only know that he is a young fellow, not much older than I am myself. His was a life sentence. He was concerned in a burglary in the country, in which two old ladies were killed. Two of his accomplices were hung for it, but in consideration of his youth, and as it was not proved that he took an absolute part in the murder, he got off with a life sentence. I heard about the case from Captain Wilson.

"He came out here about a year after I did. He had not been here a month when he killed one of the guard, and made his escape. Since that time he has been a scourge to the colony. Not a week has passed without complaints of his bailing up and robbing teamsters on their way down to Sydney. He soon gathered two or three others about him, and his daring and impudence soon made him a noted character. Several times he, with two other men, rode into good-sized villages and, pistol in hand, went from house to house, and carried off every shilling in the place. He has ridden into large stores single handed, and compelled the storekeepers to hand over the contents of their tills. Sometimes they bring spare horses with them, and ride off laden with groceries and stores. He has committed at least a score of murders, always using his pistol at the slightest show of opposition; and sometimes murdering, apparently, from pure love of the thing."

"Do you know his name?" Kate asked.

"His real name? No, I don't know that I ever heard it. He is always spoken of as Fothergill."

"I will tell you his real name, presently," Kate said. "As my sister and I came into the kitchen, he took off his hat and made a deep bow and said:

"'Ladies, me and my mates are sorry to put you to any inconvenience; but as we happen to be hungry, we must trouble you to get us some supper. You need not bother to make tea, wine is good enough for us.'

"Of course, as we were in their hands there was nothing to do but to obey his orders; so we spread the cloth, and brought out what there was in the larder. Then we fetched in the wine, and I brought several bottles of spirits; for, as I whispered to Alice, 'If they get drunk, we may be able to get away from them.'

"Before they sat down, the captain told two of his men to go upstairs with us and fetch down our watches and jewelry, and the money there was in the house. Mr. Donald had already told them where they would find that.

"We lit four candles, and put them on the table. The captain ordered Mr. Donald to sit down facing him, saying with a sort of mock politeness that they should not really enjoy their food, unless their host took the head of the table. Several times, while they were eating, I saw the captain looking hard at Alice and me. Presently he said:

"'I have it now. Why, you are the Ellison girls, ain't you?'

"I was astonished, as you may suppose, but I said:

"'I am Miss Ellison, and Mrs. Donald is my sister.'

"'By Jove, who would have thought it!' he said. 'Do you know who I am?'

"I said I didn't, although really I seemed to have some sort of recollection of his face.

"'Why,' he said, 'don't you remember Tom Thorne, whose father the squire turned out of the public house? And to think, now, that the squire's daughters are waiting on me. This is a piece of luck.

"'Well, my dears,' he went on, with a horrible grin, 'you need not tell me how you came here now, you will have plenty of time for that. We have made up our minds to take you both with us, for it's a horrible lonely life in the bush, without the pleasure of ladies' society. But I never dreamt that I was in for such a slice of luck as this.'

"Mr. Donald jumped from his seat as the fellow spoke, but in a moment he levelled a pistol at him and shouted:

"'Sit down or I fire.'

"Alice rushed to her husband, and pushed him down into his seat.

"'I had rather die than go with you,' I said to him quietly.

"'Perhaps so, my dear,' he replied; 'but you see, you haven't got the choice.'

"Then he went on taunting us about old times, and especially reminding me that I had got him a thrashing, over breaking the school house window. When I went out to get them some more wine, for they wouldn't touch the spirits, I got a knife and hid it in my dress; for I made up my mind to kill myself, rather than that.

"A little later I stole upstairs and brought down a brace of pistols, which Mr. Donald kept under his pillow, and slipped one into Alice's hand. Presently they began to get noisy, and the captain ordered me to come and sit on his knee. Then Alice and I showed the pistols, and said we would shoot ourselves, if one of them laid a finger on us.

"The captain muttered some order to his men, which I didn't hear; but I guessed it was to leave us alone, for the present. I had no doubt what they intended to do was to catch us off our guard, and wrench the pistols from us; and I was glad I had the knife hidden away, for if they did carry us off, I was sure to be able to find some opportunity for using that.

"It was awful!" the girl said, putting her hand to her face. "Awful to be standing there and hearing them laughing and shouting and cursing. I was tempted to go behind him, and shoot him suddenly; but the others would have been just as bad, and we should have gained nothing by it. I would not go through that half hour again, for all the money in the world.

"The men had just finished and were getting up from the table, and I knew the moment was coming fast, when we heard a sudden shout outside. My heart gave a bound, as they rushed to the door. The captain fired a shot at Mr. Donald, just as he was getting up; and as he ran out, shouted to me:

"'I will come back for you, missy.'

"If it had not been for Mr. Donald falling to the ground, I should have fainted; but Alice called me as she ran to him, and I think I was trying to lift him up when the constable ran in, and I knew we were saved."

Reuben had given a sudden start, when Kate Ellison mentioned the name of Tom Thorne, but he had not interrupted her.

"I had a score against that scoundrel before," he said, as she finished; "and by heavens, I will settle accounts with him when I meet him. I could have forgiven him for the wrongs he did me; but now—" and his fingers closed on the hilt of the pistol in his belt.

Kate, who had been looking down as she told her story, raised her eyes at the tone of intense passion in the young officer's words; and a sudden flush of colour mounted into her cheeks, which were pale from the terror and excitement through which she had gone.

"I say ditto to Captain Whitney," Mr. Barker said. "I don't know anything about his previous doings against him; but I know that, if ever I come across the scoundrel, I will shoot him as a dog.

"Even you can't say anything against that, wife, though you are always on the side of mercy."

"No," Mrs. Barker agreed. "I would say nothing to stay your hand there, John. Even putting this aside, he has committed a score of murders; and there will be no more wrong, in shooting him, than there would be in killing a wild beast.

"That is the sound of a horse coming, at a gallop. Perhaps it is the doctor."

Hurrying to the door they found, to their great satisfaction, that Mrs. Barker's guess was verified. The surgeon had been at home when the messenger arrived, and had started five minutes later, arriving three or four hours earlier than they had even ventured to hope.

Mrs. Barker at once led the way into the next room and, a few minutes later, came out again for hot water and sponges. Kate had stolen away upstairs, when the surgeon had entered the house. The two men remained to hear the verdict.

"He is going to probe the wound. He can give no opinion, yet, till he discovers what course it has taken; but he says that it is a favourable symptom that the pulse is so strong and regular. He wishes you both to come in, as it will be necessary to hold his patient's hands, while he is making the examination."

"I cannot give any positive opinion," the surgeon said, when he had finished the examination. "I can't find the ball, and I cannot tell for certain what course it took, after entering; but I think, judging from the pulse, and I may say from the expression of his face, that no vital part is injured."

An exclamation of thankfulness broke from Mrs. Donald.

"We must not be too sanguine," Mr. Ruskin went on; "but there is certainly strong ground for hope. I shall be able to give a more definite opinion, in the course of a few hours. He must, of course, be kept perfectly quiet; with no more nourishment than is absolutely necessary, and that in the shape of beef tea. I should make him a bed here. We will manage to slide a door under him, and lift him on to it, with as little movement as possible.

"At any rate, madam," he said, turning to Mrs. Donald, "I can congratulate you upon the fact that the bullet did not strike a couple of inches higher. Had it done so, my ride would have been a useless one."

A bed was at once brought from a room above and made up, and Mr. Donald was placed upon it, in the manner which Mr. Ruskin had suggested. Then with lightened hearts the party, with the exception of his wife, left the room.

Kate and Mrs. Barker at once set to to prepare a meal for the surgeon; while Reuben went over to give his companions the good news, that the surgeon had strong hopes that Mr. Donald would recover.

In the afternoon all the party, with the exception of Mr. and Mrs. Barker and the constables, rode off to their respective stations; assuring Reuben of their readiness to assemble again, at once, should he obtain news which would afford a hope that the gang could be traced.

A few hours later, the other four constables for whom Reuben had sent rode up. An outhouse was now prepared for the reception of the police, Reuben himself taking up his abode there, although Mrs. Donald strongly urged him to come into the house; but with Mr. and Mrs. Barker and the surgeon there, and the time of one of the ladies taken up with the wounded man, Reuben thought that their hands were perfectly full, and said that he should prefer to mess and sleep with his men.

"You see, Mrs. Donald," he said, as she tried to induce him to alter his determination, "I shall have to be sending out men and receiving reports, and may be obliged to ride out in the middle of the night; therefore, you see, as absolute quiet is ordered for your husband, it will be far better for me to be outside the house; as the coming and going would be sure to disturb him, and he would naturally want to know what is going on."

"You will not, I hope, take all your party away in pursuit of these men, Captain Whitney," she said anxiously. "They might get up some false alarm, to take you away, and then come down upon the house again. I have been too much taken up with my husband to think much about it; but although Kate keeps up bravely, I know that she is greatly shaken, and terribly anxious. I don't know whether she told you; but it was to her, chiefly, that horrible man spoke; and it was she he told, as he rushed out, that he would come back to fetch her. She will never have a moment's peace, or tranquillity, till we hear that he is either killed or taken."

"Nor shall I," Reuben said. "I do not think that the scoundrel will dare to attempt to carry out his threat to come back again; but with so daring a villain, it would be rash to omit the smallest precaution. You may be quite sure, Mrs. Donald, that in no case will I leave the house unprotected; and that if I should be called away I will leave two men here who, during my absence, will remain in the house; and with them, Mr. Barker, and the doctor, you may feel perfectly assured that no open attack will be made.

"But I cannot impress too strongly upon you that, seeing the man with whom we have to deal, your sister should not stir outside the house; until we have caught him, or until Mr. Donald is so far recovered as to be able to be removed. I will not tell her so myself; because I see that, now the strain is over, she is greatly shaken, and I would not add to her anxiety; but if you could break it to her, as if it were your own idea, that she had better keep within doors until this fellow's caught, I am sure that it will be well."

"You will come in this evening, I hope; and always of an evening, Captain Whitney. It will make a change, and cheer us up; besides, we want to hear all about your adventures, since we saw you last."

This Reuben gladly promised and, after it was dark, and he had placed a sentry, he came into the house. Mrs. Barker was on duty in the sick room; and Reuben, at Mrs. Donald's request, gave them an account of the voyage out, and of the circumstances which had led to his entering the police.

He would have passed very briefly over the affair at the Cape, but by many questions Mrs. Donald succeeded in eliciting from him all the details of the story.

"It was a gallant action, indeed," she said warmly. "You certainly saved the lives of those two girls, at a terrible risk of your own."

"To make the romance complete, Whitney," Mr. Barker remarked, "you ought to have married Miss Hudson."

"Unfortunately, you see," Reuben said with a smile, "in the first place I was only a boy, and she was two years my senior; in the next, and much more important place, she happened to be in love with someone else; and I did not happen to be in love with her, though she was, I admit, a very charming young lady, and had been extremely kind to me."

"How was that, Whitney?" Mr. Barker asked. "Eighteen is a susceptible age. I can only account for your coldness on the supposition that you had left your heart in England."

"I fancy my heart was, then, where it is now," Reuben rejoined, with a slight smile.

"In the right place, eh, Whitney?"

"In the right place," Reuben repeated quietly.

At this moment Mrs. Barker entered, and said that Mr. Donald would be glad if Reuben would come and sit with him, for a little time.

"Don't let him talk much," Mr. Ruskin said. "The less he talks, the better; but your talking to him, for a time, will cheer him up and do him good."

"I am glad to see you going on so well, Mr. Donald," Reuben said heartily, as he entered. "The doctor says you are not to talk much; but you are to play the part of a listener."

"Do you think you will catch these fellows?" was Mr. Donald's first question.

"I will catch them, sooner or later," Reuben said. "I will run them down if they are above ground; but I can take no steps in the matter until I hear from my black boy. I have been expecting him to turn up, ever since I got here; and shall begin to be afraid that those scoundrels have ill treated him, if he does not turn up before long."

"My wife has been telling me that they knew you at home, Whitney; and that she and her people did you some terrible injustice, somehow. But she wouldn't go into the matter. Curious, isn't it, your meeting at this end of the world; and that, too, at such a moment?"

"It is curious," Reuben said; "what people call a coincidence. But Mrs. Donald is mistaken in telling you that her people did me an injustice. Her father was one of the kindest friends I ever had, and although Mrs. Ellison somewhat misjudged me, and her daughter naturally shared her feeling, they were not in anyway to be blamed for that; for they only thought as ninety-nine people out of a hundred did."

"Whitney, Whitney," Mr. Donald muttered to himself. "I seemed to know the name, though I cannot recall where.

"Ah!" he said suddenly, "of course I remember now, for I was in the court when—" and he stopped.

"When I was tried," Reuben put in quietly. "Yes, that was me. I was acquitted, as you know, principally from the way in which Mr. Ellison stood up for me. Thank God that he never, for an instant, believed that I was guilty."

"And to think it should be you!" Mr. Donald said. "How strange things turn out! I remember I could not make up my mind about it. It seemed so strange, either way."

"We had better not talk about it now," Reuben said quietly. "I said then, and I say now, that I knew the people who did it and, strange as the circumstances have already been, you may think them stranger still, some day, if I bring one of them before you, alive or dead."

At this moment there was a knock at the door, and Mrs. Donald came in and said that one of the constabulary wished to speak to Reuben.

"Then I will say goodnight. I hope I shall find you getting on nicely, in the morning, Mr. Donald.

"Will you say goodnight to Miss Ellison and Mrs. Barker for me, Mrs. Donald? And tell Mr. Barker that I shall be ready, in five minutes, to smoke that pipe we talked about with him, outside."

Chapter 16
Jim's Report

"Jones, what is it?"

"Your black has just come, sir. I would not let him come in; for the fact is, he ain't a figure to introduce among ladies."

"What's the matter with him, Jones? Not hurt, I hope?"

"He has been knocked about a bit, sir; and he is done up with travelling. The poor fellow can hardly crawl, and was half starved; so I set him to work eating, and came off to fetch you."

By this time they had arrived at the door of the shed. Jim was sitting by a fire, eagerly devouring a hunch of cold meat. The men were standing round, waiting till he had appeased his hunger before they asked any question. He looked up and nodded, when Reuben entered.

"Well, Jim, I am glad to see you back," Reuben said heartily. "I was beginning to be afraid about you. I hope you are not hurt?"—for the black had a handkerchief tied round his head.

Jim gave a grunt, but continued stuffing great lumps of meat into his mouth. Reuben saw that he must wait till the black's hunger was satisfied, and stood quietly looking on until, having devoured some five pounds of meat, he gave a sigh of contentment, and then took a long draught of rum and water, which Constable Jones handed to him.

"Jim better now," he said.

"That's right, Jim; now tell us all about it."

Jim's story was a long one, and it took more than an hour in the telling; for his English was not always distinct, and it often required much questioning, on Reuben's part, before he could quite make out its meaning. The substance was as follows:

On leaving, some ten days before, on the mission of discovering the haunt of the bush rangers, he knew that it was of no use to go among the wild blacks, their allies; as the hostility against their semi-civilized fellows was so great that he would, at once, have been killed. He resolved to go back to the spot where the track had been obliterated, by that of the flock of sheep;

to make a wide circuit, and pick it up beyond and, if possible, follow it until he found them. The difficulties were great, for the bush rangers had spared no pains in hiding their trail; keeping always upon hard, high ground, and at one time getting into the bed of a running stream, and following it for two miles before they again struck for their rendezvous.

However, step by step Jim had tracked them; sometimes losing the trail altogether, sometimes guided merely by a fresh-made scratch on the surface of a stone, or by a broken twig or bruised blade of grass. At last, he traced it far out into the bush, many miles beyond the furthest range of settlements, and then he lost it altogether. There had been a halt, for some time, at this spot.

Beyond this, Jim was entirely at fault. He made circle after circle round the spot, but could find no trace whatever of their passage, and returned to the point where he had missed the trail. He relit the embers of the fire which the bush rangers had made, cooked some food, and laid himself down— first to think it over, then to sleep, for it was now just the close of day.

It was clear to him that here, more than anywhere else, the bush rangers had made a great effort to throw anyone who might be pursuing them off the trail. He had no doubt that the bush rangers had muffled their horses' hoofs with cloth, and had proceeded with the greatest care through the bush, so as to avoid breaking a single twig in their passage; and the only reason for such greater caution could be that it was here, and here only, that they wished to throw the pursuers off the trail. It would have seemed, to a white man, that they had done this before, especially when they had kept in the water course; but to black Jim's perception, it appeared that they had been more careless than would be expected; and that, while apparently doing their utmost to conceal their tracks, they had really left sufficient indications to allow a practised tracker to follow them.

Why then, now that they were far beyond the settlements, and fairly in the country of their native allies, should they, for the first time, so hide their trail that he could not discover it?

The result of Jim's thoughts was that, when he awoke at daybreak, he started back towards the settlements. When he came to the river which the party had passed, in pursuit of the natives, he kept along its bank, scrutinizing the ground with the greatest care. After six miles' walking he suddenly stopped, at a point where the soft turf near the margin was cut up by the passage of the party of horsemen. Here was the confirmation of his ideas.

Arguing the matter out with himself, Jim had arrived at the conclusion that, hitherto, the trail had been a false one, the bush rangers' object being to lead their pursuers to believe that they had gone far out into the native country; whereas, in fact, their hiding place was somewhere among the settlements. Should this be so, the only way to find them was to search for their back track. This he had now found and, with a shout of triumph at his own cleverness, Jim forded the river and followed the track of the horses.

This was now clear enough, the horsemen taking no pains whatever to conceal their traces, feeling perfectly confident that any pursuers must now be thrown off the scent. Jim followed it till sundown, when he had made some thirty miles; and then, withdrawing some little distance from the tracks, he made his fire and camped for the night.

He was now inside the line of the outlying stations, and had approached to the edge of a bit of wild and broken country, which offered so few inducements to settlers that it had been passed by for the better land beyond; although occasionally, when herbage was scarce, the settlers in the neighbourhood drove the animals up to feed among its hills. The black had no doubt that the gang, of which he was in pursuit, had their haunt somewhere in the heart of this wild and little-known tract.

In the morning he again started and, after travelling several miles, entered a narrow valley with very steep sides, with trees and brushwood growing wherever they could get a foothold. He now adopted a careless and indifferent carriage and, although he kept a sharp lookout, no one who saw him would have supposed that he had any particular object in view.

Presently he noticed that the tracks turned sharply off from the line he had followed, in the centre of the valley; and entered the trees, which grew thickly here at the foot of the hills. He made no halt, even for an instant, but walked straight on. Half a mile further he sat down and lit his fire, and began to cook some food. He had no doubt that he was watched for, just after he passed the point where the track turned off, he heard a very low whistle among the trees.

As he sat by the fire, he kept his back towards the direction from which he had come; and when he presently heard footsteps, no change in his attitude betrayed that he was conscious of the fact that persons were approaching him, until two men stopped beside him. Then, with a cry as of sudden alarm, he leapt to his feet.

"Lor' a mussy!" he exclaimed, "de white man frighten me bery much. What for dey no say dey come?"

"Who are you, nigger, and where do you come from, and what are you doing here?"

"My name Jim," he said; "me going tro' the country looking for place to tend hosses. Me bery good at hosses. Me look arter de hosses ob Mr. Hudson."

"What did you leave him for?" one of the men asked, sternly.

"Someting lost from de house," Jim said quietly. "Massa Hudson tink me took it. He make bobbery, so Jim ran away and look for nodder place."

"Um," the man said; "I wonder whether you are speaking the truth? If I thought you weren't, I would put a bullet through your head, in double-quick time."

"No, sah," Jim said in great terror; "dat de truth, sure 'nough. Jim try to get work at Sydney. Couldn't get; so start away, and ask at all de stations. No one want black boy for hosses, so keep on and tink dere more chance out furder. Does massa want a boy for hoss?"

"What do you think, Bill?" the man who had spoken asked his companion. "Shall we put a bullet in this fellow's head, at once, or make him useful?"

"I dussay he is a liar," the other replied; "but then all these black fellows are liars, so that does not make much difference. A black fellow would certainly be useful for the horses, and to look after the fire. We can always shoot him when we have done with him. We shall soon see, by the way he handles the horses, whether he has been accustomed to them."

"All right," the other said. "You come along with us then."

"What wages massa pay?" Jim asked.

"Anything you may be worth. Don't you fret about wages."

Jim pretended to hold out for a fixed sum; but the man said, in stern tones:

"Come along, we don't want no more jaw, so you had best hold your tongue."

No other words passed till they got back to the trees, and then turned off where the horses had previously done so. Two minutes' walk brought them to a roughly-made shed, built against the almost perpendicular side of the hill. It was built of logs, and there was nothing to show that it was inhabited. No smoke curled up from the chimney. The door and shutters were closed. Anyone who, passing through the valley, had turned among the trees and accidentally come upon it, would have taken it for some hut erected by a wood cutter.

One of the men knocked three times at the door, and it was at once opened. Jim was pushed inside, the men followed him, and the door was shut.

"Who have you got here?" a man, sitting by the side of a large fire some distance inside the cottage, asked angrily.

"It's a nigger who wants work. He says he is accustomed to horses so, as it was the choice between shooting him and bringing him here, we thought we might as well bring him to you. It would be handy to have a fellow to look after the horses, and cut the wood, and make himself useful. If we find he is of no use, there will be no great trouble in getting rid of him."

"That is true enough," the other said, "and I don't think there's much risk about it.

"Come here, you fellow, and let me look at you."

Jim stepped forward towards the fire. He saw now that the hut was built against the entrance to a cave of considerable size. In the centre was a great fire, the smoke of which probably made its way to the surface through crevices in the rock above. Four other men, besides the one who had addressed him, were lying on sheepskins against the wall. There was an opening at the further end of the cave into an inner chamber; and here Jim knew, by an occasional snort or an impatient pawing, the horses were stabled.

The chief of the party asked a few more questions as to where Jim had come from, and how he chanced to be passing through so unfrequented a country. As the black had already decided upon his story, the questions were answered satisfactory enough.

"I think he's all right," the man said, at last. "At any rate here he is, and he's not likely to go out again. We have been talking of getting a black fellow, for some time; and as here is one ready to hand, we may as well make the best of him.

"Look you here," he went on sternly, to the black; "you come of your own free will, and here you have got to stop. You will have as much to eat as you can stuff, plenty of rum to drink, and 'bacca to smoke; and if there's anything else you fancy, no doubt you can have it. Only look you, if you put your foot outside that door, unless you are ordered to do so, I will put a bullet through your black brain."

"All right," Jim said. "Plenty eat, plenty drink, plenty smoke; dat suit Jim bery well. He no want to go out of de house, if massa say no."

"That's settled then. Now, put some more logs on that fire."

Jim at once assumed his new duty, and the bush rangers, who all hated the slightest work, were soon well satisfied with their new acquisition. There were several carcasses of sheep, hanging from hooks placed in the roof, where they were slowly smoked by the fumes from the wood. A pile of logs were heaped up in one corner, and these had to be cut up into sizes and lengths suitable for the fire. At one end a space was roughly partitioned off, and this was filled with groceries, flour, and cases of wine and spirits which had been taken from waggons going up country.

In the stable were several sacks of oats; and a barrel filled with water, which was drawn from a spring, a short distance from the hut. The first time Jim went into the stable the captain accompanied him, and soon saw, by the black's handling of the horses, that his account was so far accurate, and that he was thoroughly accustomed to stable work.

The cooking was also handed over to him, and the gang passed their time in sleeping, drinking, playing cards, and discussing plans of robbery. For the first few days a sharp watch was kept up on the black, and the men went out themselves to chop wood, or bring in water when it was required. After a few days, however, they relaxed their vigilance, and Jim gradually took these tasks also upon himself.

He was perfectly aware, although he pretended to be unconscious of it, that the first few times he went out one or other of the bush rangers stole quietly after him, and watched him at work; but as nothing suspicious was observed in his conduct, this supervision was gradually given up.

"It's time to be moving again," the leader of the band said, about a week after Jim had joined them. "We settled the next job should be Donald's station. We know for certain that he generally has money by him, and there will be the watches and trinkets of the women. That fellow Thompson, who worked for them at first, says he has got a first-rate cellar of wine; and that the women were both out-and-outers. If they are as pretty as he says, we will have them here, lads, to do the housekeeping. We want something to liven us up; besides, we shall forget our company manners, if we don't get some ladies to keep us up to the mark a little."

There was a burst of coarse laughter.

"What do you say, boys; shall we start tomorrow? It's a long ride, and we had best leave about noon. We must get into the neighbourhood before dark, so as to give the horses twelve hours' rest before we begin; for we may have to ride for it.

"It ain't likely. Barker's is the nearest station, and it would be hours before they could get together men enough who would dare to follow us;

but still, it's just as well to be prepared, and since that confounded new police officer has been on the station, there's never been no certainty about things. We owe him one for that last affair, which cost Smith, Wilson, and Mulready their lives; but we will pay him out yet. Who would have thought of his being there, just on that very night? I swear, if I ever catch him, I will roast him alive."

"He is no fool," one of the others said. "He gave it those black fellows hot, and no mistake. The sooner he's put out of the way, the better. He's a different sort of chap than the last fellow. I sha'n't feel comfortable till he's got either a spear or a pistol bullet in him."

Jim, who was squatting in the corner, apparently half asleep, was listening intently to every word. They did not heed his presence in the slightest; for indeed he had, since his arrival, so mixed his talk with native words that the bush rangers had no idea that he could follow their conversations.

He was thinking, now, what was his best course to adopt. In the first place, he had gathered from their talk that this was only one of their hiding places, and that they seldom stayed very long in one neighbourhood. The question, therefore, was whether they would return. It was of no use his going to give the alarm, unless he could return before his escape was suspected; or they would have made off before he could get back again.

As for the Donalds, whose station was to be attacked, it gave him no concern whatever; for the Australian blacks had little or no regard for life, except those of people to whom they were attached. It was Reuben's mission to capture the bush rangers and, had it been necessary, Jim would have remained quiet while a dozen families were slain, until he found an opportunity of bringing the police down upon them.

He listened now, intently, for any word which might afford an index to their intentions. Presently the question he hoped for came.

"I suppose you will not come back here again, Tom?"

"No, I thinks it's getting too hot to hold us, in these parts. We might ride back here, give our horses a rest, and load up with a few things we may want. We can bring two or three spare horses from Donald's. The weather is pleasant now, and we might very well put in a few weeks with the blacks. That last haul we made of traders' goods—cottons, and beads, and trumperies for the gins, and brass rings and such like for the men—will put them in the best of humours. You may be sure there will be a hot chase after us, after this business; and I should propose that we try our luck down south, for a bit."

"I agree with you," one of the others said. "We have had a very good spell here, for the last ten months; and it don't do to tempt luck too long. That losing three of our number, last week, looked as if it was going to turn."

"What's it matter?" the captain laughed. "So much the more for us to divide. We have got a goodish bit of brass, now, to say nothing of the goods we have got at each of our places. We can fill up their places easy enough, any time; and those who come in are free to their share of what there is, in the way of grub and goods, but they only share in the brass from the time they join."

Jim had heard what he wanted, and he now lay down and thought it out. They were only coming back for a short time. Possibly they might change their minds, and not return at all. It would be a risky thing to depend upon it; besides, his master might be blamed if this attack on the Donalds succeeded.

It would be better, then, to try to get word to him, in time for him to be there before the bush rangers arrived. He himself would return to the hut; so that, if the police arrived too late, he would be able to continue with the bush rangers till some fresh opportunity occurred for bringing his master upon them. It was possible, of course, that one of the men would be left in the hut, in which case he had only to wait.

The next morning the men busied themselves examining and cleaning their arms, and after dinner they went to the inner cave, and led out their horses.

"Now, look here," the leader said to him, "we are going away, you see."

Jim nodded.

"We come back again tomorrow. I lock this place up, you stop quiet till we come back. If anyone comes and knocks, while we away, don't Jim answer. Let them think place empty."

"All right," Jim said shortly, and went and sat down by the fire, as if he had no further interest in their proceedings.

The windows, he had already noticed, had not only shutters outside; but they were firmly closed within, with massive planks, securely nailed and fastened. Jim heard the last of the party go out, and then the door was shut, and the lock turned. Jim heard the party ride off, and then threw himself on the ground and listened, to assure himself that they kept steadily on their way.

The moment he was sure they were gone, he began to search the place for a tool which would fairly suit his purpose. Presently he found a large butcher's knife, with which they cut up the carcasses; and with this he set to work to dig a hole in the ground, close to the wall of the hut. The bottom log was only sunk a few inches in the soil, and in two hours he had burrowed under it, and made his way out beyond; then he crept back again, scraped the earth into the hole again as tightly as he could, crawling out backwards. He then placed a piece of turf over the outside hole, and stamped it down flat.

It was possible that, after he had started, they might change their mind and send one of their number back again; that, however, had to be risked, and at a steady run he set off for the settlements. He did not make for the nearest; for he had gathered, from the talk of the men, that the convict labourers of most of the settlements in the neighbourhood were in league with them.

After three hours' steady running, in which he had covered over twenty miles, he saw a shepherd's cottage and, making for it, gave the man the message which he had taken to Reuben. He had no sooner done so, and had found that the man was willing to set off with it at once, than he turned and retraced his steps to the hut, as rapidly as he had come. It was already dusk when he reached it.

Instead of approaching boldly, he made a circuit and crawled up to it on his belly; and lay for some time, listening intently, with his ear to the door. He felt convinced that no one was there; but to make sure he knocked, and then withdrew among the trees. But all was still and, feeling sure now that the place was untenanted, he removed the piece of turf from the hole and made his way back into the hut again; carefully replacing the piece of turf, and then packing earth under it, so that it would not give way if trodden upon. This, however, was a very unlikely occurrence, as he had made the opening where some bushes screened it from view.

He swept up every scrap of soil from the floor inside, filled up the hole there and trampled it down; and then, after indulging his appetite to the fullest, threw himself down and went to sleep.

When he awoke, a few streaks of light streaming through the cracks of the door showed that it was day; and he made up the fire, and awaited the return of the bush rangers.

It was four or five hours before they returned, and the instant they opened the door and entered, Jim was sure that they had failed; but to his disappointment all were there, and his plan of taking them in a trap had not succeeded. At this he was not surprised; for his own calculations, as to the distance to be traversed, had shown him that it was very questionable whether, even under the most favourable circumstances, Reuben could have got there in time with his men.

Without speaking a word to him, the men led their horses through to the inner cave, and then threw themselves down by the fire. Jim at once proceeded to unsaddle the horses, and rub them down; keeping an ear open, all the time, to what was being said by the bush rangers. Their remarks however were, for a time, confined to terrible curses as to their luck.

"How did it come about, that's what I want to know?" the leader said. "This is the second time that accursed police fellow has turned up, and put a spoke in our wheel. Why, it was not more than half an hour after the first shot was fired before they was down upon us; there must have been pretty nigh twenty of them. How could they have got such a lot of men as that together, if they hadn't known that we were coming? It beats me altogether."

"So it does me!" was the general exclamation.

"They seemed regularly to jump out of the ground, just when all was going pleasant. Never knew such a bit of luck—that is, if it was luck, and not done o' purpose—and yet, I don't see as they could have known, possible, as we was going there. Why, we didn't know ourselves till yesterday, not what day it was to be; and except ourselves, and that black fellow, no one could have known it."

"Well, it's certain none of us blabbed; and I don't see as how he could have told anyone."

"Not exactly," the leader said, "considering he's been shut up here, ever since we have been away; besides, I don't believe he knew anything about it. He don't make out half we say to him and, when we are talking together, he minds us no more than if he had been a black monkey; but if he did, it's no odds, he could not have passed through these walls and back again; and if he could, who was he to tell it to? The men round here are all our pals, and would have cut his jaw short with a bullet. But there, it's no use talking about it, he's not been out, and there's an end of it.

"Still, it beats me altogether. That police fellow seems to know what we are up to, just as well as we do ourselves. I would give all my share of the swag we have made, for the last six months, for a shot at him."

"I don't like it," one of the others said, "I don't; blest if I do; and I says as the sooner we are out of here, the better. After what's happened, I sha'n't feel safe till I am well out in the blacks' country. If he knows what we are going to do, there ain't any reasons why he shouldn't know where we are."

"Why, Johnson," his leader sneered, "you don't really believe the fellow's a sort of conjurer, do you?"

"I don't know," the man said doggedly. "After he has turned up twice as he has, I shouldn't be surprised at nothing—not if I heard the sound of him and his men galloping up outside, now."

There was a moment's silence, as each involuntarily listened.

"We are getting to be like a pack of gals," the leader said savagely, "and I agree with you, the sooner we are out of this, the better. As soon as it gets dark, we will be on the move; but I tell you, directly we get out among the blacks, I shall come back again. I am going to carry off that gal, somehow. I've owed her one for years and years, and I always pays my debts—at least, that sort of debt.

"Now then, you black, just leave them horses for the present, and come and cook us some food; the quicker, the better."

Jim hurried about, but in the bush rangers' present state of temper, nothing would satisfy them; and when, in his hurry to satisfy their angry orders, he stumbled and upset a glass of spirits and water he was handing to the captain, the latter caught up a brand from the fire; and struck him so violent a blow on the temple, with the glowing end, that he fell senseless on the ground.

He must have lain there a long time. He was brought to his senses by a bucket of water being dashed over him; and he found, when he staggered to his feet, that the band were preparing to depart. They had already packed up the bales of presents for the blacks, and placed them on the horses. Some of their more valuable belongings were packed away in a secret hiding place, the rest were left to take their chance till they returned; and indeed, except by their friends among the shepherds, there was little probability of anyone paying a visit to the hut, however long their absence might be.

Had it not been that Jim had proved himself a really useful fellow, for the last week, they would have shot him at once and tossed his body in the wood; but they found it so pleasant, having all their work taken off their hands, that after a short discussion they decided to take him with them.

The door was locked, and they started at a trot; but evening was closing in, their horses had already performed two long journeys in the last twenty-four hours, and they soon settled into a walk. They travelled for some hours and, it being then evident that the horses could proceed no further, a halt was called. No fire was lighted, for they were scarcely beyond the settlements and, for aught they could tell, an active search might still be carried on for them.

So anxious were they, that they agreed to keep watch by turns; but when morning broke, it was discovered that the black was missing. The next quarter of an hour was spent in angry recriminations; but as none could say in whose watch he made his escape, their quarrel ceased.

"It's no use bothering about it," the leader said. "There's one thing, he knows nothing, and can tell nothing against us. He may guess what he likes, but people don't waste time in listening to black fellows' stories. I expect he has only given us the slip because of that lick across the head I gave him, last night. I admit I was a fool to do it, but I wasn't in the best of tempers.

"However, if the worst comes to the worst, he can only lead them to the hut; and they won't find much worth taking, there. When we once get out to the blacks, we can snap our fingers at them."

It was, indeed, about midnight when Jim had stolen away. He was still faint and giddy, and his face was terribly burned by the blow which had been dealt him; but when once fairly away from the bush rangers, he set out in the direction in which he knew the Donalds' station lay; and never halted until he arrived there, on the following evening, utterly wearied and worn out, for he had eaten nothing on the previous day.

"Then they have got away after all, Jim," Reuben said, when he had listened patiently to the long narration. "You have done all that was possible, Jim. You have done splendidly, my poor fellow, and although we were just too late to catch the bush rangers, we saved the people here; but it is indeed unfortunate that they should have got off."

"Jim knows where dey hab gone," the black said. "Dey hab gone to de country of Bobitu—I heard dem say de name. Jim know dat country well—he come from der."

Further question showed that Jim had, indeed, belonged to Bobitu's tribe; and had come with a party of his people down to the settlements, where he was taken ill and left to die, but was picked up and nursed by Mr. Hudson.

"And you could take us there?"

Jim nodded.

"Bery long march, massa. Tree days, with horses. Plenty bad people; much fight."

"I don't care how far it is, or how much fighting we have got to do; I am bound to hunt down that fellow, however far he's gone. I suppose there is no trouble about water. If they can go there, we can."

"Four, six water holes," Jim said. "No trouble about dat—trouble from de black fellow."

"Well, we must risk it, anyhow. We can't start for a day or two. I must send and fetch up all the police, and I daresay some of the colonists will join. The news of this business here has maddened everyone, and as it is not likely that the blacks will give any trouble for some time, and as we know the bush rangers have left for the present, no one need be afraid of leaving their station for a week or two."

The next day mounted messengers were sent off in all directions, giving notice that the police would start, in three days' time, for a hunt after the bush rangers; and that there was, this time, every prospect of success, as their hiding place was known.

On the day named, no less than thirty settlers assembled; together with the whole of the police force. All were well armed, and had brought several days' provisions with them. Mr. Donald had made marked progress, and the surgeon had now every hopes of his recovery; but as he could not be moved, and it was just possible the bush ranger might return to carry out his threat, during their absence, two constables were left in the house; and Kate was charged, on no account, to put her foot outside the door.

Chapter 17
In Pursuit

The last thing before the party started, Reuben went into the house. Mr. Barker was going to remain behind. He was past middle life, and the expedition was likely to be a very toilsome one; and Reuben was glad when he said that he thought six days' severe riding would be rather too much for him, and that he should constitute himself the guardian of the ladies.

"My wife has arranged to stay here, while you are away; so I shall ride over to my place and see that all is going on straight, every day, and sleep here at night."

"Well, ladies," Reuben said, as he entered the room, "we are just off. So I will say goodbye to you; and I hope that, on my return, I shall find Mr. Donald much better. I am sure that Mr. Ruskin would not have left, this morning, unless he felt that he had quite turned the corner. Pray take care of yourselves, while we are away. You know I don't want to alarm you, but pray be careful. I shall not feel comfortable, as to your safety, till I have that villain safely in my hands."

"Goodbye, Captain Whitney. You know you have all our best wishes," Mrs. Barker said. "We will take care of ourselves, till we hear that you have destroyed the band; and above all, its leader."

"The news that you have done so," Mrs. Donald said, "will do more, I think, for my husband, than anything in the way of doctoring. But take care of yourself, Captain Whitney. I know from what Mr. Barker said that, although you make light of your expedition, it is a dangerous one. He said the police had never ventured so far in the bush, and you may expect sharp fighting with the blacks."

"We may have a brush with them," Reuben said lightly; "but do not be anxious about us. We are a very strong party, and you need have no fear of the result.

"Goodbye, Miss Ellison; pray be careful till I return."

The last words were said in an undertone, as he held her hand.

"Goodbye, Captain Whitney," she said. "God bless you all, and bring you safely back."

Two minutes later, the party rode off. Jim was, like the rest, mounted, as they would travel fast. Four led horses carried provisions; for they would not, as before, find food by the way. It was two o'clock in the day when they started, and they rode thirty miles before they halted, for the night, at a water hole. They had seen no signs of natives during the day, but Reuben at once posted four men as sentries.

It was a merry party round the fire, for all were in high spirits at the prospect of an expedition to a point far beyond that to which any white men, with the exception of fugitives from justice, had penetrated; and they were delighted with the thought of putting a stop, at last, to the operations of the band who had so long been a scourge to the settlement.

Mr. Blount, Dick Caister, and several others who had formed part of the last expedition were of the party; and the confidence which these felt in their young leader, and in the sagacity of his native follower, communicated itself to those who had not formed part of the previous expedition.

"Must start early," Jim said to Reuben, the last thing. "Long way to water. Ride all day, not get dere before dark."

They rode rapidly for some time, after starting, so as to allow the horses to take it easily, during the heat of the day, when there was a halt of three hours; but in the afternoon they quickened their pace again, and men and horses were jaded and done up when, just as the sun was setting, they arrived at their destination.

"How that black fellow of yours finds his way through this bush is a perfect marvel to me," Dick Caister said. "The country has become more undulating, this afternoon; but the first thirty miles were almost perfectly level, and I could see nothing, whatever, that could serve as an index, except of course the sun. Still, that is only a guide as to the general direction. It must have been nine or ten years since that fellow was here, and yet he led us as straight as if he was making for a church steeple."

"It seems to be a sort of instinct," Reuben said, "although possibly, for the last part of the distance, he may have seen signs of the passage of the natives. As far as I can understand, he tells me at this time of year there is no other water hole, within a long distance; so that naturally there will be many natives making for it. I am glad there are not any of them here, now.

"Why isn't that horse hobbled like the rest?" Reuben asked suddenly. "Whose is it?"

"That is the one your black fellow rode, sir," Sergeant O'Connor said.

"Jim, where are you?" Reuben called, but no reply came.

"What has become of him, I wonder?" Reuben said. "Has anyone seen him, since we rode up?"

"He jumped off, the instant we came here," one of the policemen replied; "and said to me, 'Look after captain horse,' and I haven't seen anything of him since."

"There has been somebody here, sir," another policeman said, coming up. "Here's the remains of a fire, behind this bush."

"Yes," Mr. Blount said, examining them, and pulling out a brand that was still glowing. "Do you see, a lot of sand has been thrown over it. Whoever was here must have seen us coming, and tried to extinguish the fire when they caught sight of us."

"That is most unfortunate," Reuben said. "The fellows must have made off, to carry the news of our coming to their friends. However, it's too late to do anything now. It's already getting dark, and they must have got a quarter of an hour's start. We have taken quite enough out of the horses, and can do no more with them, if they have to travel tomorrow; but I would give a year's pay if this hadn't happened.

"Well, there's nothing to do for it but to light our fires, and camp."

The knowledge that they had been seen, and that the news would be carried to those of whom they were in search, acted as a great damper on the spirits of the party; and the camp was much more quiet and subdued than it had been, on the previous evening.

"All is not quite lost," Reuben said when, two hours later, he found that Jim was still absent from the camp. "I can only account for his stealing away from us, in that manner, by supposing that he must either have caught sight of the natives, or come upon their trail; and at once set off in pursuit. I don't see what it could be, otherwise."

"But if he saw them, why didn't he tell you, Whitney?" Mr. Blount said. "Tired as our horses were, they could have got up a gallop for a bit."

"Yes, but for a very short distance," Dick Caister put in; "and as it was getting dusk, if the blacks had had anything like a start, we could not have overtaken them before it had got quite dark. Those blacks can run like the wind. It takes a well-mounted man to overtake them."

An hour after the party had lain down, one of the sentries challenged; and the answer which came back, "All right, me Jim," at once brought everyone to their feet.

"Well, Jim, what is it? Where have you been?" Reuben asked.

"Jim hungry."

"That you may be quite sure," Dick Caister said, with a laugh. "Was there ever a native who wasn't hungry; unless he had stuffed himself, half an hour before?"

"Yes, I kept some supper for you, Jim," Reuben said; "but before you begin to eat, just tell me if everything is all right."

"Everyting all right," Jim said, squatting himself beside the still glowing fire, and beginning to eat.

Reuben knew, by experience, that it was of no use questioning him until he had finished; and he therefore waited patiently, although one or two of the settlers grumbled at being kept waiting for the news. When Jim had finished his meal, he looked round. Reuben knew what he was expecting, and handed him a hornful of rum and water. The black took a draught; and then, without any further delay, began to tell his story.

He had, while still some distance from the halting place, seen a light smoke coming up, and was sure that a party was already there.

"But why did you not tell us, Jim?" Reuben interrupted. "We might have galloped on, and caught them."

"No, sah, no catch dem; horses too tired, black fellow run away, when see white men coming. Dat no do at all. Only one way to do. Let 'em tink dat no one saw dem, else dey run and run, all de way to Bobitu.

"When get near camp, Jim see dat smoke not come up, know de black fellow see white man and put out um fire. When Jim come here he jump off hoss, find fire, and follow de track. Dey four men; one go one way, one go anoder, two men go straight on. Dey go on to tell Bobitu, de oders go to black fellows in de bush. Jim not care for dem, follow de two."

"But how could you follow them, in the dark?"

"Jim were sure de way dey go, dat enough for Jim. He suppose dat dey 'top after a bit; and when dey see de white men all 'top quiet at de water hole, and light fire, dey tink it all right. No make hurry, perhaps 'top and light a fire demselves.

"So Jim go on quiet for two, tree hour; den at last he see fire, sure 'nough. He crawl up quiet and see two black fellow dar, and hear what 'em say. Dey tired, make long walk today to water hole; say no hurry, white men all go sleep round fire, not go on till sun get up, so dey stop for two, tree hour to rest demselves.

"Jim get quite close and jump up, den cut off one black fellow head with sword, run sword through de body of other, finish 'em both, and den come back to camp."

"Well done, indeed, Jim!" Reuben exclaimed, and a chorus of satisfaction rose from all the party at hearing that the men—who, had they reached the bush rangers, would have given the alarm, and so enabled them to make their escape before the expedition arrived—had been killed. The news, however, that two of the party had escaped, and might bring the blacks down upon them before morning, necessitated an increase of precautions.

Reuben at once divided the force into four parties, each consisting of five constables and seven settlers. One party were at once placed on watch, and were to be relieved in two hours' time.

"I not tink dey come before morning, sah," Jim said. "No water hole near here. Tomorrow plenty black fellow come."

"All right, Jim. We don't care for them, in the daylight; and now that I know the bush rangers won't be alarmed, I don't mind."

Jim's prediction proved correct. The night passed off quietly, and the party again started at daylight. The country became more and more broken, as they proceeded. The undulations became hills. Some of these were so steep that all had to dismount, and lead their horses up.

"Is Bobitu's camp among these hills, Jim?"

"Ober toder side, sah. Him place in valley, toder side; bush, plenty game for black fellow."

"How far is it to this valley, Jim?"

Jim's ideas of figures were but vague, and he could only say that they would get there somewhere about sunset.

"That would be a bad time to get there, Jim. We must halt, a mile or two this side of them; and you must lead half the party round, so as to cut off their retreat, even if we don't attack them till the morning. On their fresh horses, those fellows will gallop right away from us, if they once get a start.

"There is no fear, I hope, of any of the other blacks getting there before us, and giving the alarm?"

Jim shook his head.

"No. We come straight from water hole. Black fellow go round long way. No fear dey get dere. Dey fight when we go back."

"That's all right. Bobitu's fellows, and the bush rangers, will be quite enough to tackle at once. As for the others, we will make short work of them, if they venture to attack us on the march back. They fight pluckily enough against men on foot, because they know they can make off when they like; but they can't stand a charge of horsemen."

Although not so long as the journey on the preceding day, the men were heartily glad when, at about four o'clock in the afternoon, the halt was called, and they heard that the place where the bush rangers were supposed to be was but four miles away. After some consultation, it was decided that Jim should lead half the band—consisting of ten constables under O'Connor, and fifteen colonists—round through the hills, to a position near the mouth of the valley in which the blacks and bush rangers were likely to be; and that, when he had posted them there, he should come back again to their present halting place, and lead forward the party under Reuben.

"Mind," Reuben said, before the others started, "we don't want to attack the blacks, unless they show fight. Our object is the bush rangers. Jim says that, by what he heard, they have got some sort of houses they have built there. Let us make straight for them. If the blacks attack, drive them off; but we can settle with them, afterwards. The great point is to capture or kill the bush rangers."

All agreed to this, for although the blacks gave great trouble, by driving off the sheep and cattle, and sometimes killing the shepherds, there was not the same feeling of hatred entertained for them as for the bush rangers. It was felt to be natural that the natives should resent the occupation of their hunting grounds; and although they were shot down without mercy in fair fight, or if overtaken while carrying off cattle, there was no active feeling of animosity against them; and they were generally kindly treated, when they called unarmed at the stations, and asked for food.

Against the bush rangers, on the other hand, a deadly hatred was felt by the colonists; and the fact that these were constantly aided, by the ticket-of-leave labourers, increased the hostility with which they were regarded.

Jim left his horse behind him, when he started with his party; saying that coming back at night, in the dark, he would rather be without it. After their comrades had set out, those who remained behind posted two men as sentries; and then, as soon as they had cooked and eaten a meal, laid themselves down to sleep, until the time should come for their advance.

It was just midnight when Jim returned. He reported that he had seen no blacks by the way, and that he believed he had posted his party without their being observed. He himself, instead of returning by the same route that he had taken them, had come straight up the valley.

There were, he said, two huts which had been built by the bush rangers; and these were now occupied by them. There were great fires blazing, and he thought that the natives had probably only arrived there that evening. He had got near enough to find that they were in a high state of delight, at the presents which their white friends had brought them.

"Did you catch sight of any of the bush rangers, Jim?" Reuben asked.

"Two ob dem came out and spoke to black fellows at fire, but too far off to see which dey were."

An hour before daybreak the party moved forward, and halted within half a mile of the bush rangers' camp. There they stopped, till they could see the sunlight touch the top of the hill at the right-hand side of the valley. This was the signal agreed upon and, mounting, they rode forward at full speed.

Just as they got within sight of the huts, they heard a wild shouting, followed instantly by the crack of rifles. Another minute, and they had reached the scene and joined the other party, who had made straight to the huts. The blacks, awakened suddenly as they were sleeping round the embers of their fires, had hastily thrown a volley of spears, and had darted away among the bushes.

"Surrender, in the queen's name!" Reuben shouted, "and I promise you that you shall be taken down, and have a fair trial."

The answer came in the flash of a rifle, from the window of one of the huts; and a constable immediately behind Reuben fell dead, with the ball through his head.

"Dismount!" Reuben shouted, "and break in the doors."

With a shout, the men threw themselves from their horses and rushed at the doors of the huts.

"Sergeant O'Connor," Reuben said; "do you, with six of your men, keep up a fire at the windows. Don't let a man show himself there.

"Let ten of the others look after the horses. We shall have the blacks back, in no time."

So saying, he ran forward and joined those who were battering at the doors. Several of them had brought stout axes with them, and the doors speedily gave way. There was a rush forward.

Mr. Blount fell dead, and Dick Caister's shoulder was broken by a bullet; but there was no check, as the colonists poured into the huts. There was a short sharp fight, but in two minutes it was over. Three of the gang had been shot, as they leapt from the windows. Four more lay dead, or dying, in the huts.

One of them had thrown down his arms, and shouted for mercy. He had been knocked down and stunned, by the butt end of a rifle; but was otherwise unwounded.

Short as was the fight, it had given time to the blacks to rally. Their shouts were ringing in the air, and the spears were flying thickly as the party, having finished their work, rushed outside again, to assist the constables who were guarding the horses.

"Pour a volley into the bushes," Reuben shouted; "then mount, and charge them."

The order was executed and, in a minute, the horsemen were dashing hither and thither among the bushes, shooting down with their pistols the blacks who resisted, or dealing tremendous blows among them with their hunting whips. The charge was irresistible, and in five minutes the main body of the blacks were flying, at full speed, up the steep hillsides.

The victors soon gathered round the huts. Several men and horses had been wounded with spears, but none of the injuries were of a serious character.

"Well, how about the prisoners?" Reuben asked the sergeant, who had arrived before him.

"There's only one prisoner, sir. All the rest are accounted for."

"Is it their captain?"

"I don't know, sir. I have never set eyes on him; but if he's a young chap, as they say, it ain't him."

"Jim," Reuben said, "just go round and examine the bodies, and see which of them is the captain."

Jim returned in a couple of minutes.

"None of dem ain't him, sah. He not dere."

Reuben started.

"Are you quite sure, Jim?"

"Quite sure, sah."

"Are you sure none of them escaped, sergeant?"

"I am quite sure of that, sir. No one came out of either of the doors, and there were only three who tried to bolt through the windows, and we accounted for them all. Perhaps that chap who is prisoner can tell you where to find the captain. It's a bad job, indeed, if he has escaped."

"Is the man recovering his senses?"

"Yes, sir, he's just coming round."

Reuben stepped into the hut. The escape of Thorne destroyed all the satisfaction which his success would have given him. He had good reason to know the fiendish malignity of the man and, in spite of the warnings he had given Kate Ellison, and his strict orders to the police on guard, he felt a thrill of anxiety, now that he was aware her enemy was still at large.

The prisoner was sitting up, in a corner of the hut; a policeman, with drawn sword, standing near him.

"Where is your leader?" Reuben asked sternly. "The man you call Fothergill."

"He went away yesterday morning," the man said, with a grin of satisfaction. "You haven't caught him yet; and you will hear more of him, before you do."

"Where was he going?" Reuben demanded.

"You won't get nothing out of me," the fellow said. "He's been a good mate, and a true, and I ain't going to put you bloodhounds on his scent. He's gone a-wooing, that's where he's gone, and that won't help you much."

Reuben at once went outside, and called the settlers round him.

"I am sorry to say," he said, "that the leader of the party has got away. He rode off yesterday morning, and although the prisoner we have taken did not say where he has gone, I have not the least doubt he has ridden back to the Donalds, to try and carry out his threat to return for Miss Ellison.

"Therefore, gentlemen, may I ask you to start homeward, at once. The horses have only done a few miles and, if we press forward, we may manage to get to our camp of the evening before last. We have no more to do here, except to see if there are any valuables hidden in the huts, and set fire to them.

"I expect that we shall have fighting with the blacks, on our way back. Those parties the two fellows who got away went to fetch will, likely enough, bar our way. If it were not for that, I should ride on by myself; but my duty is to stop with my men until, at any rate, we have passed the place where the blacks are likely to attack us. That done, I shall push on. It is annoying, indeed, to think that that fellow must have passed us somewhere on the way, yesterday."

The settlers agreed, at once. They all sympathized with Reuben, in his disappointment at the escape of the leader of the bush rangers; and regretted the matter deeply, on their own account. They were, too, now that the work was done, anxious to be off; not only because they wished to return to their stations, but because they felt that their position was a dangerous one. They had penetrated, to a distance hitherto unattempted, into the country of the natives; and they knew that these would gather round them, like hornets, on their return march.

Ten minutes were spent in the search of the huts. The police probed the ground with their swords, and closely examined the walls. They found, under some sheepskins in one corner, a bag containing upwards of two hundred pounds; which was doubtless the amount which the bush rangers had brought back with them, from their last plundering expedition, and had not yet been added to their main store, wherever that might be. This, however, was a welcome find to the police, and they abandoned the idea of searching further; and were about to set fire to the hut, when the prisoner said:

"Lookee here! I may as well tell you where the lot is hidden. It may do me good, when it comes to the trial; and you may as well have it, as for it to lay there. You dig up the ground in front of that tree, behind the hut, and you will find it."

Five minutes later a large leather bag, containing a considerable quantity of gold and notes, and a number of watches, chains, and other trinkets, was brought to light.

"Don't stop to count the money now," Reuben said. "Fasten it on one of the horses, and let us be off.

"Sergeant, let Jones ride beside the prisoner, and be responsible for his safety. See that his hands are tied behind him, and his ankles tied securely to stirrup leathers. Let four men take charge of the eight horses of these bush rangers. Do you ride ahead with four others, and keep a sharp lookout as you go. Don't press the horses, but we must go at a smart pace, for we have a long day's march before us. It is fully sixty miles to the water hole where we camped, the night before last."

A few minutes later, the party were in motion. Although disappointed at the escape of the leader of the band, they were well satisfied with the result of the expedition, and at the small amount of loss at which it had been accomplished. There was general regret at the death of Mr. Blount; but two lives were considered to be but a small loss, for the capture of so strong a body of bush rangers; who, knowing that they fought with ropes round their neck, always made a desperate resistance.

Half the journey was accomplished without incident, and Reuben felt satisfied that they would, at least, have no trouble with the tribe they had scattered in the morning. The speedy start that they had made had taken them beyond their pursuit; and if attacked, it would be by other tribes.

After an hour's halt, to feed the horses and cook some meat for themselves, the party proceeded again. Another fifteen miles were passed; then Reuben saw the sergeant, with the little party ahead, suddenly draw rein. He galloped forward to them.

"What is it, sergeant?"

"I am pretty sure I saw a black fellow's head, over that rock, sir. It's a nasty piece of ground. I noticed it yesterday, as I came along. It would be the worst place to be attacked in of any we have passed. If the blacks are here in force, they know what they are doing."

Reuben examined the position. It was certainly a nasty place to be attacked in. The valley was narrow, and thickly strewn with boulders of all sizes, which had rolled down from the hillsides. Among these the bush grew thickly, and it was only down a narrow path in the centre, formed by a winter stream, now dry, that horsemen could pass.

"I don't think it would do to make a bolt through that, sir," the sergeant said, shaking his head. "We could only ride two abreast and, if they are strong, we should be riddled with spears before we got through; and there's no charging them, among those stones and bush."

"That is so, sergeant. We shall have to dismount, and drive them out foot by foot. There's nothing else for it."

By this time all the party had come up, and Reuben explained to them the situation. All at once agreed that they could do nothing on horseback, on such ground.

The whole party therefore dismounted. The horses were tied to bushes, and the prisoner securely fastened to a tree. Then, rifle in hand, they moved forward.

The sergeant's eye had not deceived him for, as they approached the spot where the boulders and bush grew thickest, a shower of spears was thrown, and the native cry rose shrill in the air. The party were advancing in skirmishing order; and most of them threw themselves down, or dodged behind rocks, as the blacks rose to throw their spears and, a moment later, the rifles cracked out. Several of the blacks fell, and the rest disappeared among the bushes.

"Make your way forward, steadily and carefully. Let each man watch his neighbour, to the right and left, and keep in line as much as you can."

The fight now commenced in earnest, but the settlers and police gradually made their way forward. Not only had they the advantage in weapons; but the fact that they were able to fire while lying down, or stooping, gave them an immense advantage over the blacks; who had to expose themselves when rising to throw their spears, or take aim with their bows.

Several times, emboldened by their superior numbers, the blacks attempted a rush; but the heavy fire from rifle and pistol which greeted them, each time, sent them back in diminished numbers. At last the resistance became feebler, as the natives, seeing that they were being driven out of their shelter, began to slink off; so as not to be exposed to the fire of the white men, in the comparatively open ground beyond. Many, however, were not quick enough, and were shot down as they scaled the steep hillside.

The party of whites gathered, and compared notes. Many had received wounds more or less severe, but none of a nature to prevent them from continuing their journey. They quickly returned to their horses and, mounting, continued their way.

"There is no fear of any farther attack, I should think, sergeant."

"I should think not, sir. The beggars must have had enough of it. They must have lost from forty to fifty men."

Two hours later, the party arrived at the halting place.

"Now, sergeant," Reuben said, "I shall hand over the command to you; and shall ride on at once, with my boy. I am most anxious about the man who has escaped. I shall take four of the bush rangers' horses. They have not been ridden and, having had three or four days' rest, are comparatively fresh. The fellow has had only one day's start and, if I push straight on, I may be there before him."

Reuben briefly bade adieu to his friends, while Jim was transferring the saddles to two of the bush rangers' horses and, leading two others, they started together in darkness. Changing saddles every ten miles, they rode on till past midnight, when they halted; for the horses, accustomed as they were to long journeys, were now completely broken down, and Jim and his master could scarce keep their seats.

"Too much long," Jim said, as he threw himself down, after taking off the saddles and hobbling the horses; "too much long, sah."

"It is long, Jim," Reuben replied. "People in England would hardly believe horses could go a hundred miles in a day, even if led a part of the distance. Another fifty miles will take us to Donald's. It is about twenty miles to the water hole where we camped, the first night; and that was about thirty miles from the station."

"Shall Jim light a fire, sah?"

"No, Jim, it isn't worth while. There is some cold meat in my haversack, if you are hungry; but I am too tired to eat. If there are any natives prowling about, a fire might bring them round on us."

"No tink black fellows near, massa."

"I don't think so either, but I don't want to run the risk, Jim; besides, I am sure neither of us can be trusted to keep watch."

Reuben, in spite of his fatigue, was some time before he could get off to sleep. The thought that probably Tom Thorne was, at that time, camped at the water hole twenty miles ahead; and that, in the morning, his horse would be far fresher than those he had ridden, was maddening to him. At one time he thought of getting up, and pursuing his way on foot; but he was stiff in every limb, and felt that the journey was beyond him. Moreover, if the bush ranger had taken some other line, and was not camping there, he would have no means of pursuing his journey.

At the first gleam of daylight they were afoot. The saddles were put on the horses, and they continued their way. Reuben soon found, however, that the five hours he had rested had been insufficient to restore the horses and, even by riding them alternately, he could get them but little beyond a walk.

On arriving at the water hole, the remains of a fire were found. Jim examined the ground carefully, and found the tracks of a horse; and was of opinion that the rider had started three or four hours previously. Reuben carried a large flask of spirits and, having poured what remained in it down the throats of the horses, and given them a drink at the pool, he again pressed on.

Ten miles farther, he arrived at the first outlying station. The owner of this had not joined in the expedition, being a married man, and unwilling to leave his wife in such an exposed position. But upon Reuben's arrival he at once agreed to lend him two fresh horses, and to take care of those which Reuben brought with him.

While the settler was driving them in from the paddock, his wife busied herself in preparing two huge bowls of bread and milk. These were thankfully swallowed by Reuben and Jim and, five minutes later, they started on the fresh horses.

It was indeed a relief, to Reuben's anxiety, to find himself again flying over the ground at a rapid gallop, after the slow and tedious pace at which he had travelled since morning. His spirits rose, and the fears which had oppressed him seemed lifted, as if by magic. He assured himself that he had no cause for anxiety, for that the two constables would assuredly be on the watch, and Kate had promised not to venture beyond the doors of the house until his return.

Chapter 18
Settling Accounts

Reuben soon checked the speed of his horse. Anxious as he was to arrive as soon as possible, he might, for aught he knew, yet have occasion to try the animal to the utmost; and he therefore reduced the almost racing pace, at which he had started, into an ordinary steady gallop. The horses were fresh and in good condition, and for several miles kept up the pace without flagging. Then they were allowed to ease down into a walk, until they got their wind again; and then started at the pace, half canter, half gallop, which is the usual rate of progression of the colonial horses. They drew rein at last on a slight eminence, from which the Donalds' station, a mile or so distant, could be perceived.

"Thank God," Reuben muttered to himself, "I am back here, at last. There is no occasion for further hurry;" and the horses were allowed to go at an easy walk.

"Man on horseback," Jim suddenly said, touching Reuben's arm.

"Where—where, Jim?"

"Gone from de house, sah, trough dem trees. Dare he go again, he gallop fast."

Reuben had not caught sight of the figure, but he pressed his spurs against the horse's sides.

"I will see who it is, at any rate. Jim, do you ride straight on to the house, and say I shall be there in a few minutes."

As Reuben rode, at a headlong gallop, towards the point where his course would probably intersect that of the horseman, riding in the direction Jim had pointed out, he turned over rapidly, in his mind, the thought whether his anxiety for Kate Ellison was not making a fool of him. Why should he turn from his course, just at the end of a long journey, to start at full speed on the track of this figure, of which Jim had caught only a glance? It might be a stockman, or someone who had ridden over from one of the neighbouring stations to see how Donald was getting on; but even so, he told himself, no harm was done by his assuring himself of that.

It was not the way Mr. Barker would take to his station. Had it been a neighbour who had come over, he would not be likely to leave again, so early. Neither of the constables would be riding away, in defiance of his orders on no account to stir any distance from the house.

Presently he caught a glimpse of the horseman. He was not more than half a mile away now, but the view he obtained was so instantaneous that he could not distinguish any particulars.

"He is riding fast, anyhow," he said. "Faster than a man would travel, on ordinary business. He is either a messenger, sent on urgent business; or it is Thorne."

He slightly altered the direction of his course, for the speed at which the horseman was travelling must take him ahead of him, at the point where Reuben had calculated upon cutting him off. In a short distance he would get a view of him; for the trees ended here, and the plain was open and unbroken, save by low bush.

When the figure came clear of the trees, he was but a quarter of a mile away; and Reuben gave a start, for he recognized at once the uniform of his own corps. It could only be one of the men left at Donald's and, with an exclamation of anger, Reuben pressed his horse to the utmost in pursuit of the man, who was now almost directly ahead, at the same time uttering a loud call.

The man glanced back but, to Reuben's surprise, instead of stopping waved his hand above his head, and pressed forward. Two miles were traversed before Reuben was beside him.

"What do you mean, sir?" he thundered out.

But the man pointed ahead.

"He has carried off Miss Ellison, sir, and has shot Brown dead. I will tell you, afterwards.

"There, do you see, sir, over that brow there?"

At the moment, Reuben saw a figure on horseback rise against the skyline, fully two miles in front.

"Ride steadily, Smithson," he said. "Keep me in view, and I will keep him. We must overtake him in time, for his horse is carrying double. I shall push on, for I am better mounted than you are; and he may try to double, and throw us off his traces. If anything happens to me don't stop for a moment, but hunt that fellow down to the end."

Reuben had been holding his horse somewhat in hand, during the last mile, for he thought there must be some reason for the constable's strange conduct; but he now let him go and, urging him to his full speed, soon left the constable behind. He knew that, for some distance ahead, the country was flat and unbroken; and that the fugitive would have no chance of concealment, whichever way he turned.

Upon reaching the spot where he had seen the bush ranger pass, the wide plain opened before him; and he gave a shout of exultation, as he saw that he had gained considerably. The fugitive, indeed, had evidently not been pressing his horse.

"He thinks he has a long journey before him," Reuben muttered. "I fancy he's mistaken. He thinks he's only got a constable after him, and that he can easily rid himself of him, whenever he comes up to him. No doubt he learned from some of the convicts that everyone is away, and therefore thinks himself safe from all pursuit, when once he has wiped out Smithson. All the better. I shall overtake him all the sooner."

Such indeed was the view of the bush ranger, who kept along at a steady canter, troubling himself very little about the solitary constable whom he believed to be in pursuit of him. When, indeed, on glancing round, he saw that his pursuer was within a quarter of a mile of him, he reined in his horse and, turning, calmly awaited his coming.

Reuben at once checked the speed of his horse. He knew that the man was said to be a deadly shot with his pistol, but he was confident in his own skill; for, with constant and assiduous practice, he had attained a marvellous proficiency with his weapon. But he did not care to give his foe the advantage, which a man sitting on a steady seat possesses, over one in the saddle of a galloping horse. He therefore advanced only at a walk.

The bush ranger put down the change in speed to fear, caused by his resolute attitude, and shouted:

"Look here, constable. You had best turn your horse's head, and go home again. You know well enough that one constable is no match for me, so you had best rein up before I put a bullet in your head. If you shoot, you are just as likely to kill the young woman here, as you are me; and you know I don't make any mistake."

Reuben was already conscious of his disadvantage in this respect, for the bush ranger held the girl on the saddle in front of him, so that her body completely covered his. She was enveloped in a shawl, which covered her head as well as her figure. Her captor held her tightly pressed to him with his left arm, while his right was free to use a pistol.

Reuben checked his horse at a distance of some fifty yards, while he thought over the best course to pursue. As he paused, Thorne, for the first time, noticed that it was an officer with whom he had to deal, and not with the constable; who, as he believed, was the only one in the district. He uttered a savage exclamation, for he felt that this materially altered the conditions of the affair.

"Oh, it's you, is it?" he said. "I thought it was only one of your men; but the advice I gave is as good, for you, as for him. I advise you to turn back, before all my mates are down on you."

"Your mates will never be down on anyone again, Tom Thorne," Reuben said sternly. "We have wiped out seven of them, and the other is a prisoner."

"It's a lie!" the bush ranger said, furiously. "They are two hundred miles away, in the bush."

"With your friend Bobitu, eh? Yes, they were, but they are not now, Thorne. They are lying under the ashes of that hut of yours, close to the tree where you buried your treasure; and it's I who am going to have help, not you. My man will be up in a few minutes," and he glanced round at the constable, whom the bush ranger now perceived, for the first time, less than half a mile away.

Reuben's words had the effect they were intended to excite. They filled the bush ranger with fury, and desire for vengeance; while the sight of the approaching constable showed him that, unless he took prompt measures, he would have two adversaries to fight at once.

Without a moment's hesitation, he set spurs to his horse and dashed at Reuben. When within twenty yards, he fired.

Reuben felt a sharp pain, as if a hot iron had been passed across his cheek. Thorne uttered a shout of exultation as he saw him start but, as he kept his seat, again raised his hand to fire. In an instant Reuben discharged his pistol, and the bush ranger's weapon dropped from his hand, for Reuben's bullet passed through his wrist.

Throwing the burden before him headlong to the ground, Thorne drew a pistol with his left hand; and the two shots rung out again, at almost the same instant. Reuben, however, was slightly the quickest, and this saved his life. His bullet passed through the bush ranger's body, while Thorne's pistol was diverted somewhat from its aim, and the bullet struck Reuben's left shoulder, instead of his head. In an instant, he had drawn another pistol.

"Surrender or I fire!" and then seeing, by the change in the bush ranger's face, and by his collapsing figure, that he was badly hit; he waited, still keeping Thorne covered with the muzzle, for the bush ranger had a charge left in the pistol which he still grasped in his left hand.

Twice Thorne tried to raise it, but in vain. Then he reeled in the saddle, the pistol dropped from his hand, and he fell heavily over on to the ground.

Reuben at once leaped from his horse, and ran to raise Kate Ellison; who lay motionless on the ground, as she had been thrown. Removing the shawl wrapped round her head, he found she was insensible. Kneeling beside her, he raised her head to his shoulder and, a minute later, the constable galloped up.

"Badly hurt, captain?" he asked, as he leaped off his horse; for the blood was streaming down Reuben's face, and his left arm hung useless.

"Nothing to speak of, Smithson. See to Miss Ellison, first. There is some water in my flask in the holster. Just bring it here, and sprinkle her face. I hope she is only stunned; but that scoundrel threw her off with such force, that she may well be badly hurt."

"Is he done for, captain?" the man asked, glancing at the prostrate figure of the bush ranger, as he proceeded to obey Reuben's instructions; "because if you ain't certain about it, I had better put a bullet into him. These fellows are very fond of playing 'possum, and then turning the tables upon you."

"There is no fear of that, Smithson. He's hard hit. I hope he's not dead, for I would rather that he were tried for his crimes."

It was some time before Kate Ellison opened her eyes. For a moment she looked vaguely round; then, as her eyes fell upon Reuben's face, she uttered a little cry, and raised herself into a sitting position.

"What is it, Captain Whitney? Are you badly hurt?"

"Thank God you have recovered, Miss Ellison. You began to frighten me horribly. I was afraid you were seriously injured.

"Do not look so alarmed. I can assure you I am not much hurt; only a flesh wound, I fancy, in the cheek, and a broken collarbone."

"And you have saved me again, Captain Whitney?"

"Yes, thank God I have had that good fortune," Reuben said quietly; "and this time for good, for Tom Thorne will never molest you again."

"But can't I do something? Your face is bleeding dreadfully. Please let me bind it up;" and tearing a strip off the bottom of her dress, she proceeded to bandage Reuben's face.

The constable took off the black silk handkerchief which he wore round his neck.

"I think, miss, this will make a sling for his arm; and when that is done the captain will be pretty right.

"Do you think you can ride back, sir?" he asked, when he had fastened the handkerchief, "or will you wait till I ride back to the farm, and fetch help."

"I can ride back well enough," Reuben said, trying to rise to his feet; but he found himself unable to do so.

The ball, after breaking his collarbone, had glanced downwards, and the wound was a more serious one than he had imagined.

"No, I don't think I can ride back, Smithson."

"There is a light cart at the farm," Kate Ellison said. "Please fetch that. I will stop here, with Captain Whitney, till you come back."

"I think that will be the best way, miss," the constable agreed and, mounting, he rode off at once.

It was an hour and a half before he returned, bringing the cart; but before he arrived, Mr. and Mrs. Barker had ridden up on horseback, the former having returned from his visit to the farm, just as the constable rode in. While they had been alone, Reuben had heard from Kate what had taken place.

"I did as you told me, Captain Whitney, and did not go once outside the door. The constables kept a very sharp lookout, and one of them was always on guard by the door; so there really did not seem any possibility of danger.

"This morning, as I was washing up the breakfast things with Mrs. Barker, a shot was suddenly fired outside the door and, before I had time to think what it meant, that man rushed in. He caught me by the wrist, and said:

"'Come along, it's no use your screaming.'

"Mrs. Barker caught up something and rushed at him, but he knocked her down with the butt end of his pistol. Then he caught up her shawl, which was lying on the chair close by, and threw it right over my head; and then caught me up, and carried me out.

"I tried to struggle, but he seemed to hold me as if I were in a vice. I heard Alice scream, and then I must have fainted; for the next thing I knew was that I was being carried along on horseback. I was so muffled up, and he held me so tight, that I felt it was no use to struggle; and I made up my mind to lie quite still, as if I was still insensible, till he put me down; and then—I think I intended to try and seize his pistol, or to get hold of a knife, if there was one and, if I could not kill him, to kill myself.

"There did not seem the least hope of rescue. Mr. Barker was away, and would not be back for hours. I supposed that the constables were shot, and all the men round were away with you; and from the distance you said you were going, I did not think you could be back for days.

"Presently I felt him stop and turn his horse; and then, when he spoke, I knew that he had not killed both the constables, and that one of them had followed him. When you answered, I thought it was your voice, though it seemed impossible; but I could not be sure, because I could not hear plainly through the shawl. Then the pistols were fired, and I suddenly felt myself falling; and I did not know anything more, till I saw you leaning over me.

"But where are all the others, and how is it you are here alone? Of course, you must have turned back before you got to where the bush rangers were."

"No, I am glad to say we succeeded with that part of the work, Miss Ellison, and have wiped out the bush rangers altogether. We have got one of them a prisoner, but all the rest of the gang are killed.

"The distance is not quite so far as we thought it was. It was a thirty miles' march, and two sixties. We attacked them at daybreak, on the third day after leaving."

"But it is only the fourth day today, is it not? At least, it seems so to me."

"It is the fourth day, Miss Ellison. When we found that the leader of the gang was not with them, and I learned from the man we had taken prisoner that he had started to ride back here, twenty-four hours before, I was naturally very anxious about you; knowing, as I did, what desperate actions the man was capable of. So we started at once and, after a sharp fight with the blacks, got down in the evening to the water hole, sixty miles on our way back, where we had camped the second night out.

"Of course the horse I had ridden could travel no further, but I pushed on with my black boy, on two of the horses which we had taken from the bush rangers, and which had been led so far. We made another forty miles by midnight, and then halted till daybreak, to give the horses rest; but they were so done up, this morning, that we could not get them much beyond a foot pace. When we came to the first settlement we exchanged them for fresh ones, and galloped on; and, thank God, we are just in time."

The tears were standing in the girl's eyes, and she laid her hand on his, and said quietly:

"Thank you. Then you have ridden a hundred and fifty miles since yesterday morning, besides having two fights; and all because you were uneasy about me?"

"I had, as you see, good reason to be uneasy, Miss Ellison."

At this moment a horse's hoofs were heard approaching, and Jim galloped up. He had, on arriving at the station, been unable to obtain any information as to what had taken place. Mrs. Donald was in a dead faint. Mrs. Barker had, just before he arrived, ridden off to meet her husband; but the dead body of the constable, by the door, and the disappearance of Kate, showed him what had taken place; and he at once started after his master.

His horse, however, was a very inferior one to that ridden by Reuben, and until he met the constable returning, he had been obliged to follow the track of the horses in front; so he did not arrive at the scene of the fray till half an hour after its conclusion. He uttered exclamations of dismay, at seeing his master's condition; for Reuben had been gradually growing faint, and could now scarcely support himself on his elbow.

Jim, however, had taken the precaution to snatch a bottle of spirits from the shelf, before he started; having an eye to his own comforts, as well as to the possibility of its being required. He now knocked off the neck, and poured some into the cup of Reuben's flask, and put it to his lips.

"Thank you, Jim; that is just what I wanted."

"Massa lie down quiet," Jim said. "No good sit up;" and, gathering a large bunch of grass, he placed it under Reuben's head; and Reuben lay quiet, in a half dreamy state, until Mr. and Mrs. Barker rode up.

Kate rose to her feet as they approached; but she was so stiff and bruised, with her fall, that she could scarcely move forward to meet Mrs. Barker; and burst into tears, as her friend threw her arms round her.

"That's right, my poor child," Mrs. Barker said. "A cry will do you good. Thank God, my dear Kate, for your rescue."

"I do indeed, Mrs. Barker. It seems almost a miracle."

"Captain Whitney seems to spring out of the ground, whenever he's wanted. He seems hurt badly. The constable said it was a broken collarbone, but it must be something a good deal worse than that."

"Oh, don't say so, Mrs. Barker, after what he's done for me. If he were to die!"

"There, there, don't tremble so, child. We must hope that it is not so bad as that; but he would hardly be looking so bad as he does, for only a broken collarbone. My husband broke his—one day the horse ran away with him, among some trees—and he was up and about again, in a day or two.

"Is he badly hurt, do you think, John?" she asked her husband, who was kneeling beside Reuben.

"I hope not," the settler said. "He ought not to be like this, only from a wound in the collarbone; but of course it may have glanced down, and done some internal mischief. I am inclined to think that it is extreme exhaustion, as much as anything—the reaction after a tremendous nervous excitement."

"He has ridden a hundred and fifty miles, since yesterday morning," Kate said, "and has had two fights, besides this. Directly he knew that the leader of the bush rangers had escaped, he came on by himself."

"Oh! They caught the bush rangers, did they?" Mr. Barker said, joyfully. "I was afraid, by his getting back here so soon, that they must have missed them somehow, and found they were on the wrong scent.

"And he has ridden all the way back, has he? A very zealous officer, Miss Ellison, a very zealous young officer, indeed."

But Kate was too anxious, and shaken, to mark the significance of Mr. Barker's tone.

"Don't tease her," his wife said, in a low voice. "She is terribly upset and shaken, and can hardly stand.

"Ah! What is that?"

The interruption was caused by a low groan from the fallen bush ranger.

"Shoot him dead, sah," Jim, who was supporting his master's head, exclaimed. "Don't let dat fellow come 'live no longer."

"I can't do that, Jim," Mr. Barker said, moving towards the fallen man. "The man is a thorough scoundrel, a murderer, and a robber; but he is harmless now. One cannot wish he should recover, even for his own sake; for there is enough against him to hang him, ten times over. However, we must do what we can for the poor wretch."

So saying, he mixed some brandy with a little water in the cup, and poured it between the bush ranger's lips.

"Is it mortal?" Mrs. Barker asked, as he rejoined her.

"I think so," he said. "I fancy he is shot through the lungs.

"You must really sit down, Miss Ellison. You look as white as a ghost, and we cannot have you on our hands, just now. We have got them pretty full, as they are.

"Ah! Here comes the cart."

The constable had put a quantity of straw in the bottom of the light cart, and Barker and Jim raised Reuben, and laid him in it.

"We must take the other, too," Mr. Barker said. "The man is alive, and we can't leave him here."

"Yes," Kate said; "he must go, too. He did Reuben a great wrong, years ago. I hope he will confess it, before he dies."

Mr. Barker glanced at his wife, as Kate used the young officer's Christian name; but she was not thinking of Captain Whitney of the police, but of the boy Reuben, who had been accused of poisoning her father's dog, and of committing a burglary from his house.

"You had better get up in front, with the constable, Miss Ellison," the settler said, when the two wounded men had been placed in the cart. "You certainly are not fit to ride.

"Or, look here, the constable shall take my horse, and I will drive; and then I can look after you, and you can use me for a prop, if you feel weak; but before we start, I must insist on your taking a sip of brandy and water.

"It is no use your saying no," he persisted, as the girl shook her head. "We shall have you fainting before you get home, if you don't."

Kate did as she was ordered. Mr. Barker then helped her up to her seat. As she got up, her eyes fell upon Reuben's face.

"Oh, Mr. Barker!" she said. "He looks dead. You are not deceiving me, are you?"

"Bless me, no!" the settler said, cheerfully. "My opinion is that he's dead asleep. The loss of blood, the sudden reaction after the long excitement, and the exhaustion of his ride have completely overcome him; and my opinion is that he is sound asleep.

"Jim, do you lead your master's horse, while the constable takes the other; and then you two had better ride on, and help Mrs. Donald get things ready. Get a bed up at once, for Captain Whitney; and get some clean straw in the outhouse, with one of the rugs over it, for the other."

So saying, he touched the horse with the whip, and the cart moved slowly on, with Mrs. Barker riding beside it. She would have gone on ahead, to have assisted in the preparations; but she expected, momentarily, to see Kate faint, and thought it better to remain with her, in case her assistance should be required.

The journey occupied some time, for Mr. Barker picked the way carefully, so as not to jolt the cart. Mrs. Barker endeavoured to keep Kate's attention fixed, by asking her questions as to what she had heard about the expedition, wondering when it would return, and whether any of the settlers were hurt. When they got within half a mile of home, she said:

"I think, dear, you are looking a little better now. I will ride on. Fortunately there is the beef tea we made, last night, for Mr. Donald. I will get it made hot, and I will get a cup of strong tea ready for you. That will do wonders."

When the cart arrived Mrs. Donald ran out and, as Kate descended, clasped her in a long embrace.

"Come straight in here, my dear," Mrs. Barker said. "I have got a basin of cold water, and a cup of strong tea, and the two together will do marvels. We will attend to your wounded hero."

Reuben remained perfectly quiet and inert, as he was lifted out and carried into the house, where a bed had been made up for him in a room on the ground floor.

"Just lay him down. Throw a blanket over him, and let him lie perfectly quiet."

"Do you think he is really asleep?" Mrs. Barker asked, as she looked at the quiet face.

"I do, really," her husband replied. "Put your ear close to his mouth. He is breathing as quietly as a child.

"And," he added, placing his fingers on Reuben's wrist, "his pulse is a little fast, but regular and quiet. Twenty-four hours of sleep will set him up again, unless I am greatly mistaken. I don't expect that his wound will turn out anything very serious.

"Let me think. Was it not this afternoon that Ruskin said he would be back again?"

"Yes, either yesterday or today."

"That is lucky. He will be surprised at finding two new patients on his hands, now.

"I will go and have a look at that poor wretch in the shed. Give me a cupful of beef tea. I will pour a spoonful or two between his lips. You had better go and look after Kate. You will not be needed here, at present.

"If your master wakes, Jim, let us know directly," he said to the black, who had seated himself on the ground by the side of Reuben's bed.

"I can't call the poor fellow away from his master," he added to his wife, as he closed the door behind them; "but I am really anxious to know what has taken place, out in the bush; and whether many of our fellows have been killed. If, as Kate said, she heard the captain tell the bush ranger that all his band had been killed, except one who is a prisoner, it has indeed been a most successful expedition; and we colonists can hardly be sufficiently grateful, to Whitney, for having rid us of these pests. What with that, and the thrashing the blacks have had, we shall be able to sleep quietly for months; which is more than we have done for a long time."

Kate came out of the room, with Mrs. Donald, a minute later. The basin of cold water and the tea had had the effect Mrs. Barker predicted. A little colour had returned into her cheeks, and she looked altogether more like herself.

"How is he?" Mrs. Donald asked.

"In my opinion, he's doing capitally, Mrs. Donald. His pulse is quiet and even, and he's breathing as quietly as a child; and I believe he is simply in a state of exhaustion, from which he is not likely to wake till tomorrow morning; and I predict that, in a few days, he will be up and about. Indeed, if that bullet hasn't misbehaved itself, I see no reason why he shouldn't be up tomorrow."

"That is indeed a relief, to us both," Mrs. Donald said, while Kate could only clasp her hands in silent thankfulness.

"And now, how is your husband? I hope he is none the worse, for all this exertion."

"He was terribly agitated, at first," Mrs. Donald said. "I fainted, you know, and he got out of bed to help me up; and it was as much as I could do, when I recovered, to get him to lie down; for he wanted to mount and ride after Kate, although, of course, he is as weak as a child, and even with my help he could scarcely get into bed again.

"Fortunately Mrs. Barker ran in, before she started on horseback to fetch you, to say that the constable was off in pursuit, and that quieted him. Then I think he was occupied in trying to cheer me, for as soon as he was in bed I broke down and cried; till the constable came back to say that Captain Whitney had overtaken, and shot, the bush ranger."

Three hours later, to the great relief of all, the surgeon arrived. He was first taken in to look at Reuben, having been told all the circumstances of the case; and he confirmed Mr. Barker's opinion that he was really in a deep sleep.

"I would not wake him, on any account," he said. "It is a great effort of nature, and he will, I hope, awake quite himself. Of course, I can't say anything about the wound, till he does.

"Now for his antagonist."

The bush ranger was still unconscious, though occasionally broken words came from his lips. The surgeon examined his wound.

"He is shot through the lungs," he said, "and is bleeding internally. I do not think that there is the shadow of a chance for him, and no one can wish it otherwise. It will only save the colony the expense of his trial.

"And now for my original patient."

He was some time in Mr. Donald's room and, when he came out, proceeded at once to mix him a soothing draught, from the case of medicines he carried behind the saddle.

"We must get him off to sleep, if we can," he said; "or we shall have him in a high state of fever, before morning. A man in his state can't go through such excitement as he has done, without paying the penalty.

"And now, I suppose, I have done," he said with a smile, as Mrs. Donald left the room with the medicine.

"Yes, I think so," Mrs. Barker said. "If you had come an hour earlier, I should have put this young lady under your charge; but I think that the assurance of my husband, that Captain Whitney was doing well, has been a better medicine than you could give her."

"No wonder she is shaken," Mr. Ruskin remarked.

"Mrs. Barker tells me you had a heavy fall, too, Miss Ellison."

"Yes," she replied. "I was stunned for a time but, beyond being stiff and bruised, I am none the worse for it."

"Look here, Miss Ellison," the doctor said, after putting his fingers on her wrist, "I suppose you will want to be about, tomorrow, when our brave army returns. Now, there is nothing you can do here. Mrs. Donald can nurse her husband. The other two require no nursing. Mrs. Barker, I am sure, will take charge of the house; and therefore, seriously, I would ask you to take this draught I am about to mix for you, and to go upstairs and go to bed, and sleep till morning."

"I could not sleep," Kate protested.

"Very well, then, lie quiet without sleeping; and if, in the evening, you find you are restless, you can come down for an hour or two; but I really must insist on your lying down for a bit.

"Now, Mrs. Barker, will you take this medicine up, and put this young lady to bed."

"I hope she will get off to sleep," Mrs. Barker said, when she came downstairs again.

"I have no doubt whatever about it," Mr. Ruskin replied. "I have given her a very strong sleeping draught, far stronger than I should think of giving, at any other time; but after the tension that the poor girl must have gone through, it would need a strong dose to take effect. I think you will hear nothing more of her, till the morning."

Indeed, it was not until the sun was well up, the next morning, that Kate Ellison woke. She could hardly believe that she had slept all night; but the eastern sun, coming in through her window, showed her that she had done so. She still felt bruised and shaken all over, but was otherwise herself again. She dressed hastily, and went downstairs.

"That's right, my dear," Mrs. Barker, who was already busy in the kitchen, said. "You look bonny, and like yourself."

"How are my brother and Captain Whitney?" Kate asked.

"I don't think Mr. Donald is awake, yet," Mrs. Barker replied; "but Captain Whitney has just gone out to the shed, with my husband and the surgeon."

"Gone out to the shed!" Kate repeated, in astonishment.

"Yes, my dear. That poor wretch out there is going fast. He recovered consciousness about two hours ago. The constable was sitting up with him. He asked for water, and then lay for some time, quite quiet.

"Then he said, 'Am I dreaming, or was it Reuben Whitney I fought with?'

"'Yes, it was Captain Reuben Whitney, our inspector,' the constable replied.

"For a time he lay quiet again, and then said: 'I want to see him.'

"The constable told him he was asleep, and couldn't be woke.

"'Is he badly wounded?' the man asked. 'I know I hit him.'

"'Not very badly, I hope,' the constable answered.

"'When he wakes ask him to come to me,' the man said. 'I know I am dying, but I want to see him first. If he can't come, let somebody else come.'

"The constable came in and roused the doctor, who went out and saw him, and said he might live three or four hours yet.

"Soon afterwards, just as the sun rose, Jim came out, to say that his master was awake. Mr. Ruskin went in to him and examined his wound, and probed the course of the bullet. It had lodged down just at the bottom of the shoulder bone. I am glad to say he was able to get it out. When he had done, he told his patient what the bush ranger had said; and Captain Whitney insisted upon going out to him."

"It won't do him any harm, will it?" Kate asked anxiously.

"No, my dear, or Mr. Ruskin would not have let him go. I saw him as he went out, and shook hands with him and, except that nasty bandage over his face, he looked quite himself again. As I told you, a broken collarbone is a mere nothing and, now we know where the bullet went and have got it out, there is no occasion for the slightest anxiety.

"Here they come again, so you can judge for yourself."

A very few words passed between Reuben and Kate; for Mrs. Barker, who saw how nervous the girl was, at once began to ask him questions about what the bush ranger had said.

"He has made a confession, Mrs. Barker, which your husband has written down, and Mr. Ruskin and Smithson have signed. It is about a very old story, in which I was concerned when a boy; but it is a great gratification for me to have it cleared up, at last. I was accused of poisoning a dog, belonging to Miss Ellison's father; and was tried for a burglary, committed on the premises, and was acquitted, thanks only to Miss Ellison's influence, exerted on my behalf—

"I fear," he said with a slight smile, "somewhat illegally.

"However, the imputation would have rested on me all my life, if it had not been for Thorne's confession. I thought that he did the first affair. I knew that he was concerned in the second, although I could not prove it; but he has now made a full confession, saying that he himself poisoned the dog, and confirming the story I told at the trial."

"Oh, I am glad!" Kate exclaimed. "You know, Captain Whitney, that I was sure of your innocence; but I know how you must have longed for it to be proved to the world.

"What will you do, Mr. Barker, to make it public?"

"I shall send a copy of the confession, properly attested, to the magistrates of Lewes; and another copy to the paper which, Captain Whitney tells me, is published there weekly.

"It is curious," he went on, "that the sight of Whitney should have recalled those past recollections; while, so far as I could see, everything that has happened afterwards, his career of crime and the blood that he has shed, seem altogether forgotten."

"I suppose there is no hope for him?" Kate asked, in a low voice.

"He is dying now," Mr. Barker said. "Ruskin is with him. He was fast becoming unconscious when we left him, and Ruskin said that the end was at hand."

A quarter of an hour later the surgeon came in, with the news that all was over.

"Now, Captain Whitney, you must come into your room, and let me bandage up your shoulder properly. I hadn't half time to do it, before."

"But you won't want me to lie in bed, or any nonsense of that sort?" Reuben asked.

"I would, if I thought you would obey my orders; but as I see no chance of that, I shall not trouble to give them. Seriously, I do not think there is any necessity for it, providing always that you will keep yourself very quiet. I shall bandage your arm across your chest, so there can be no movement of the shoulder; and when that is done, I think you will be all right."

There was only one more question which Reuben had to ask, with regard to the event of the preceding day—why it was that Smithson did not go to his comrade's assistance. He then learned that Thorne rode quietly up to the back of the house and dismounted, then went to the stable, where Smithson was asleep—having been on guard during the night—and pushed a piece of wood under the latch of the door, so that it could not be raised. Having thus securely fastened Smithson in, he had gone to the front of the house, and had apparently shot down the constable there before the latter was aware of his presence.

Smithson, awakened by the shot, tried in vain to get out; and was only released by Mrs. Barker, when she recovered from the effect of the stunning blow which the bush ranger had struck her. He had then mounted at once, and followed in pursuit.

In the afternoon the party returned from the bush, having experienced no further molestation from the natives. Nothing occurred to interfere with the progress of Reuben's wound and, in the course of a fortnight, he was again able to resume his duties.

The complete destruction of the gang of bush rangers, and the energy with which they had been pursued into the very heart of the bush country, made a vast sensation in the colony; and Reuben gained great credit, and instant promotion for his conduct.

A month after the return of the party from the bush, Mr. Donald was about again and, as the danger was now past, he abandoned his idea of selling his property. The course which events took can be judged by the following conversation, between Mrs. Donald and her sister, three months later.

"Well, Kate, after all he has done for us, of course I have nothing to say against it; and I don't suppose you would mind, if I had. Still, I do think you might have done better."

"I could not have done better," Kate said hotly, "not if I had had the pick of the whole colony."

"Well, not in one way, my dear; for you know that, personally, I like him almost as well as you do. Still, I do think it is a little unfortunate that we ever knew him before."

"And I think it's extremely fortunate," Kate said stoutly. "If it hadn't been that he had known us before, and cared for me—he says worshipped, but that's nonsense—ever since I was a child, he would never have made that terrible ride, and I—"

"Oh, don't talk about it, Kate; it's too dreadful even to think of now."

"Well, my dear, no doubt it's all for the best," Alice said philosophically. "At any rate, you are quite happy, and he is a noble fellow. But I hope, for your sake, that he won't stay in the police. It would be dreadful for you when he was riding about, hunting after bush rangers and blacks; for you know, my dear, there are plenty of others left in the colony."

"I told him so yesterday," Kate said shyly. "I said, of course, that I didn't want to influence him."

Alice broke into a laugh.

"You little goose, as if what you say doesn't influence him."

Three weeks later, Reuben received a letter from Mr. Hudson.

"My dear Whitney, I am glad to hear, from you, that you are engaged to be married; and the circumstances which you tell me of make it a most interesting affair. If I were you, I should cut the constabulary. I enclose a paper from Wilson, giving you three weeks' leave. Come down to Sydney at once, and talk it over with me. You know I regard you as my son, and I am going to have a voice in the matter."

Reuben went down to Sydney and, after ascertaining his views, Mr. Hudson went into town and forthwith arranged for the purchase, for him, of a partnership in the chief engineering firm in the town. When he told

Captain Wilson what he had done, the latter declared that he had robbed the colony of its best police officer. Reuben protested against the generosity of the old settler, but the latter declared he would have no nonsense on the subject.

"I am one of the richest men in the colony," he said, "and it's hard if I can't spend my money as I choose."

There is little more to tell. Reuben became one of the leading citizens of Sydney and, twenty years afterwards, sold his business and returned to England, and bought an estate not far from Lewes, where he is still living with his wife and family. He was accompanied from Australia by his mother; who, in spite of her strong objections to the sea, went out to live with him, two years after his marriage.

The only point upon which Reuben Whitney and his wife have never been able to come to an absolute agreement is as to which owes most to the other.